IN THE SERVICE OF THE EMPEROR

ITALIANS IN THE AUSTRIAN ARMED FORCES
1814–1918

Lawrence Sondhaus

EAST EUROPEAN MONOGRAPHS, BOULDER
DISTRIBUTED BY COLUMBIA UNIVERSITY PRESS, NEW YORK

1990

EAST EUROPEAN MONOGRAPHS, NO. CCXCI

Copyright © 1990 by Lawrence Sondhaus
ISBN 0-88033-188-7
Library of Congress Catalog Card Number 90-83777

Printed in the United States of America

Contents

PREFACE	v
1. BEFORE THE RISORGIMENTO The army and navy, to 1814	1
2. "WE MUST NOT EXPECT MORE ... THAN IS REASONABLE" The army, 1814–1848	12
3. DISCIPLINE AND IGNORANCE The army, 1848–1866	34
4. AUSTRIA'S ITALIAN NAVY The navy, 1814–1848	62
5. DENOUEMENT AT SEA The navy, 1848–1866	82
6. UNDER THE DUAL MONARCHY The army and navy, 1867–1918	96
EPILOGUE	117
NOTES	123
BIBLIOGRAPHY	161
APPENDIX Biographical Index Statistical Tables	171 177
MAPS	197
INDEX	203

PREFACE

Throughout the period of the Risorgimento and up to the incorporation of Trieste and the Trentino into Italy in 1918, the Austrians quite accurately were considered to be the principal roadblock to the unity and national aspirations of the Italian people. For historians writing on this period of Italy's past, the Austrians have continued to fill the traditional villain's role. Consequently, the subject of the hundreds of thousands of Italians serving in the Habsburg armed forces during and after the era of the Risorgimento has received little coverage. The dramatic activities of a patriotic minority—General Carlo Zucchi in 1831, the Bandiera brothers in the 1840s, the leaders of the Venetian resistance in 1848-49, and the irrendentist martyrs of later years—are relatively well known, and would give one the impression that Italians pressed into Austrian service were all good nationalists who fought tirelessly to sabotage the Habsburg army and navy. Italian history written in the patriotic vein has encouraged this view, irrespective of its accuracy.

From a far different perspective, Austrian military and naval historiography has also given us a biased account of Italian service in the Habsburg armed forces. The *schlaue Italiener* are among the villains of Habsburg military history; reflecting their own traditional sentiments, the Austrians have been in the vanguard of those promoting the myth that Italians, by their very nature, were bad soldiers. Austrian military historians, like their Italian counterparts, have emphasized incidents of Italian disloyalty and desertion, but for the purpose of justifying their prejudice against Italian soldiery. Just as the Italian tendency is to paint these men with a patriotic brush, the Austrian inclination has been to condemn them as a liability, an "enemy within the gates," whose military record by far was the worst of any of the Habsburg nationalities. For their own reasons, the Austrians, as much as the Italians, have had little interest in breaking from their traditional views of the subject.

In fact, the record shows that Italians in the Austrian armed forces were not markedly less loyal than soldiers or sailors of the other nationalities. Instances of what the Italian historian would call patriotism, and the Austrian would characterize as treachery, were the exceptions (albeit dramatic exceptions) to the customary complacent or even loyal service that Italians provided. The coincidence of a number of historical factors created for the Austrians a base of Italian manpower which was largely indifferent to Italian nationalism and predisposed to serve the Habsburg monarchy dutifully if not enthusiastically.

Italian domination of the Austrian navy and the presence of a substantial minority of Italians in the Habsburg army should have made both institutions highly vulnerable to the patriotic movements of the Risorgimento, but other factors prevented a full scale revolution in the ranks. In the years between the Napoleonic wars and the revolution of 1848, the relatively limited scope of subversive proselytizing enabled the Austrians to contain and limit its effects. After 1814 the Carbonari gained some adherents in the army but few, if any, in the predominantly Italian Austrian navy. Conversely, in the 1830s and 1840s, the Young Italy movement came close to destroying the navy but made few converts in the Italian regiments of the Habsburg army. Even in the chaotic years of 1848 and 1849, when the authority of the Habsburgs was at its weakest, attempts to paralyze the army and navy in the interest of Italian national aspirations met with failure both on the peninsula and in the Adriatic. As a result, the Austrians were able to retain their hold on Lombardy until 1859, Venetia until 1866, and Trieste, Istria, and the Trentino until 1918. In each of these territories, the conscription of Italians for Austrian service continued right up to the time of their cession.

The bulk of the present work concerns the period from 1814 to 1866, when Austria ruled much of northern Italy and drafted large numbers of Italians into her army and navy. This half-century has been subdivided into the relatively tranquil years between 1814 and 1848, when the Habsburg armed forces usually were on a peacetime footing, and the years of warfare between 1848 and 1866, when they were active in five campaigns (1848, 1849, 1859, 1864, and 1866) and one armed intervention (in the Danubian Principalities, 1855–1857). Because the experiences of Italians in the Austrian army were significantly different from those of their counterparts in the navy, their respective stories are treated in topical chapters within this chronological framework. The relatively small number of Italians in the Habsburg armed forces prior to 1814 permits the background material to be dispensed with in a single chapter. The same approach has been applied to the years after 1866, when the Italians of the Tyrol, Trieste, and the eastern Adriatic littoral were the only Habsburg subjects of their nationality.

The shortcomings of the traditional Austrian and Italian literature on the subject at hand already have been noted. The more recent works of Gunther Rothenberg provide detailed coverage of the Habsburg army during the years 1814–1918 but include little original research on the nationality question in the armed forces.[1] A good deal of the motivation behind the present manuscript has come from Alan Sked's provocative monograph on Field Marshal Radetzky's army during the revolution of 1848, which points out the weaknesses of earlier works but still leaves enough loose ends to inspire further research.[2] On the narrower topic of Italians in Austrian service, Raimondo Luraghi has published a paper under the title "Italians in the Habsburg Armed Forces, 1815–1849."[3] This piece is useful in some respects but focuses on the service and achievements of Italians in positions of higher responsibility and limits coverage of the rank and file to a few general remarks. While the personal stories of a number of Italian commanders and officers are included in the present work, an effort has been made to keep the purely biographical material to a minimum in both the text and notes. Sketches of the lives and careers of some of the more significant figures have been included in the appendix.

As for sources, the collections of the Kriegsarchiv and Haus–Hof– und Staatsarchiv in Vienna, Austria were invaluable to my research. The library of the Kriegarchiv includes a number of works on Habsburg regiments, which I found very useful in my effort to reconstruct the experience of Italians in the Austrian army. Though such histories normally are too partisan to be of much value to the serious researcher, the German–language accounts of the former Lombard and Venetian units are an exception to the rule. Part of a genre of Habsburg regimental chronicles from the years 1867–1914, all were written by German, Magyar or Slavic officers after the units in question were transferred from their lost Italian recruiting grounds to new districts in Hungary or Galicia. While typically partisan in covering their regiments after they became Hungarian or Polish, the authors treat the performance of their Italian precursors with a great deal of frankness, reporting desertions and other problems, obviously with no intent in glorifying the exploits of Lombards or Venetians. The authors invariably show some surprise when recounting a respectable performance of a regiment during its Italian period and are forced to admit, somewhat reluctantly, that the Italians were not such bad soldiers after all.[4] Unfortunately, memoirs and letters of Italians describing their personal experiences in Austrian service are in short supply, and the works that are available have considerable biases and must be used with caution. Moriz von Angeli's writings reflect the views of a second generation Italian officer born in Vienna, *kaisertreu* and with no hint of a national consciousness; on the other extreme, Carlo Alberto Radaelli's work reflects his involvement in the Young Italy movement within the Austrian navy.[5] By necessity as well as design, I have produced an "external" rather than "internal" treatment of my subject, in which the fluctuating attitudes of the Austrians toward their Italian soldiers and sailors provide the general framework as well as much of the evidence.

The archival research for the present project was funded by a Fulbright-Hays Training Grant from the U. S. Department of Education. I would like to thank *Oberrat* Dr. Peter Broucek, *Amtssekretär* Herr Karl Rossa, and *Marine Referent* Herr Peter Jung, all of the Kriegsarchiv, and Dr. Anna Benna and her staff at the Haus- Hof- und Staatarchiv, for help and guidance during my year in Vienna. In my secondary research I benefitted from the collections and staff assistance of the Austrian Nationalbibliothek, the library of the Kriegsarchiv in Vienna, Alderman Library at the University of Virginia, and Krannert Memorial Library at the University of Indianapolis. A summer research grant from the University of Indianapolis helped support the final preparation of the manuscript.

I am grateful to Professor Alan Reinerman of Boston College for reading an earlier version of the manuscript and for always encouraging my Austro-Italian interests. I benefitted from comments and audience response at the spring meeting of the New England Historical Association in Salem, Massachusetts, where I presented a brief synopsis of chapters 3 and 5 in April 1988, and the annual meeting of the Consortium on Revolutionary Europe in Charleston, South Carolina, where my paper in February 1989 summarized chapters 2 and 4. I offer my sincere thanks to family, friends, and colleagues for the moral support that has sustained my efforts.

Lawrence Sondhaus
Indianapolis, 1989

Chapter 1

BEFORE THE RISORGIMENTO

The record of Italians in the Habsburg armed forces reaches back at least as far as the sixteenth century, when Charles V, holding the titles of Holy Roman emperor and king of Spain, extended Habsburg hegemony over much of the Italian peninsula. His Spanish and Imperial armies included regiments raised in Italy, but during the subsequent wars of religion Italian leadership was far more important to the Habsburg cause than Italian manpower. In the eyes of the rest of Europe, the political decline of Italy had not tarnished the Italian reputation for excellence in the art and technology of war. Long after the Renaissance, young Italians with the requisite social or educational backgrounds had no trouble obtaining officers' commissions from the major continental powers. The Habsburg armies were no exception. Charles V had a great number of Italians in his officer corps, among them the brothers Prospero and Fabrizio Colonna, two of his most distinguished generals.[1]

After Charles's abdication and the division of the Habsburg domains between the Austrian and Spanish branches of the family, the latter attracted far more Italian talent than their eastern cousins. By the time of the Dutch wars for independence, the Parmesan Duke Alessandro Farnese and the Genoese Ambroglio Spinola were among the most prominent Spanish commanders.[2] Because the Spanish Habsburgs also received the family possessions in Italy, Italian common soldiers served Spain rather than the Holy Roman Empire.

In the Thirty Years' War, the Imperial and Spanish armies fought as partners against the Protestant forces and eventually, France. The nature of their common effort makes it difficult for the historian to distinguish between army units raised for the king of Spain and those formed for the Holy Roman emperor. There is firm evidence that at least ten regiments of Italian infantry served in the Imperial army, as well as one regiment of curassiers (heavy cavalry).[3] But again, the role of Italians in the upper echelons of the Habsburg army overshadowed their significance in the ranks. The Pisan–born Ottavio Piccolomini entered Imperial service in 1619, after twenty years in the Spanish army, and amassed a tremendous amount of power by becoming a protégé of the powerful Wallenstein. Eventually, he enhanced his position still more by helping to engineer the downfall and death of his mentor. By the end of the Thirty Years' War he had risen to the position of supreme commander of all German Habsburg forces.[4]

A number of other prominent Italian generals fought for the Habsburgs in the wars of the seventeenth century. The Modenese Raimondo Montecuccoli, a child of nine at the start of the Thirty Years' War, was a well respected commander by its end. He went on to serve Leopold I against the Turks and organized the first Habsburg standing army. By the time of his death, in 1680, he was also known for his writings on the art of war.[5] Three years later, the battle to save Vienna from the Turks provided the forum for the first exploits of Prince Eugene of Savoy, the most celebrated Italian general ever to serve the Habsburgs. In 1697 Eugene became supreme commander of the Habsburg army and in 1703, president of the Hofkriegsrat (Court War Council). He held both offices until his death in 1736.[6]

But the army Montecuccoli created and Eugene commanded contained few Italian soldiers.[7] Eugene himself forbade the hiring of Italians for the "German" Habsburg regiments, which were supposed to be recruited from the hereditary crown lands and the Holy Roman Empire. In 1715 he placed them on a list of so–called "forbidden nationalities" which included Frenchmen, Swiss, Poles, Hungarians, and Croats. Seven years later, recruiting regulations drawn up by Field Marshal Ludwig Andreas Khevenhüller stipulated that *Welschen* should be barred from the regiments, because "they do not adjust easily to our brand of *Kameradschaft*."[8]

Nevertheless, the Habsburg defeat in the War of the Spanish Succession brought an influx of Italians into the Imperial army. The peace settlement of 1713, while confirming Bourbon possession of the throne of Spain, awarded the former Spanish Italian territories to the Austrian Habsburgs. Lombardy, Naples, and Sardinia came under

Austrian rule, the latter being traded for Sicily in 1720, and the army of Emperor Charles VI absorbed several Spanish Italian regiments. By the early 1720s elements of a dozen such units had been combined into two regiments of infantry and one of marines. The Regiment Marulli, under the control of the *Inhaber* or proprietary colonel Cavaliere Francesco Marulli, had a mixture of Neapolitan and Lombard manpower. The Regiment Alcaudete, under the Spanish Count Antonio Alcaudete, had a core of Catalans but after 1713 raised all of its recruits in Lombardy. Both participated in the Austro-Turkish war of 1737-39, fighting in Bosnia, Serbia, the Banat of Temesvar, and Transylvania.[9]

Meanwhile, the third regiment served as the infantry of a new Habsburg navy, created in 1718 by Charles VI. The original Neapolitan and Sardinian marines were joined after 1720 by a contingent from Sicily. The regiment never left Naples and Sicily and was disbanded in the 1730s, when the Bourbons conquered these territories. There is no record of the composition of the officer corps or crews of Charles's navy, but they must have been overwhelmingly Italian. The ships were mostly Neapolitan, supplemented by others built later at Trieste. In 1738, after losing Naples and Sicily, the emperor disbanded the fleet rather than attempt to maintain it on the resources of the Adriatic alone.[10]

By the 1740s, natural attrition and years of fresh recruitment combined to give the two remaining Italian regiments a predominantly Lombard character. In the War of the Austrian Succession, both saw action first against the French and their German allies in Bavaria, then against France in the Italian theater, before spending the last half of the war on garrison duty in eastern Slavonia.[11] Their assignment to a quiet front may have been an indication of unreliability in battle, but the Habsburg army had no reservations about forming a third unit in Lombardy during the war. In early 1744 Marquis Girogio Clerici raised a regiment which, according to one historian, consisted of "2,300 vagabonds and ruffians." Irrespective of their background, they were good soldiers and fought with distinction later the same year against the French at the Battle of Cuneo. Unlike the other two Italian regiments, Clerici's troops spent the rest of the war in Italy. They were not sent to garrison duty in Hungary until after the last campaign.[12]

Austria survived the war of the 1740s because Maria Theresa had been able to mobilize the resources of the Habsburg lands to a greater extent than any of her predecessors. The performance of Hungarian regiments after their debut in 1741 helped dispel old notions about the unsuitability of non-Germans for the Imperial service. Thereafter, regiments from outside of the Holy Roman Empire and hereditary crown lands became a permanent feature of the regular standing army, alongside the older "German" regiments. Postwar reductions claimed one of the units from Lombardy, the Regiment Marulli, disbanded in 1751. Some of its men joined the remaining two regiments, both of which enjoyed a more stable existence. When Habsburg army units received numeric designations in the 1760s, the Clerici became the 44th Infantry and Alcaudete's old regiment became the 48th.[13]

Maria Theresa's Italian troops were active throughout the Seven Years' War. The two regiments saw considerable action against the Prussians, most notably in 1757 at Schweidnitz and Leuthen, in 1758 at Hochkirch, and in 1762 at Döbeln. At Schweidnitz, the Clerici fought with special distinction and one Lieutenant Omati was singled out for his bravery. In the same battle, the other Lombard regiment lost its commander, Colonel Guido di Bagno, the first Italian officer of higher rank ever to die for a purely Austrian cause. At Hochkirch the following year, the Clerici suffered heavy losses after their commander, Colonel Francesco Valentiani, requested that his men have the honor of leading the first assault on fixed Prussian positions. Valentiani himself was mortally wounded during the charge but lingered long enough to receive a deathbed promotion to general and elevation to the ranks of the hereditary nobility. The two regiments were together again in 1762 at the Battle of Döbeln, where the Clerici once more absorbed the greater losses. A Prussian ambush resulted in the capture of their new commander, Colonel Francesco de Feretti, and 300 of his men, losses which crippled the regiment for the remainder of the war.[14]

Following their respectable showing against the Prussians, the Italian troops were rewarded with extended terms of garrison duty in their native Lombardy. After the return to peace, the "German" regiments of the army all received recruiting districts in the hereditary Habsburg crown lands, an important step in the evolution of the Holy Roman imperial army into a truly Austrian army. The Hungarian diet prevented the drawing of districts in Hungary on the grounds that the measures interfered with local rights and prerogatives. The reforms were not applied to Lombardy, either, but by the 1780s it became customary for the 44th Infantry (the former Clerici) to take its recruits from the duchy of Milan in western Lombardy, while the 48th recruited in the eastern areas belonging to the duchy of Mantua.[15]

The Italian component within the Habsburg armed forces remained small throughout the second half of the eighteenth century. In an army consisting of between fifty-five and sixty infantry regiments, dozens of cavalry units, and various other battalions of supporting troops, the two regiments of foot soldiers formed a relatively insignificant minority. The populous province of Lombardy remained undisturbed by conscription, and the number of men actually enlisted in the two regiments (just over 2,000 in each) represented a fraction of a percentage of the overall population, which stood at 900,000 in mid-century.[16]

While the Italians were under-represented in the rank and file of the army, they continued to be over-represented in the officer corps. In the five decades following 1740, two dozen Italians reached general's rank in Habsburg service; half were from states or provinces other than Lombardy, and all but four were of noble birth.[17] At the same time, the ample supply of Italian officers below the generalcy, combined with the small number of Lombard soldiers, enabled the Austrian army to avoid the problem of having non-Italian commanders in charge of Italian units. Prior to being disbanded in 1751, the Regiment Marulli had an Italian commander for twenty-four of the thirty years of its existence. Between 1722 and 1789, the 48th Infantry likewise had an Italian commander for sixty out of sixty-seven years, while Italian colonels led the 44th continuously from 1744 until 1801.[18]

By the last years of Maria Theresa's long reign, all of the parties involved were generally satisfied with the position of Italians in the Habsburg army. The officer corps provided the opportunity for well-to-do Lombards to pursue a military career. The ranks, still operating on the traditional life term, were filled both by enlistees who preferred the military life to civilian society and by an assortment of convicted or paroled men whom civilian society preferred to have in the military. In any event, the light demands of recruiting in Lombardy all but ensured that the unwilling, innocent civilian would not be pressed into service. The army hierarchy, the Italian officers, the Lombard soldiers, and the people of Lombardy all had no reason to criticize the existing state of affairs.

This atmosphere of mutual contentment changed somewhat after 1778, when Austria and Prussia squared off in the War of the Bavarian Succession. The record of the 44th Infantry from the Seven Years' War earned it a place in the northern army, but after one of its three battalions reached the front in Bohemia the officers and men did not live up to the reputation of their predecessors. Because the two sides fought no major battles and spent much of their time foraging for food, the winter campaign of 1778–79 has been labeled the "Potato War." Nevertheless, the weeks of marching and counter-marching included a number of skirmishes, and in one such encounter, the battalion from the 44th was cut off from the rest of the Habsburg army and its colonel, regimental commander Marquis Giovanni Bossi, surrendered without offering resistance. After the return of peace in 1779, a courtmartial found fault with Bossi's conduct and forced him to resign his commission under threat of having it revoked. Of the sixteen other officers with the battalion, fifteen were discharged for their part in the surrender. After these proceedings, the dishonored battalion was disbanded and its men dispersed among other regiments.[19]

The apparent disloyalty of the battalion left a bad taste in the mouth of the Habsburg leadership. Emperor Joseph II, whose opinion of Italian soldiery was not very high to begin with, placed no emphasis on military recruiting in Lombardy.[20] After the Potato War, when an expansion of the peacetime army raised the strength of all German and Hungarian regiments to just over 3,000 men, he kept the two Italian regiments at the previous level of 2,000 apiece. But Joseph did not completely exclude the Lombard units from his military reforms. His new system of regimental schools (*Regiments-Knaben-Erziehungshäuser*), established to care for the neglected children and orphans of soldiers, included a school at Cremona. It served the Italian regiments from 1782 until the collapse of Austrian rule in Lombardy in 1796.[21]

The Lombards themselves certainly did not object to the continuation of the old recruitment policies and the freedom from conscription, but by the end of the 1780s the disruptive effects of Joseph's various reform programs had weakened their sympathy for Austrian rule.[22] Despite the souring of Austro–Lombard relations, the army did not hesitate to employ its Italian units when the emperor went to war against the Turks later in the decade. The 44th and 48th Infantry each sent two battalions to the front in the Balkans, where a fifth Lombard batallion of grenadiers, drawn from both regiments, also saw action.

While the 48th was relatively inactive for most of the campaign, the 44th redeemed its tarnished image somewhat by fighting with distinction from 1788 to 1790. The most heroic of its exploits came early in the war in the Banat of Temesvar, after a Lieutenant Lopresti and two dozen Lombards were detached to guard Rama Castle on the cliffs above the Danube. An unexpected Ottoman advance isolated their position, and some four to five thousand Turks then tried to take the castle by storm. Lopresti and the tiny garrison held out for three hours, fending off four assaults before succumbing to a fifth. Needless to say, there were no survivors. Two years later the regiment again distinguished itself in the siege of Giurgevo, where a Captain Mauro and Lieutenant Baron Colli won accolades. By the end of the war, seven officers and men from the 44th had received silver medals for bravery.[23]

Following the death of Joseph II, the new emperor Leopold II withdrew the Habsburg army from the Balkans and negotiated an end to the Turkish war. The Italian troops returned once more to garrison duties in Lombardy, only to be called to action again just two years later against revolutionary France. As in the Turkish war, the 44th and 48th Infantry each contributed two battalions, joined by their common grenadier battalion. All were employed in Piedmont as part of an Austro–Sardinian force holding the line of the Alps against the French from 1793 through 1795. These early years of the war in Italy, before General Bonaparte arrived on the scene, featured little in the way of decisive battles. The opposing armies clashed in countless skirmishes, however, and as in the past, the men of the 44th saw far more action and performed much better than those of the 48th. The Milanese also suffered heavy casualties during these years, which could not have been good for their spirit. The greatest bloodbath came in 1795 at Sambucco and Loano, sharp actions in which their Mantuan counterparts also participated. While the 44th again distinguished itself amid great losses, the 48th Infantry suffered a complete breakdown of morale. The collapse was so serious that the regiment had to be disbanded later in the year, leaving the army with only a single regiment of Italians, along with one grenadier battalion.[24]

These remaining troops did not fare very well over the next two years, when Bonaparte's Army of Italy racked up its impressive string of victories. At the end of 1796, all three battalions of the 44th Infantry joined the grenadiers as garrison of the fortress of Mantua, which the French subsequently besieged. Early in 1797, after the city fell to Bonaparte, the men were exchanged for French prisoners and evacuated to Austria.[25] In the postwar Treaty of Campoformio the Austrians recognized the transformation of Lombardy into the Cisalpine Republic, receiving in return the former lands of the Venetian Republic. Meanwhile, the 44th went on garrison duty in Trieste, its first peacetime station outside of Lombardy since before the Seven Years' War. Assignment to an Italian city failed to compensate for the seemingly permanent separation from home, though, and the morale of the regiment suffered a serious decline.

Despite the deteriorating conditions within the unit, the 44th Infantry again saw action in the next round of warfare, between 1799 and 1801. By then its spirits had reached such depths that it was practically useless; the grenadiers fought with distinction throughout the war but the rest of the regiment could not be trusted to do its duty. The regimental commander, Count Giovanni Strassoldo, had to ask for volunteers to participate in the Battle of Novi (November 1800) and only 150 men—less than 10 percent—answered the call.[26] Early the following year, after the Treaty of Lunéville reinstated the provisions of Campoformio (including the Austrian cession of Lombardy), the bulk of the 44th deserted and returned home.

Later that year the regiment received new recruiting grounds in Venetia, heretofore untapped as a source of army conscripts. From 1801 to 1805, two other regiments also reinforced themselves with Venetians: the 46th Infantry, transferred from the Tyrol, and the 63rd, made up of Walloons from the former Austrian Netherlands. The 13th Infantry, a predominantly German and Slovene unit from neighboring Inner Austria, also took some Venetian recruits. But of these four regiments, only the 44th ever had a predominant Italian character. This, consequently, also meant that it was the least trusted by the Habsburg leadership. After 1801 non-Italian commanders ran the regiment, and when Austria went to war again in 1805, its three battalions spent the entire campaign on garrison duty in Venice. Meanwhile, the grenadiers managed to participate in the Archduke Charles's victory at the Battle of Caldiero. The men of this battalion won two gold medals for their performance in the campaign, as the last Italian regulars to fight for Austria in the Napoleonic wars.[27]

After the Peace of Pressburg and the Austrian cession of Venetia, the army gave the 44th Infantry a recruiting district in Galicia and converted it to Polish manpower. The other units reinforced with Venetians likewise were reassigned to other provinces. Aside from two volunteer battalions of Jägers (light infantry sharpshooters) which joined in Archduke John's abortive invasion of Venetia in 1809, no Italians served under Habsburg colors until the final campaign against Napoleon.[28]

As the number of Italians in the Austrian ranks dwindled to an insignificant level, their traditional influence in the Habsburg military leadership also started to wane. In the 1790s and early 1800s, Count Camillo Lamberti was the most visible Italian in the higher circles of the army. Named tutor and adjutant to the Archduke Francis in 1784, he became an important military advisor in Vienna after his young charge was crowned emperor eight years later. Lamberti soon mastered the art of court politics, aligning himself closely with Baron Franz Amadeus Thugut, Francis's chief minister. But Thugut's ouster in 1801 also brought the fall from grace of Lamberti; he remained in the emperor's entourage through the war of 1805, only to be criticized and ridiculed by Archduke Charles, who considered him an incompetent intriguer and a bad influence on Francis.[29] Though he rose to the rank of general, Lamberti left behind no great record of accomplishments and must be characterized as a poor successor to the tradition of Piccolomini, Montecuccoli, and Eugene of Savoy.

Austria's defeat in the War of 1809, which left her temporarily landlocked, also brought the release from Habsburg service of the small number of Italians in the Austrian navy. After Charles VI disbanded his Austro-Neopolitan fleet, the Habsburgs in the late 1760s tried unsuccessfully to build a navy in the Adriatic.[30] In 1786, Joseph II finally created a small permanent force for the upper Adriatic, based at Trieste. This "Trieste navy" initially had only two small ships, six officers, twenty-nine non-commissioned officers and other skilled men, and sixty-five seamen. None of the original officers was Italian, but there were nine among the non-commissioned personnel: two from Trieste, two from Dalmatia, one Venetian, and four from outside the Adriatic. Over half of the seamen were South Slavs, but Italians made up most of the rest of the ships' crews.[31]

After conquering the Venetian Republic in 1797, Napoleon, in the Treaty of Campoformio, ceded most of its territory to Austria; the French also left behind roughly half of the Venetian fleet when they evacuated Venice. These ten ships of the line, seven frigates, and countless smaller vessels dwarfed the "Trieste navy" and suddenly thrust Austria into the ranks of the maritime powers. The Habsburgs made little use of this windfall before their defeat in 1805 forced the cession of Venetia to the Napoleonic kingdom of Italy. Nevertheless, it was during this brief period that the precedent was set for the predominantly Italian Habsburg navy of the post-Napoleonic years. For most of the time that the forces of Venice and Trieste were united as a single navy, the Italians (in particular the Venetians) made up the largest single group in the officer corps and among the seamen. Of 119 naval officers active in May 1802, seventy-one (or 60 percent) were Italian, and of these, fifty were veterans of the Venetian navy. But at least during these years, sheer numbers did not ensure a Venetian-Italian domination of the Austrian navy. Aside from a brief period in 1805, the Habsburgs never entrusted the command of their navy to a Venetian officer.[32]

The peace treaty of 1805 required the Austrians to turn over to the French all ships originally built by the Venetian Republic and to release from their service all officers and men of Venetian origin. The Habsburg Monarchy was left once again with a limited coastline, guarded by a small navy based at Trieste. Despite the departure of the Venetians, the officer corps of this restored "Trieste navy" still had an Italian plurality: in early 1809, 44 percent of its officers were Italian, most of them from Trieste, Istria or the ports of Dalmatia. The Austrian defeat at the hands of France later that year led to the harsh Treaty of Schönbrunn, in which the Habsburgs had to relinquish the rest of their coastal territories. Austria subsequently disbanded her "Trieste navy." The seamen were sent home and the officers were absorbed by the Habsburg army.[33]

After 1809, the Italian contingent in the Austrian armed forces was limited to these and a few dozen other career officers who decided to remain in Habsburg service even though all of Italy had fallen under some form of Napoleonic rule. At this stage, contemporary Austrian observers would not have given the Italian performance very high marks. The navy had come and gone before any conclusions could be drawn about the merits of its Italian seamen, while the most recent conduct of the army's Italian regiments, under the strain of war, had been far from encouraging. The latter development obscured the fact that, prior to the 1790s, Habsburg military authorities had had few complaints about the Lombard units. Their success story throughout most of the eighteenth century had three basic causes: the regiments spend most of their time on garrison duty at home in Lombardy, their commanders usually were Italian, and the number of men in their ranks stood at less than 5,000, of a population that reached

1.3 million by the time of the French Revolution.[34] Civilian–military relations in northern Italy were not to be so congenial after 1814, when Austria again ruled in both Lombardy and Venetia. In addition to supporting the Habsburg navy, the provinces would be expected to provide their share of regiments to the army, and these units more often than not would be stationed away from home and commanded by non-Italians.

Chapter 2

"WE MUST NOT EXPECT MORE . . . THAN IS REASONABLE"

In August 1813 Austria reentered the war against France, sending armies into action in both Germany and Italy. Unlike the dramatic War of Liberation in the north, the southern theater of 1813–14 featured sluggish campaigning by relatively small armies; nevertheless, Napoleon's enemies pursued their cause in Italy using some of the same methods and strategies that worked in Germany. As in the north, the allies in the south sought to supplement their regular forces with formations of volunteers. Undeterred by its most recent experiences with Italian soldiers, the Habsburg army in February 1814 organized an Italian *Freikorps* in Venetia. This force, which grew to a strength of three battalions, included men from an "Italian Legion" formed by the British the previous fall, deserters from the Napoleonic Italian army, and other volunteers. In March the Austrians created a "Jäger corps" for Lombardy, but it failed to attract more than a few hundred recruits. Neither of these units saw action in the campaign and the Jägers were soon disbanded.[1]

The viceroy of Italy, Prince Eugene de Beauharnais, put up a gallant fight for eight months and did not conclude an armistice with the allies until 16 April 1814, more than two weeks after Napoleon's own capitulation in France. He abdicated shortly thereafter, leaving behind the remnants of a proud army that had served alongside the French from Spain to Russia. Once Austrian troops had occupied both Lombardy and Venetia, the Habsburg leadership acted quickly to tap this course of veteran military manpower. Ten days after the Italian armistice, Emperor Francis decreed that "in order to give the Italian troops and especially the officer corps the means for their future existence," four regiments of line infantry, four light infantry battalions and one regiment of light cavalry (chevaux-legers) were to be formed from the troops of Eugene's army. In mid-May the Hofkriegsrat appointed Feldmarschalleutenant Marquis Annibale Sommariva, a Lombard with decades of experience under Habsburg colors, to oversee the creation of the new Habsburg units.[2]

Within the framework of an unrealistic deadline of 15 June for the completion of the project, the army went out of its way to accommodate Sommariva's efforts. All officers of the army of the Napoleonic kingdom of Italy born in Lombardy or Venetia were to be eligible for Habsburg commissions. Common soldiers, drafted for four years under the old French-sponsored Italian conscription code, continued to serve under its terms. New Italian recruits were offered enlistment under the same conditions, which were far more lenient than the fourteen-year service required in the Austrian provinces of the empire or the life conscription still employed in Hungary. Other gestures included the retention of the old Italian articles of war, with punishments far less draconian than their Austrian counterpart, and a translation of Habsburg service regulations into Italian, at the request of Italian officers wishing to ease their transition to the German language of command. The Austrians even moved with caution in dismantling the Italian military bureaucracy, waiting until 1 July to replace Eugene's war ministry with their own administrative structure.[3]

The first of July became the official date of creation for all of the units called into existence by Francis's decree of 26 April, but even after the additional two weeks' grace Sommariva could not call his task complete. On paper the defunct Italian army provided plenty of raw material—fifteen regiments and two battalions of infantry, along with seven regiments of cavalry—but regiments on the Franco-Italian model were far smaller than those of traditional German-Austrian size. Furthermore, most of the Italian regiments had consisted of raw recruits at the beginning of the last campaign and all had suffered losses in action. In units where a majority of the officers opted to enter Habsburg service and enough of them approached the transition with enthusiasm, the process went smoothly. For example, by the middle of June, Colonel Count Ferdiando Ceccopieri of the old Fourth Line Infantry Regiment of the Italian army had transformed this unit and the defunct Fifth Italian regiment into the new Third Austro-Italian

Infantry Regiment, with a full compliment of three regular batallions and two companies of grenadiers, a total strength of just over 3,600 men.[4] But the story of the Second Austro–Italian regiment was far more typical. Drawing upon three old Italian units for its manpower, it mustered out only 1,500 men in July and still had only 2,200 in the fall of 1815.[5]

The light–handed approach toward the Italians did not survive past the initial guidelines to Sommariva. On 3 July 1814, long before most of the new regiments were ready for service, the emperor resolved that all would have peacetime garrison duties outside of Lombardy and Venetia.[6] During the second half of the year Francis further undermined the atmosphere of good will by ordering mass transfers of Italian officers away from the new regiments. The casualties included the industrious Ceccopieri, who ended up in command of the 9th (Galician) Infantry.[7] With few exceptions, the departing officers were replaced by commanders of other nationalities from the established regiments of the Habsburg army. The emperor initially decreed that all officers transferred to the Italian regiments should be fluent in Italian, in order to gain the trust and confidence of their men, but this guideline soon broke down because of the dearth of Italian–speaking officers in the German–dominated corps.[8] Thus, the Habsburg troops of Lombardy and Venetia were to be exposed to non–Italian commanders and far–away provinces virtually from the onset of their service. Francis, in his eagerness to hasten the process of integration, created a prematurely tense atmosphere; more important, his apparent distrust of the Italians, before they had had the opportunity to prove or disprove their loyalty, laid the groundwork for greater problems in the long run.

In the fall of 1814 the emperor's impatience with Sommariva's project led them to order the activation of all of the new units regardless of whether they had reached their authorized strength. The four light battalions were the first to take up garrison duty, their ranks filled out at the eleventh hour by manpower from the Italian *Freikorps*, which disbanded in October. In November, Francis dispatched the four infantry regiments and the new cavalry regiment to their new stations outside of Italy.[9] As a further sign of their integration, each infantry unit received a number in the regular order of the Habsburg line, assuming those conveniently left vacant by an earlier reduction of the number of regiments following the defeat of 1809. The First Austro–Italian regiment became the 13th Infantry, with garrison duty at Brünn (Brno) in Moravia; the Second became the 23rd, assigned to Prague; the Third became the 38th, garrisoned at Graz in Styria; and the Fourth became the 43rd, stationed at Ofen (Buda) in Hungary.[10] In recognition of their common identity, however, the army dressed all of the troops in what were to become the traditional colors of Austrian-Italian infantry: red trim and facings on the white Habsburg coat. In future years, only the Italians (and a handful of non-Italian regiments, whose uniforms had been trimmed in red since the days of Maria Theresa) would wear these colors. Gestures of this sort, relatively meaningless to the modern observer, mattered as much in the Habsburg army as in other European armies of the era.

On the order of gestures, the Italian grenadier battalion (consisting of two companies from each of the four regiments) went to the imperial capital for its first posting. While their comrades in the line infantry marched to their new northern stations in the dead of winter, the grenadiers received a warm and ceremonious welcome in Vienna. In January 1815, Prince Alois Leichtenstein presided over a fête attended by a number of aristocrats and other representatives from Lombardy and Venetia. Those present included the generals Count Achille Fontanelli and Count Luigi Mazzucchelli, two of the highest-ranking officers of the Napoleonic Italian army to be granted Habsburg commissions.[11] The honeymoon ended soon enough, however, and the grenadiers went on their way to less glamorous quarters in Pest.

Within weeks, Napoleon's escape from Elba gave Francis another opportunity to express his distrust of the new Italian troops. The return to a war footing meant that the Italian units, like the rest of the army, had to be reinforced with men from their home recruiting districts, a process complicated by the great distance between their current stations and northern Italy. Fearful that deserting Italians would form a dangerous sort of "Fifth Column" behind Austrian lines, the emperor ordered that reinforcements should leave Lombardy and Venetia in groups no larger than 200 men and only under the command of German officers. The only Italians to see action with the Habsburg armies were from the Italian minority in the southern Tyrol serving in the German dominated Tyrolese Jäger Corps, later renamed the Kaiser-Jäger Regiment. After deciding initially not to send his new Italian regiments to the front, Francis belatedly experienced a change of heart. In mid-July 1815, four weeks after

Napoleon's defeat at Waterloo, the Hofkriegsrat decreed that "in order to give the Italian troops a renewed indication of His Majesty's trust," contingents from each of the units would be sent to France to participate in the campaign.[12] The order came so late, however, that only the cavalry regiment—recently designated the Seventh Chevaux-Legers—was en route to the front when a general order came for all troops not already in France to return to their peacetime garrisons.[13]

The Hundred Days sparked a great paranoia over the loyalty of Italian officers that permanently poisoned the atmosphere for their transition to Habsburg service. Those already admitted to the corps came under suspicion, and the veterans of Eugene's army who had declined Austrian commissions found themselves on even shakier ground. After Napoleon's return from Elba, the Hofkriegsrat gave all officers in the latter category a deadline of 1 April 1815 to swear an oath of loyalty to the emperor. Hundreds complied, thus placing themselves under the jurisdiction of Austrian military law regardless of whether they actually accepted commissions. All officers suspected of having sympathies with France or with Joachim Murat's Neapolitan regime ultimately were arrested and called before a courtmartial in Mantua. In November several were sentenced to death or hard labor for alleged revolutionary activity. A year later, Francis commuted all of the death sentences and pardoned many of the other prisoners but left a total of twelve former Napoleonic officers to serve out terms at hard labor.[14]

Although the proceedings involved few of the officers taken into Habsburg service in the summer of 1814, the outcome no doubt discouraged those hoping to be accepted on equal terms by their new government.[15] Austrian suspicions were based entirely upon their nationality and past Napoleonic service, two facts that none of them could do anything to change. The social background of the infantry officers provided additional grounds for criticism, as Austrian commanders noted with dismay that most of the subalterns taken in from Eugene's Italian army came from among "the lower classes of the people." By Habsburg aristocratic standards they were not particularly well–educated; to make matters worse, they were slow to learn German and in spite of all that had happened, many remained sympathetic toward Napoleonic ideals. Not surprisingly, the burdens of pursuing a military career under such circumstances were more than many of the officers could bear, and a significant number resigned their commissions after only a few years (or in some cases months) of service. This, of course, only meant that more non-Italians had to be brought in to fill the resulting vacancies in the leadership of Italian regiments.[16]

The Italian non-commissioned officers, while not politically suspect, also became targets of criticism soon after their entry into Habsburg service. Their problem was simpler but from a practical standpoint, more serious: the Italian sergeants proved to be even less adept at learning German than their superiors. Given the fact that good NCOs historically have provided the backbone for every successful military force, the failure of so many of them to learn the Habsburg language of command created a dangerous missing link in the cohesion of the new units. In the summer of 1815 the Hofkriegsrat attempted to remedy the problem by transferring German-speaking NCOs with a strong "textbook" knowledge of their language to the Italian regiments, to assist their Italian counterparts in learning German.[17] But once the precedent was set for supplying the Italian regiments with non-Italian NCOs, it proved far easier to teach these men Italian than to teach the Italian NCOs German. Though Italians still accounted for the majority of the sergeants, this practice brought many Italian soldiers into contact with a "foreign" commander at an even more intimate level than before.

None of the new Italian units participated in the occupation of France (1815–18) and because all were stationed so far from home, none saw action against Murat's Neapolitans in the abbreviated Italian campaign of 1815. The return to peace gave the Austrians the opportunity to establish their military infrastructure in Lombardy and Venetia. Army officials set up recruiting depots and converted the Napoleonic Italian army's orphanage in Milan (the *Istituto degli Orfani militari*) into a common *Erziehungshaus* for all of the Italian units.[18] Meanwhile, the continuing process of integration brought the gradual introduction of the Austrian articles of war, starting with an imperial decree of December 1815 which introduced corporal punishment in the Italian regiments. Henceforth, those guilty of indiscipline were subjected to the traditional running of the gauntlet or to the *Stockstreichstrafe*, lashes with a wooden cane. Six months later, the old Italian military law was abolished altogether.[19]

While the infantry regiments experienced their share of problems, the Italian cavalry quickly became a model regiment. The cavalry officers taken in from the Italian army were aristocratic enough to satisfy the most snobbish of Austrian commanders, and the combination of seven old Italian mounted regiments into a single Austrian one left the Seventh Chevaux-Legers with more than enough manpower. Count Bartolomeo Alberti de Poya, a Habsburg veteran of a Galician Uhlan (lancer) regiment, commanded the cavalry from the summer of 1814 and fashioned an esprit de corps that stood in sharp contrast to the morale of the Italian infantry. Yet even Alberti's unit was not immune from the general discouragement that led a number of Italian officers to resign shortly after obtaining their Habsburg commissions. By the end of 1817 early retirements, combined with a number of transfers to non-Italian mounted units, left the Italian cavalry regiment with only half of its original officers.[20]

Despite the early difficulties, the Hofkriegsrat soon laid plans for the creation of still more Italian infantry regiments. In August 1816 the four light battalions raised in 1814 were combined to form the 45th Infantry, garrisoned at Padua. Three non-Italian regiments— the 16th (Styrian), the 26th (Carinthian), and the 44th (Galician since 1807, after being Italian from 1744 to 1806)—subsequently were transferred to northern Italy and assigned new recruiting districts in Lombardy and Venetia.[21] Once the conversion of the latter three units began (in 1817), the Habsburg army had eight Italian infantry regiments (out of a total of fifty-eight), which supported three of the army's twenty grenadier battalions. A garrison battalion was raised at Peschiera in 1816, but no artillerymen were recruited in Lombardy or Venetia (or ever would be) and for the present, no Jäger battalions were formed in the Italian provinces. By 1818 the eight regiments had been assigned to permanent recruiting districts, four in Venetia and four in Lombardy. The Venetian units were the 13th (recruiting center: Padua), the 16th (Treviso), the 26th (Udine), and the 45th (Verona), while the Lombard regiments were the 23rd (Lodi), the 38th (Brescia), the 43rd (Como), and the 44th (Milan). The Seventh Chevaux-Legers remained the only Italian cavalry regiment, drawing the bulk of their recruits from Lombardy and a smaller number from Venetia.

In September 1817, with the occupation of France and Naples winding down, the Austrian army moved closer to a peacetime footing. Regiments already stationed in their home districts remained there, while in the rest of the army the third battalion of each infantry regiment returned home. These orders, which left only the first and second ("field") battalions of the latter regiments on an active footing, applied to all but the Italian units. The emperor still wanted to have as few Italians as possible stationed in Lombardy and Venetia, and allowed the original four Italian regiments to maintain only a nominal force of two companies apiece in their designated recruiting headquarters.[22] As for the four newer Italian regiments garrisoned in northern Italy, only the 45th was as yet truly "Italian"; the Germans and Slovenes of the 16th and 26th and the Poles of the 44th would be replaced only gradually by new Italian recruits. While these three transplanted units were still undergoing this transition, the army hierarchy commonly referred to them as the "half-Italian" regiments.[23]

In contrast to the speed with which the Austrian army created the new Italian regiments, Vienna after 1814 moved slowly and indecisively in determining the political future of Lombardy and Venetia. The viceroy Archduke Rainer, a younger brother of Francis, did not arrive in northern Italy until January 1818, and in the interim Milan and other cities became hotbeds of speculation and discontent over the postwar order. In this atmosphere Austria hesitated to promulgate new conscription laws for the provinces, and the matter did not come to a head until the four-year enlistments of 1814 and 1815 were due to expire. A recruiting law, not officially embodied in an imperial patent until October 1820, went into effect in the spring of 1819.

The new code reaffirmed the division of Lombardy and Venetia into eight recruiting districts, one for each of the infantry regiments. Service was extended to eight years, with all men aged twenty to twenty-seven liable for conscription. Provisions for exemptions and the hiring of substitutes were similar to those in effect for the hereditary Austrian provinces, with one important exception: the nobility of Lombardy and Venetia, unlike their counterparts throughout the rest of the empire, were not automatically exempt from service. Young noblemen fell under the same obligations as the common man, with the lone provision that, if conscripted, they could enter the service as regimental cadets.[24]

The eight-year obligation, though double the previous requirement, was still far more lenient than the terms of service in effect in the rest of the empire. In the Austrian provinces fourteen years remained the rule, followed by the additional liability, until the age of forty or forty-five, of service in a Landwehr battalion. Hungary still had conscription for life, with assignment to a reserve battalion coming only after a soldier became too old or infirm to serve in the line. But since the Hofkriegsrat determined that the Italian regiments should have only the three regular battalions with no Landwehr or reserve, the conscripts of Lombardy and Venetia were under no further obligation once their eight years ended.

The liberal aristocracy of Lombardy and the educated elite of Milan hastened to condemn the new law, unimpressed that it was, at least by Habsburg standards, quite lenient. Although none of the criticism was blatantly self-serving, the rules regarding exemptions—including the service liability for sons of the nobility—became their principal target. Count Ferdinand Bubna, the Austrian commander in Lombardy, reported to Metternich that the conscription law had had an immediate bad effect on "public" opinion, strengthening the hand of opponents of Habsburg rule.[25] But Metternich, writing on the eve of the adoption of the Carlsbad Decrees, compared the unrest in northern Italy to the situation he faced in the German Confederation. In his reply to Bubna he urged a similar hard line against all liberal agitation in Lombardy and Venetia.[26] Austria would proceed to raise troops under the terms of the new law, letting the chips fall where they may.

Given the long history of resistance to conscription in Italy, which had plagued native Italian rulers and even the Napoleonic armies, Bubna had good reason to expect trouble. Yet by late summer he was able to report to Metternich that the initial levy had been a surprising success. "In spite of public opinion [in Milan], the conscription has proceeded in a quiet and orderly manner, and with such a good will among the people . . . ." He admitted that he was "more than a little amazed by the cheerfulness and high spirits of the recruits," especially those being marched off to "the interior of the monarchy," among whom "almost no desertions have occurred." Bubna noted that such loyal compliance "is completely unknown in the history of Italian recruiting under any government, including the [Napoleonic] kingdom of Italy." He concluded that "the mass of the people from which the recruits are drawn . . . are not so unfavorably disposed toward His Majesty's service as the leaders of the liberal faction expected, and wanted to make us believe."[27]

Economic conditions no doubt were a leading factor in the early success of conscription. Throughout northern Italy, and especially in Venetia, a postwar depression created great hardship which, while not making the army life appear attractive, must have made it easier for many conscripts to acquiesce in their fate. Austrian officials may have been surprised at the great inaccuracy of the liberal party's predictions, but this was only another manifestation of the traditional division between urban and rural Italy and of the gulf between the peasantry and the higher classes, factors which plagued the efforts of Italian nationalists throughout the Risorgimento. In rural areas, lack of education and a strong attachment to the simple farm life further immunized the agricultural lower class from the anti-Austrian arguments of the urban liberals. As one historian has noted in describing the peasants on the plain of Lombardy, "the majority seem to have lived in a bovine stupor."[28] Such a state of social and political consciousness could only work to Austria's favor. Bubna, an astute observer who always kept one eye on the future, made a number of suggestions to Metternich in the wake of the successful levy but proposed nothing that would take advantage of these social divisions. It took another three decades, and a great revolutionary upheaval, to inspire Field Marshal Radetzky to advocate a course as radical as that.[29]

A descendant of the ancient Czech nobility, Bubna concerned himself most with reconciling the Italian aristocracy to the idea of Habsburg service. He called for an increase in the number of scholarships (*Stiftplätze*) allotted to Lombardy and Venetia at the Wiener Neustadt Military Academy, where the 107 reserved for the rest of the non-Hungarian provinces and 304 for the sons of officers dwarfed the twenty set aside for Italian boys. Recognizing that "the aversion of the Italians toward the idea of a German education is still much too great," Bubna contended that the establishment of another Austrian military academy in Italy "would not be superfluous." For the time being, he suggested reforms for the *Erziehungshaus* in Milan that would enable the regimental school to attract children from the "educated classes" of Italian society. As for the general role of Italians in the armed forces of the monarchy, he observed that Austria had five million Italian subjects, a number "too great for it to be permissible . . . to allow them the passivity to which they are inclined."[30] For the good of the empire Austria had to treat them like any other nationality, and this included using them within the military, irrespective of whether they would make good soldiers.

In contrast to the success of the first conscription, a campaign to reenlist Italians already in the ranks failed miserably. Throughout the infantry regiments, soldiers and NCOs serving under the provisional four-year obligation abandoned the army in droves after completing their term, leaving behind few veterans to balance the influx of raw recruits.[31] Affected as well by the fact that so many of their officers were either transferred to non–Italian units or had chosen early retirement, the regiments created from the remnants of Eugene's Italian army (the 13th, 23rd, 38th, 43rd, and 45th) quickly lost what was left of their Napoleonic roots. As in so many other respects, the cavalry regiment did not conform to the rule. In the Seventh Chevaux–Legers, the popular Colonel Alberti managed to get half of his men to reenlist, a feat that won him the praise of the Hofkriegsrat.[32]

In the wake of the Neapolitan revolution of 1820, Austria's decision to overthrow the liberal regime in Naples raised the question of the role the Italian units would have in the operation. Unlike in 1815, when the resumption of hostilities against Napoleon and Murat found all of the new regiments stationed far from the theaters of war, the onset of unrest in Naples came with four of the eight infantry regiments headquartered in their home districts: the 45th (formed from the merger of the light battalions) in Verona and the three "half–Italian" units—the 16th, 26th, and 44th—in Treviso, Udine, and Milan, respectively. Ever thinking in terms of the long range consequences, Count Bubna advised Metternich that the Italian troops should be given active and visible roles in the campaign. If Austria were to maintain her position in Italy under any circumstances, he concluded, sooner or later her Italian troops would end up having to fight other Italians. Bubna believed that the traditional particularism and regional animosities in Italy would keep most northern Italians from sympathizing with the Neopolitans, and he saw no risk in sending Austria's Italian regiments southward in the upcoming operation.[33]

The count's suggestions were far from bold, calling for a token force of two Italian units (the 45th and one of the four then stationed outside of Lombardy–Venetia) to participate in the invasion of Naples. "A clever division" of the troops would serve to contain them if any problems occurred, but Bubna did not consider this a possibility, especially "because the officers are mostly German." Meanwhile, the "half–Italian" regiments would be used to help keep order in northern Italy. The use of the Italians would be a valuable demonstration of trust, and Austria certainly had little to lose by giving it a try.[34]

Bubna did not have the first word on the matter, however, nor was he to be the man in charge of the campaign. Count Johann Frimont, his counterpart as commander of the army in Venetia, received command of the invading forces. A Lorrainer by birth, Frimont's career as an officer in the Hungarian hussars had left him somewhat magyarized;[35] in any event, he had no special sympathy toward the Italians in Habsburg service and did not heed Bubna's advice regarding their use. The proposals also fell on deaf ears in Vienna, where the imperial leadership had yet to recover from recent revelations that during the Austrian army's occupation of Naples following the fall of Murat, Neapolitan Carbonari had attempted to win converts even among its non-Italian officers.[36] When Frimont crossed the Po in February 1821, there were no Italian units among his fifty-two battalions of infantry and forty squadrons of cavalry.[37]

Just as it appeared that no Italians would see action in 1821, Piedmont succumbed to revolution and the Austrian army had to undertake a second campaign of intervention. With Frimont still in the field against the Neapolitans, Bubna received command of the operation against the Piedmontese rebels. Short of troops to begin with, the count had a good excuse to include in his invasion force the "half-Italian" 44th Infantry, the only Italian regiment under his jurisdiction. The third battalion of the 44th entered Piedmont on 10 April 1821, the second day of the campaign, and by early May the remaining two battalions had followed. The revolution was crushed before any of the troops came under fire, and the regiment ended up as part of the Austrian occupation of the Piedmontese fortress of Alessandria. The 44th returned to Lombardy in 1822, but parts of two of its battalions went back to Alessandria during the first three months of 1823 for further occupation duty.[38]

While there was nothing heroic or glamorous about the service of the 44th Infantry during or after 1821, at least the regiment was more active than the other Lombard and Venetian formations. Frimont's "half-Italian" regiments, the 16th and 26th, remained in their Venetian garrisons throughout the invasion and occupation of Naples, while his 45th Infantry—all Italians—went to a new station in Hungary in October 1821.[39] Meanwhile, the Italian units already posted outside of Lombardy and Venetia remained far from any action. When the 13th Infantry returned to Venetia at the end of 1822, it marked the first time since late 1814 that any of the original four regiments had set foot in northern Italy.

At that, the reassignment of the 13th came under special circumstances. While stationed in Carinthia earlier in 1822, an eye disease of unknown cause hit the regiment and soon reached epidemic proportions. After a number of soldiers were blinded or left unfit for service, the Hofkriegsrat ordered the unit home to Venetia to convalesce and replenish its ranks with fresh recruits. After three years of Venetian garrison duty, the 13th went on to Olmütz in Moravia; their reassignment was somewhat premature, for the problem of eye disease lingered until 1829.[40] This and other similar cases naturally received their share of local publicity at home, with the result that the fear of contracting illness while on some far-away post eventually became a leading motive for resistance to conscription in Lombardy and Venetia, or of desertion from an Italian regiment slated for reassignment to a distant province. Indeed, on the eve of the revolutions of 1848, Italian agitators urging their countrymen to desert would play upon the fear of disease when appeals to nationalism did no good. On such occasions, the military authorities had to reassure the men that "there was no question of them being sent to an unhealthy area in Hungary or some other fortress."[41]

The hasty arrival and departure of the 13th Infantry left intact the Austrian policy of stationing as few Italian regiments as possible in Lombardy and Venetia. After the 44th Infantry completed its garrison duty in Piedmont and relocated to Prague, only two regiments, the 16th and 26th, were still stationed in their home districts.[42] An imperial order of 17 July 1825 amended the policy somewhat by finally sending home the third battalion of each of the Italian regiments, eight years after the same had been done for the rest of the army. This guaranteed that regardless of where the regiments went for garrison duty, at least eight of the total twenty-four battalions of Italian regular infantry would always be in Lombardy and Venetia.[43] The order left the regiments stationed outside of northern Italy with just their two field battalions (around 2,500 men per regiment), while the third battalions, once at home, were allowed to fall well below the paper strength of 750 men apiece. Those serving in the latter were often furloughed when no longer needed, to remain "on call" as reserves until their eight year obligation expired. Since the Italian regiments had no Landwehr, these soldiers on furlough were the closest thing they had to a reserve force.[44]

During the 1820s Austria continued to increase the number of Italians and Italian units in her army. In 1823 the 11th (Inner Austrian) and 12th (Galician) Field-Jäger battalions were ordered to draw future recruits from among the districts of Lombardy and Venetia, although neither was transferred to northern Italy in the wake of its conversion.[45] Prior to these changes, the only Italians serving as Jägers were those from the Alpine regions of the southern Tyrol, distributed among the various battalions of the predominantly German Tyrolese Kaiser–Jäger Regiment.[46] Meanwhile, the 22nd Infantry, converted from a Moravian to an "Illyrian" regiment in 1817, became heavily Italian after 1824 when its recruiting district was changed from Istria, Karlovac (in Croatia), and the environs of Trieste and Fiume (Rijeka)—two cities traditionally exempt from conscription—to the province of Trieste, Istria, and the area around Gorizia. Thus a regiment that had been predominantly Slavic (Slovene and Croatian) with an Italian minority became predominantly Italian with a Slovene minority. But because the 22nd was from outside of Lombardy–Venetia, the Austrians never considered it "Italian." It recruited under the same rules as the German Austrian regiments, had a Landwehr battalion, and formed a common grenadier battalion with two German–Slovene regiments from Inner Austria. The army also did not treat the 22nd with the suspicion characteristic of the common attitude toward the Lombard and Venetian units. From 1823 to 1848 it was stationed either in Trieste or elsewhere in Italy. The regiment vindicated this trust in 1831, during the revolutions of 1848, and in subsequent Italian campaigns.[47]

In the late 1820s the three "half–Italian" units discharged the last of their non–Italian personnel and the Italian identity of all eight Lombard and Venetian regiments became firmly established. At the same time, the common *Erziehungshaus* in Milan proved unable to keep up with the influx of soldiers' children from all eight regiments. In 1829 it was finally closed and the burden divided between a pair of new regimental schools, in Bergamo for Lombardy and in Cividale for Venetia. The new institutions remained in operation until 1852, when the Habsburg army abandoned the system of *Erziehungshäuser*.[48]

In March 1830, just months before a wave of revolution was to sweep across Europe, Francis shook the army from its peacetime slumber by transferring most of the units to new garrisons. Of the six Lombard and Venetian infantry regiments stationed away from home, only the 38th, at Graz since the end of 1814, came back to northern Italy. In 1831, when Count Frimont's army intervened against revolutions in Parma, Modena and the Romagna, its two field battalions participated in the campaign.

These central Italian revolutions took on a greater significance for Austria after General Carlo Zucchi, a former Napoleonic Italian and Habsburg officer, took command of the rebel army. Zucchi had been detained briefly by the Austrians after the end of the war in

1814, then, much to his own surprise, was offered a commission as Feldmarschalleutnant. He accepted and served briefly at three different posts in Bohemia before retiring voluntarily, bitter over the "system of distrust" of Italians that had become the Austrian policy. In the aftermath of the Carbonari hysteria surrounding the Italian revolutions of 1820, the Austrians in 1823 arrested Zucchi on suspicion of revolutionary sympathies and held him for three years.[49] His reappearance at the head of the revolt came as no great surprise to the Habsburg government, but it caused the military leadership to be far more uneasy about the entire campaign.

Frimont, the commander in both Lombardy and Venetia since Bubna's death in 1825, led those expressing pessimism about the prospects for a successful intervention; he also feared rebellion behind the lines in northern Italy. "We do not find ourselves in the situation of 1821," he wrote to Metternich, "[when] the poison of rebellion was not stirring in all hearts, [and] the peace of *our* Italy [Lombardy and Venetia] was for the moment secured . . . ."[50] The campaign, as it turned out, was a cakewalk for the Austrians, ending in the capture of Zucchi by, of all forces, the Habsburg navy. During the campaign the two battalions of the 38th Infantry dispersed some rebels at Rimini, then served on garrison duty in Ancona, but returned to Habsburg territory along with the rest of the army within a matter of months. After Frimont died late in 1831, his successor, Field Marshall Count Joseph Radetzky, crushed a second rebellion in the Romagna early in 1832. The only Italian unit in Radetzky's army was the first battalion of the 22nd (Trieste) Infantry, which occupied Bologna once the rebels were defeated.[51]

After a brief posting to Lombardy in 1833, this same battalion went to Parma in March 1834 to begin a six and a half year stint as a substitute for the tiny Parmesan army, which had collapsed in the revolution of 1831. The 1,200 men of the battalion carried out this unusual assignment at a cost to the Parmesan government of 10,000 gulden per year.[52] Meanwhile, an Austrian military mission oversaw the creation of a new Parmesan army, an operation set in motion by Frimont before his death. Because of the old Lorrainer's attitude toward Italians, officers from Lombardy and Venetia were not allowed to participate in the project. As he noted to Metternich, the instructors of the mission "naturally cannot be Italians, but must be chosen from the German or Hungarian regiments and yet be so fully fluent in the Italian language that their service can be pursued with complete success."[53] His successor, Radetzky, held a more enlightened view of the Italians. He would need it, too, for in the years to come the army in northern Italy was to contain an ever larger percentage of Italian troops.

The "italianization" of the Austrian army in Lombardy and Venetia came as a result of trends that began in March 1835, shortly after the death of Emperor Francis and the accession to the throne of his handicapped son Ferdinand, which brought to power the triumvirate of Metternich, his nemesis Count Franz Kolowrat, and the Archduke Ludwig as a governing council of regency. The overall strength of Habsburg forces in Italy reached a post-Napoleonic peak of 104,500 men in 1831, during the general European war scare sparked by the July Revolution of 1830 in France.[54] It declined considerably following the central Italian campaign of 1832, but immediately after Francis's death Radetzky still could report a strength of over 75,000 men, serving in sixty-three battalions of infantry and thirty-six squadrons of cavalry.[55]

When asked for this information, Radetzky took the opportunity to request an increase in the size of his forces; little did he know that the new regime in Vienna had the opposite in mind. Austria's active post-Napoleonic foreign policy had required a high level of peacetime military spending that helped push the state debt from just over 800 million gulden in 1815 to almost one billion at the end of 1834. Nevertheless, as long as Francis lived there could be no question of a significant reduction in the military budget. Once the regency took over, however, Kolowrat and the proponents of economy overrode the objections of Metternich, who advocated a strong army and continued active foreign policy. The military budget, 64.5 million gulden for 1835, fell to 62 million the following year. During the course of 1836 further economies brought the army and navy in well under their budget, at 55.1 million. The allocation for 1837 was only 50 million and although the armed forces overran their budget every year during the decade that followed, the annual level of spending remained below 60 million until 1848.[56]

The reductions were made by cutting the size of the field army and garrisoning more regiments in their home districts, where a greater number of the men could be furloughed without pay. For Radetzky's army the new policies had dramatic consequences. By the spring of 1837 he had only forty-four battalions of infantry and twenty-two squadrons of cavalry, around 45,000 men in all. None of the five Italian regiments still headquartered outside of Lombardy and Venetia was called home, and there were no Italians among the more than 30,000 troops he had lost. In 1835 Italians accounted for around 30 percent of Radetzky's infantry: eighteen battalions from Lombardy and Venetia and one from Trieste (the battalion in Parma) out of the total of sixty-three. Two years later he still had these same nineteen battalions, but they accounted for almost 45 percent of his new total of forty-four battalions of infantry. Even though none of his cavalry was Italian and hundreds of men from the Lombard and Venetian infantry were sent home on furlough, the field marshal nevertheless found himself in command of an army in which the Italians were by far the largest nationality.[57]

Unlike so many other Habsburg commanders, Radetzky had no prejudices against Italian troops. He thought they made good soldiers and was fond of pointing out that they had fought and died for Napoleon all the way to Moscow.[58] Though he was upset about the overall reductions, the proportion of Italians in his ranks initially did not concern him. Perhaps it should have, for in the early 1830s there were already indications that the conscripts from Lombardy and Venetia were not as immune to nationalism as they had been earlier. In 1831, during Frimont's intervention against the central Italian revolution, unrest in the 13th (Venetian) Infantry resulted in disciplinary action against several "malcontents." Since the incident occurred in the regiment's field battalions stationed at Graz, it had no effect on the campaign and was contained with little difficulty.[59] Two years later the imperial police in Milan uncovered a small sect of followers of Giuseppe Mazzini's Young Italy movement among the grenadier companies of the 43rd (Lombard) Infantry. This problem was likewise contained and eliminated, but the news prompted a former governor of Lombardy, Count Franz Hartig, to warn Metternich that "the Lombard soldier is exposed to a greater danger in Italy than elsewhere because the propagandists do not hesitate to try to subvert the soldier and the NCO, and the latter do not always know how to resist these subversions."

Even though "the conduct of the Lombard troops up till now can in no way be reproached," Hartig thought it necessary "to reduce the element of danger by having the Italian garrisons changed as often as possible and assigning them only to towns where troops from other provinces are in greater numbers than them."[60] After Francis's death, however, financial considerations carried more weight than such appeals for prudence.

Along with its more dramatic effects, the tighter military budget meant that the Italian regiments stationed outside of Lombardy and Venetia were less likely to be sent to posts in Bohemia or Hungary, where the greater distances had always made the transporting of new recruits from home an expensive undertaking. Croatia and the coastal cities of the eastern Adriatic littoral subsequently became more common stations for Italian troops. Thus the field battalions of the 43rd (Lombard) and 45th (Venetian) Infantry were reassigned from Pest and Pressburg to Zara (Zadar) and Fiume, respectively, and it became customary for an Italian regiment stationed in Venetia to send a battalion to garrison Cattaro (Kotor) at the southern tip of Dalmatia. The new posts, though geographically closer to home, were not popular with the soldiers. Because transport by sea was considered too expensive,[61] the units had to march to Dalmatia or the Croatian littoral from northern Italy, through rough terrain and on notoriously bad roads. In the case of the Cattaro posting, the distance covered almost equalled that of a march to Galicia. Italians stationed in Croatia did not get along well with the civilian population there and came to be despised as much as troops from the Croatian Military Border were in Italy; this mutual antagonism was to have important consequences in 1848, when Italian and Croatian leaders were unable to make common cause against the imperial government.[62] The recurring fear of disease, however, proved to be the greatest reason for Italians to dread assignment to Croatia. The 43rd succumbed to cholera while in Fiume in 1836, and in 1838 the 26th (Venetian) Infantry, which had been in its home district since 1817, was decimated by malaria shortly after being assigned to Zagreb. In both cases the army leadership took pity on the plight of the men and quickly reassigned the units. The 43rd, on the road since 1814, finally came home to northern Italy and the 26th went to Graz, always a congenial station for Italian troops.[63]

In addition to the reassignment of some entire regiments, the reductions in the military budget resulted in hundreds of men being sent home on furlough from every Lombard and Venetian unit. The government's determination to keep as few men as possible under arms subsequently eased the need for new levies and kept conscription from becoming an issue for the liberal nationalists to use against the Austrians. As the decade of the 1840s began, discontent in the ranks remained low and desertions became a serious problem only when units were transferred after an extended stay at one post.[64] Meanwhile, in a final attempt to win over the upper class of Lombardy and Venetia, the imperial court in Vienna created a Lombardo–Venetian *Leibgarde* to accompany two existing ceremonial regiments from German Austria and Hungary. The gesture came far too late to make any difference, however, and service in the guards never became popular with the aristocracy. After the upheaval of 1848, the unit was disbanded.[65]

Throughout the early 1840s, Radetzky's army continued to shrink while the number of Italian units within it grew to an unprecedented level. The field marshal started the decade with forty battalions of infantry (nineteen of them Italian) and twenty-two squadrons of cavalry; in 1844 his infantry reached a low of thirty-nine battalions, of which over half (twenty-one) were Italian.[66] The further influx of Italians came when the field battalions of a fourth infantry regiment were called home in 1843, in yet another austerity measure. By the following year fifteen of the twenty-four battalions of regular Lombard and Venetian infantry were stationed in northern Italy, as were both Jäger battalions, both garrison battalions, and two of the three battalions of grenadiers. The overall reduction in strength left Radetzky with only 38,500 men in 1844, 5,500 of whom were on furlough. He bemoaned the army's weakness and informed Vienna that in its present condition it would be unable to deal with any emergency. In reciting his woes, however, he made no mention of the great number of Italians under his command. He simply wanted more troops and at this stage of the game, he did not care about their nationality.[67]

Conditions in Italy changed rather abruptly in the summer of 1846, when the election of Pope Pius IX touched off a wave of nationalism that swept the peninsula. By then Radetzky had received two battalions of reinforcements but still could count on only 34,000 front line troops, even though on paper his forces numbered 49,000.[68] Expecting no further help from Vienna, he resolved to put the forces he had on a stronger footing by recalling furloughed soldiers and conscripting new ones. This time the levies were far from successful and, indeed, did more harm than good to the Austrian cause in Lombardy and Venetia. Conscripts from rural areas, when assembled for induction in various towns and cities, were berated and insulted by the townspeople and encouraged to desert. In case the recruits did not know that they had a national identity, the hecklers made them aware of it, and in no uncertain terms.[69] For the conscript from an urban or developed area of northern Italy, the economics of an industrializing society provided an additional motive to avoid the service. By 1845 an adult male spinning cotton in the Lombard textile industry earned at least four times the soldier's daily wage of five kreutzer and in some places could make as much in one day as a soldier received in two weeks.[70]

Conditions indeed were a far cry from the immediate post-Napoleonic years, when the impoverished, undereducated masses confounded the liberal elite by complying with the first Habsburg conscription, in the process showing no inkling of a national consciousness. Radetzky did not help matters when, in July 1847, he sent troops into the Romagna to occupy the Papal fortress of Ferrara. The action was perfectly legal under the terms of the Treaty of Vienna of 1815, which reserved for Austria the right to garrison Ferrara, but was criticized both within Italy and abroad as a needless provocation. Pius IX and King Charles Albert of Sardinia-Piedmont denounced the occupation in the strongest terms, while Britain and France protested to Vienna. Liberals and nationalists in Lombardy and Venetia echoed the criticism, and during the second week of September demonstrators took to the streets of Milan. Tensions reached a peak after a Milanese attempt to boycott the state-controlled tobacco industry led to the bloody Tobacco Riots of 2-3 January 1848.[71]

As the political situation in northern Italy began to deteriorate, Radetzky finally started to receive the reinforcements he had wanted for so long. After an imperial resolution of 9 October 1847 authorized the buildup,[72] troops from the neighboring provinces were ordered to new stations in Lombardy and Venetia. At the end of November 1847 the Habsburg army in Italy consisted of forty-three battalions of infantry and thirty squadrons of cavalry, a net increase of two battalions and eight squadrons over the beginning of the year. By January another eleven battalions and six squadrons had arrived, among them three battalions of Croatian *Grenzer* from the Military Border. Seven more battalions of Croats and another six squadrons of cavalry followed during February and March. By the time news of the Viennese revolution of 13 March reached Milan and Venice, touching off spontaneous demonstrations in both cities, the army consisted of sixty-one battalions of infantry and forty-two squadrons of cavalry, around 75,000 men in all.[73]

When the revolution came to Lombardy and Venetia, Radetzky still had the same twenty-one battalions of Italian infantry that he had had since 1843, but the addition of twenty-two battalions of non-Italian infantry, not to mention the cavalry (none of which was Italian), diluted their relative strength from roughly half of the army in 1844 to one-third in March of 1848. Throughout the rise in tensions Radetzky never requested the transfer of any of these troops to other provinces; he regarded their presence as the lesser of two evils, since sending them away would mean that the reinforcements would merely take their place, leaving the army still woefully under strength. In December 1847 Feldmarschalleutnant Count Laval Nugent, head of the adjacent *Generalkommando* of Graz, proposed to Vienna that the third battalion of the 13th (Venetian) Infantry, which made up part of the garrison at Venice, join the other two battalions of the regiment at their current station in Styria. He also called for a fourth battalion to be raised from among the furloughed men of the 13th and for it to leave Venetia as well, with the transferred men being replaced by the field battalions of a German Austrian regiment. The move never took place and its cancellation was to have dire consequences once the revolution broke out in Venice.[74]

The presence of some 25,000 Lombards and Venetians in the midst of an army of 75,000 attempting to restrain the forces of Italian nationalism naturally concerned Radetzky, but he chose to adopt an attitude of guarded confidence toward his Italian soldiers. "I do not mistrust these troops in the least," he informed the Hofkriegsrat late in 1847; "they will do their duty. But we must not expect more of them than is reasonable, particularly when they are being led into battle against their own compatriots." In February 1848, boldly hoping for the best, he boasted that "the Italian troops daily give me unambiguous proof of the best and most praiseworthy spirit. . . ."[75] His true feelings no doubt lay somewhere in between.

When the time of reckoning arrived, during the last two weeks of March 1848, nine battalions of Italian troops deserted en masse from Radetzky's ranks, followed by parts of three others.[76] The defections crippled his army and nearly cost Austria both Lombardy and Venetia. But the campaign of 1848 was to be only the first of four fought by the Habsburg Empire in northern Italy over a span of less than two decades; if Italian units could not be counted upon to fight there, their utility to the army certainly would be limited. Why did some regiments desert while others remained loyal, and what were to be the consequences for future Italians serving under Habsburg colors? After thirty-five years of peace, during which the reliability of the

Italian troops had remained open to debate, the questions were to be answered in a new era of war.

Chapter 3

DISCIPLINE AND IGNORANCE

The March 1848 revolutions in Milan and Venice all but shook northern Italy free from Austrian domination. In the wake of the uprisings Radetzky retreated from Lombardy with his loyal troops to the sanctuary of the Quadrilateral fortresses, setting up headquarters in Verona. Sardinian troops marched through Lombardy and crossed the Mincio into western Venetia, halting only after Radetzky, in dire straits, defeated them on 6 May at Santa Lucia. Reinforced from the adjoining provinces of the empire, the field marshal then went on the offensive and on 25 July defeated the Sardinians at Custoza in the decisive battle of the campaign. Charles Albert quickly sued for peace and the Austrians reentered Milan on 6 August.

After the Sardinian withdrawal all of Lombardy and Venetia, except for the island city of Venice, returned to Austrian control. Radetzky proclaimed a general amnesty and brought his Italian regiments back up to full strength, mostly through accepting the pardoned deserters back into their old units. Meanwhile, in September 1848 the Hungarian revolution escalated into open Austro–Hungarian warfare, and in March 1849 a further eruption in this conflict inspired Charles Albert to attempt a second campaign against the Austrians. By then, Radetzky's forces were so strong that he was able to dispose of the Sardinians in a matter of days. After the decisive battle of Novara (23 March) his troops suppressed a belated Lombard uprising in Brescia, then restored order in the central Italian duchies and intensified the siege of Venice. In late August 1849, after word arrived that the Austrians and their Russian allies had crushed the Hungarian revolution, Venice finally surrendered and the war in Italy ended.[1]

The mid-century upheaval was the single most confusing and stressful event in the long history of Italians living under Habsburg rule, and those in the armed forces naturally felt the pressure more than the civilian population. Of the twenty-one battalions of Italian infantry in Radetzky's army when the revolution broke out, all of nine and parts of three others were lost to desertion. Of the ten stationed outside of Lombardy and Venetia, one deserted in Hungary and parts of three others suffered significant losses through desertion. The great contrast between the loyal behavior of some Italian units and the poor record of others is as puzzling to the historian as it was to Habsburg military leaders at the time. Nevertheless, through a systematic review of the war records of the individual units, general patterns of behavior may be identified and explanations offered.

Of the twelve battalions (four regiments) of Venetian line infantry, only five were with the army in northern Italy in the spring of 1848. The two field battalions of the 13th Infantry (recruiting center: Padua) were stationed in and around Graz when the revolution began. Sent to the Styrian-Hungarian border, they skirmished with Hungarian rebels in 1848 before joining the army in Hungary for the campaign of 1849. News of the revolution seemed to have little effect on the spirit of the men and they performed well in Hungary. In January 1849 common soldiers Angelo Funes and Giuseppe Barison even arrested and turned in an officer who had tried to incite them to desert; the commander of the army in Hungary, Field Marshal Prince Alfred Windischgrätz, praised their loyalty and awarded them twenty-five gulden apiece. Once in action, the field battalions of the 13th listed great numbers of men taken prisoner or missing, suggesting a problem with their loyalty, but the soldiers of the regiment on occasion fought bravely against considerable odds, in some cases risking their lives for the sake of saving a regimental standard. The third battalion deserted in Venice during the March revolution and a replacement, raised by Radetzky in Venetia, was sent to join the rest of the regiment in Hungary during the summer of 1849. None of the battalions of the 13th fought in Italy in 1848-49. Four officers, none of them Italian, received distinguished service crosses for the Hungarian campaign, while the soldiers of the regiment won a total of three silver bravery medals.[2]

The first and second battalions of the 16th Infantry (recruiting center: Treviso) were quartered in Pest in the spring of 1848. Eight of their twelve companies deserted to the Hungarian rebels, the only mass defection of Italians in 1848–49 outside of Lombardy and Venetia. The remaining troops were combined into a single battalion and participated in the defense of Temesvar against the Hungarians later in 1848. The third battalion, stationed at home in Treviso, deserted in March 1848. In 1849 some of the previous year's deserters deserted the Hungarian army to return to Habsburg service; the regiment was reorganized and a new first and second battalion ended up serving in the garrison of Olmütz in Moravia, far from any action. The army did not replace the third battalion until later in 1849. None of the battalions of the 16th fought in Italy, but ten officers (including one Italian) were awarded distinguished service crosses, and the men received one gold and nineteen silver medals for bravery.[3]

The two field battalions of the 26th Infantry (recruiting center: Udine) were stationed in Innsbruck when the revolution broke out. The local commander, Feldmarschalleutnant Baron Franz von Welden, characterized their 2,400 men as "totally unreliable" and lamented that a great number of them (he listed 269) were "depraved people" with criminal records. Several of them deserted with their weapons and fought running battles with loyal troops sent into the forests and mountains to hunt them down. An attempt to move the third battalion to Innsbruck from the regiment's home base in Udine failed when most of the men deserted en route. The regiment was transferred to Salzburg in July 1848, purged of its most dangerous malcontents, then sent to the Styrian–Hungarian border in the fall. Both field battalions fought in Hungary in 1849; a reorganized third battalion joined the rest of the regiment there but proved to be unfit for duty. None of the battalions of the 26th fought in Italy in 1848–49. Two officers (neither of them Italian) received distinguished service crosses, while the men won a total of six silver medals.[4]

The outbreak of the revolution found the first battalion of the 45th Infantry (recruiting center: Verona) stationed at Bergamo in Lombardy, the second in Cattaro at the southern tip of Dalmatia, and the third in the regiment's home city. The second battalion played no part in any of the action in 1848–49, but the first fought its way through to Milan and joined Radetzky's army for the initial retreat to Verona. The third battalion remained loyal and, along with the first, fought with distinction at Santa Lucia. After spending the rest of 1848 on garrison duty in Verona, the two battalions fought "with renewed distinction" at Novara in 1849, helped suppress the revolt at Brescia after the defeat of Piedmont, and later participated in the final phase of the siege of Venice. Three officers were awarded high decorations for their performance, among them the Italian Major Federico Ferrari di Grado with an Order of Leopold. Three more officers (one of them Italian) received distinguished service crosses, and the men won a total of three gold and sixteen silver medals.[5]

Thus, altogether, eight of the twelve Venetian line battalions remained loyal, but of the five with Radetzky's army, three deserted. As a rule, desertion was less of a problem in units stationed outside of Italy; nevertheless, one of the Venetian battalions in Hungary (from the 16th Infantry) defected to the rebels, while the other field battalion of the 16th and both field battalions of the 26th suffered significant losses through desertion. The men of the four Venetian regiments won a total of forty-eight medals for bravery during the wars of 1848–49.

Of the twelve battalions (four regiments) of Lombard line infantry, ten were with the army in northern Italy in the spring of 1848. The two field battalions of the 23rd Infantry (recruiting center: Lodi) were stationed in Ofen (Buda) when the revolution in Hungary began. Unlike their Venetian compatriots of the 16th, they got along poorly with the Hungarians and in June 1848 exchanged shots with Hungarian national guardsmen. Under threat of reprisals the regiment left Buda and eventually joined the loyalist army of Baron Josip Jellačić, the Ban of Croatia. The loyalty of the regiment came under serious question only once, on a single bad day in September 1848 when 101 men deserted. The remaining troops participated in the siege and recapture of the imperial capital in October 1848, after the second Viennese revolution, then returned to Hungary where they saw action throughout the campaign of 1849. The third battalion deserted in March 1848 with the garrison at Cremona; the army eventually organized a replacement, which saw action in the spring of 1849 during the uprising at Brescia. Captain Enrico Benigni (Order of Leopold) and Lieutenant Carlo Gerelli (Order of the Iron Crown) were among seven officers of the regiment awarded high honors; another ten officers (one of them Italian) received distinguished service crosses. The men garnered a total of one gold and thirty-nine silver medals.[6]

The first and second battalions of the 38th Infantry (recruiting center: Brescia) were in Mantua when the revolution broke out and helped keep the fortress in Austrian hands in the early days of the fighting. The third battalion, at home in Brescia, made its way to

Verona but lost a third of its men to desertion en route. The first two battalions distinguished themselves at Santa Lucia and, after being combined into a single battalion, fought at Custoza under the command of Lieutenant Colonel Giuseppe Martini; they were in the vanguard of Radetzky's army when it reoccupied Milan. In 1849 the regiment was reorganized into three full battalions and participated in the campaign in central Italy, including the occupation of Bologna, before taking part in the final phase of the siege of Venice. The ingenious Colonel Count Anton Pergen, regimental commander, and his subaltern Martini were awarded both the Order of Maria Theresa and the Order of Leopold, while Major Count Leopoldo Porcia was one of two officers from the regiment to receive the Order of the Iron Crown. Six other officers (one of them Italian) were awarded distinguished service crosses, while twenty-one of the men received silver medals.[7]

The two field battalions of the 43rd Infantry (recruiting center: Como) were garrisoned in and around Bergamo when the revolution began and detachments from the regiment were sent to Milan, where they distinguished themselves in the initial street fighting. Some of the second battalion eventually deserted, but the rest of the men retreated with Radetzky's army and again fought with distinction at Santa Lucia. Meanwhile, the soldiers of the third battalion, which was dispersed on garrison duty in the Alpine towns of northern Lombardy, either deserted or surrendered after being surrounded by rebels. The field battalions saw no action in 1848 after Santa Lucia; in 1849 they participated in the invasion of Piedmont but did not come under fire. A new third battalion was raised in 1849 and stationed in Mantua. One non-Italian officer of the regiment received the Order of the Iron Crown, while another four officers (one of them Italian) were awarded distinguished service crosses. The men of the regiment won two gold and ten silver medals.[8]

The first and second battalions of the 44th Infantry (recruiting center: Milan) were in Cremona in the spring of 1848 and both deserted, the only Italian field battalions to be lost en masse during the revolution. The third battalion, at home in Milan, retreated to Verona with Radetzky's army, thus becoming one of only two Italian third battalions to suffer no significant defections. It fought with special distinction at Santa Lucia and also saw action at Custoza. In October 1848 two new field battalions were raised for the 44th; along with the third battalion, they remained with Radetzky's army in Italy. In contrast to the previous year, the regiment recorded only eleven desertions during the brief campaign against Piedmont in 1849, but also saw little action. Three officers (none of them Italian) were awarded distinguished service crosses, and nine of the men received silver medals.[9]

As in the Venetian regiments, eight of the Lombard line battalions remained loyal while four deserted. Since only two had the advantage of being stationed outside of Italy (where they suffered insignificant defections), six loyal and four deserting battalions were serving under Radetzky. Even though two of these six battalions also lost significant numbers to desertion, the overall record of the Lombard troops compares favorably with that of the Venetians. More than half of the Lombards stationed in Italy stayed with the army, while over half of the Venetians serving there deserted. Although the overall records were identical, the spring of 1848 found more of the Lombard units in situations where loyalty to the Habsburgs was a more difficult course than desertion. And the men of the four Lombard regiments won eighty-two medals for bravery during the wars of 1848-49, over 50 percent more than their Venetian counterparts.

This same pattern held up in the three grenadier battalions. The Venetian grenadiers formed from men of the 16th and 26th Infantry regiments, stationed in Venice since 1837, deserted in the revolution of March 1848. A replacement battalion was eventually raised and sent to Hungary in time to participate in the end of the campaign there in 1849. Meanwhile, the two remaining battalions, each with a composition two-third Lombard and one-third Venetian, remained loyal. The grenadiers raised from the 13th, 23rd and 44th Infantry regiments, stationed in Vienna since 1818, fought against the revolutionaries in the streets of the imperial capital in March 1848 and again in October. Late in the year they joined the army in Hungary and remained there for the entire campaign of 1849. The grenadier battalion supported by the 38th, 43rd and 45th regiments, stationed in Milan since 1830, retreated with Radetzky and fought with distinction at Santa Lucia. It spent the rest of 1848-49 on garrison duty in Verona.[10]

The pattern also held true in the two garrison battalions. The 5th (Venetian) Garrison, stationed in Venice since 1821, deserted with the rest of the Italian units there when the revolution broke out and was not reconstituted until after the war was over. Their behavior stands in sharp contrast with that of the 6th (Lombard) Garrison. At

Mantua since 1840, it defended that fortress alongside the field battalions of the 38th Infantry and spent the rest of the war in Radetzky's army.[11]

The Jäger battalions were an exception to the rule. The 8th (Lombard) Jägers were stationed at home in Lombardy in early 1848. Two-thirds of the men deserted, but Radetzky subsequently combined two companies of loyal troops with two companies from the 9th (Austrian) Jägers to form an under-strength mixed battalion that participated in many of the early skirmishes of the campaign in western Venetia. After seeing no action at Santa Lucia or any other major battle in 1848, the battalion was reorganized and in 1849 joined the reserve army in southern Hungary, where it did not come under fire. One non-Italian officer of the battalion was awarded a distinguished service cross and one man received a silver medal.[12]

The 11th (Lombard and Venetian) Jägers had a far better record. They were among the loyal units of Radetzky's army in the spring of 1848 and fought at both Santa Lucia and Custoza. In 1849 they participated in the invasion of Piedmont and fought with distinction at Novara, becoming the only Italian troops to see action in each of the three most pivotal battles of the war in Italy. One officer received the Order of Leopold and three were given the distinguished service cross (none of them Italian), while the men won two gold and thirty-three silver medals.[13] Relative to their size, they were the most decorated Italian infantry unit in the wars of 1848-49.

Thus, of the seven battalions of light and auxiliary infantry in existence in the spring of 1848, four had remained loyal, two deserted, and one suffered from substantial defections. The two deserting units were both Venetian, while the four remaining with the Habsburg armies were either Lombard or a mixture of Lombard and Venetian troops. Another battalion of light infantry, the 25th (Venetian) Jägers, was formed in August 1849 from cadres contributed by the reorganized 8th Jägers. They were ordered to Hungary after their creation but do not warrant inclusion in the calculations above, since they arrived too late to see action.[14]

In contrast to the mixed record of the rest of the Italian units, the 22nd (Trieste) Infantry was not plagued by desertions or disloyalty during the upheavals of 1848-49. Ironically, however, the regiment did not see as much action as most of its Lombard and Venetian counterparts. The spring of 1848 found the two field battalions on garrison duty in Dalmatia; the third battalion and one Landwehr battalion were sent out from Trieste to help guard the naval base of Pola (Pula). During the first weeks after the Venetian revolution, when the Austrian navy was desperately short of sailors, a number of men from the Landwehr battalion were assigned to duty aboard the ships of the fleet. In April 1849 the third battalion and Landwehr left Istria for Hungary, joined by a fourth battalion which had been raised in Trieste during the summer of 1848. The third, fourth, and Landwehr battalions saw limited action against the Hungarians during the campaign of 1849. The field battalions of the regiment eventually marched to Hungary from Dalmatia but did not arrive until after the fighting had ended. A fifth battalion, formed in Trieste during the summer of 1849, was disbanded at the end of the year. Six of the regiment's officers (one of them Italian) received distinguished service crosses, while five of the men were awarded silver medals. Though they were not put to the test against other Italians, the *Kaisertreue* of the 22nd prompted Italian patriots to give them the nickname *bastardi traditori*.[15]

The fidelity of the lone Italian cavalry regiment, the 7th Chevaux-Legers, was even more impressive than that of the *bastardi traditori*. As in the past, the horsemen recruited from northern Italy were an exception to all of the generalizations that applied to the infantry, and in 1848–49 their loyalty held firm under the most trying circumstances. They were stationed in Hungary in the spring of 1848, where they had been (aside from brief postings to Vienna in 1820–21 and 1830–32) ever since the beginning of 1815. The younger men among its fifteen Italian officers eventually resolved to quit the regiment, ten of them leaving in May 1848, but even these displayed a remarkable degree of honor as Rittmeister Luigi Moreschi, the senior officer among them, blocked attempts by his more zealous compatriots to incite the entire regiment to desert. When Hungarian officials ordered the horsemen to take the field against Jellačić in the fall of 1848, a group of officers under Major Alberto Alberti, the son of one of its former commanders, mutinied and seized control of the regiment in order to keep it from fighting against Habsburg forces. The Italian cavalry subsequently saw action against the Hungarian rebels throughout the campaigns of 1848 and 1849. According to a contemporary observer, the regiment was "feared by the enemy" and became "known throughout the army for its bravery" and for "its preference for the sword in attacking."[16] Count Guglielmo di Montenuovo took command of the regiment late in 1848, with Alberti becoming his second-in-command. In 1849 both men received Russian decorations along with the Order of Leopold from their own emperor, and Montenuovo was awarded the coveted Order of Maria Theresa as well. Fourteen other officers were honored with decorations while the troopers won three gold and forty-nine silver medals. In response to their performance in the field and the strong impression that they made on the Russians, Francis Joseph in August 1849 renamed the regiment the "Tsarevich" Chevaux-Legers, after Grand Duke Alexander, the heir to the throne of Russia.[17]

The thirty-one battalions of infantry and regiment of cavalry raised in Lombardy and Venetia accounted for a total of 30-35,000 men in the spring of 1848. In late April, five weeks after his retreat from Milan, Radetzky's deserters numbered 10,860 men and two officers.[18] Almost all of these were Italian and, since the initial desertions from his army accounted for over three-quarters of all Italian defections in 1848-49 (nine battalions plus parts of three others, out of a total ten battalions and parts of six), the final tally of army deserters from Lombardy and Venetia must have numbered well under 15,000 men. Thus, between one-half and two-thirds of the troops from these provinces remained loyal, and if the six battalions of the Trieste regiment and the hundreds of *kaisertreue* Italians in the Tyrolese Kaiser-Jägers are counted, the overall proportion of disloyal Italians becomes still smaller. It is also significant that relatively few of the deserters ever fought against the Austrians; a contemporary observer noted that "most of them . . . only wanted to leave military service."[19] Once Radetzky proclaimed an amnesty, they returned to the ranks by the thousands.

From the Habsburg point of view, even the record of the Italians stationed in northern Italy, where just over half remained loyal, compared favorably to that of Hungarian troops stationed in Hungary in 1848. Apart from a handful of predominantly-Romanian battalions (from Transylvania) and others containing Serbs (from Vojvodina), no Hungarian units fought against the Hungarian revolution and scores of Hungarian officers sided with its leadership against the Habsburgs. Among the 250 Italian officers in the Lombard and Venetian units and the dozens more in other regiments of the army, the high profile maintained by a revolutionary minority attracted more attention at the time (and has in the years since then) than the record of the loyal majority. A pair of lieutenants, Pietro Calvi of the 13th Infantry and Alessandro Monti of the 2nd (Bohemian) Chevaux-Legers, resigned their commissions with the first news of the revolution and went on to command Italian rebels in 1848. While Calvi served in this capacity again in 1849, Monti went first to the Balkans as a Sardinian diplomatic agent, then assumed command of the "Italian legion" of the Hungarian army, a body consisting mostly of deserters from the 16th Infantry. Both subsequently were hailed as great Italian patriotic heroes. A pair of former Napoleonic Italian officers who were granted Habsburg commissions after 1814, Giambattista Cavaedalis and Carlo Zucchi, reemerged to hold positions of importance in Venice during 1848–49, but a quarter century had passed since either had served in the Austrian army; indeed, Zucchi had spent the previous seventeen years in Austrian prisons.[20] As for Italian officers on active duty, Radetzky reported only two defections in 1848. The mass desertion of the ten cavalry officers in Hungary, a stain on the otherwise impeccable record of the Chevaux–Legers, appears to have been the most serious instance of Italians forsaking their commissions.

In his work on Radetzky and the revolution of 1848, Alan Sked poses the question of why so many Italian troops deserted and goes to great lengths to build a case for the role of patriotic propaganda in inciting them to leave the ranks.[21] After examining the record in detail, it appears more appropriate to ask why so many refused to desert. While recognizing that propaganda no doubt had its effects, the argument that desertion was politically and patriotically motivated weakens when one considers that only an insignificant number of deserters ultimately fought against Habsburg troops. It is also undisputed that the mass of the people of Lombardy–Venetia were functionally, or at least politically, illiterate and thus immune to such appeals. Carlo Tivaroni, author of the first Italian "critical" history of the Risorgimento, lamented that a combination of "discipline and ignorance" led a majority of Italian soldiers, especially those from rural areas, to fight loyally for the Austrians in 1848–49.[22]

It is likely, however, that propaganda and the spirit of the moment drove many to desert who were already predisposed to do so because of conditions within the service—conditions not immediately related to politics or the nationality question. It is not coincidental that the 38th Infantry, the only Lombard regiment not to lose a battalion in 1848, had a reputation for good management and fairness to the common soldier. Its commander, Colonel Count Anton Pergen, fought discontent by instituting a strict regularization of furloughs and establishing a procedure through which soldiers were offered the opportunity to become NCOs. Whereas most regiments granted furloughs and promotions arbitrarily, causing much bad blood between the men and their officers, in the 38th Pergen gave each man a definite furlough date upon his entry into service, which was honored provided that he had a good record and did not attempt to desert. A similar system offered promotions on the basis of seniority and good behavior.[23] By neutralizing the natural desire for desertion that would be present even in the quietest times, Pergen built an atmosphere of trust that helped his regiment make it through the maelstrom of 1848 in relatively good shape. His accomplishment is all the more impressive when one considers that all three battalions of the regiment were stationed in Lombardy when the revolution broke out, and that its recruiting center was Brescia, the same city that erupted in a defiant and hopeless rebellion in the spring of 1849.

In bad regiments, the district from which the recruits were drawn only compounded the standard set of problems. The 44th Infantry, which lost both of its field battalions, drew its conscripts from Milan, undisputably the most anti-Austrian city in Lombardy or Venetia. The 26th Infantry, in contrast, recruited from the rural Friulian region around Udine, home of most of Venetia's substantial Romansh-speaking minority. It must have included many soldiers who could not communicate very well even with Italian officers and NCOs. And as Sked points out, to make matters still worse the cities and towns of this district appear to have rid themselves of hundreds of their most vicious criminals by dumping them on the regiment.[24]

Italians made up only a minority of the officer corps of the Lombard and Venetian regiments, but since there were numerous instances of Italian troops fighting loyally under non-Italian officers, this factor was not the most crucial. Indeed, there is evidence that Italian soldiers did not like Italian officers, because "they had the reputation of favoring non-Italian soldiers to prove their loyalty."[25] Nevertheless, the three regiments suffering the most desertions—the 16th, 26th and 44th—also happened to be the three with the fewest Italian officers, a problem dating back to their origins as "half-Italian" regiments transferred to recruiting districts in northern Italy in 1817 from other provinces of the empire. While the differences between these regiments and the five originally raised from the old Napoleonic Italian army blurred over the years, none of them had ever had as many Italian officers as the other Lombard and Venetian units.[26] If not a decisive liability, this certainly was not asset. Taken along with the example of the 38th Infantry, such evidence suggests that the state of rapport between the men and their officers and of their general prewar spirit were the most decisive factors.

In offering an explanation for the loyalty of some Italian units in 1848, Sked proposes a connection between loyal behavior and long assignment to posts in northern Italy. This may have been true for the Lombard regiments serving in the Habsburg army during the eighteenth century, but against the more recent mirror of the post-Napoleonic period the opposite appears to have been the case, at least with the Venetians. In Venetian regiments, the units that spent the most time away from home before 1848 were the most loyal in 1848–49; those spending the most time in northern Italy suffered the most desertions. The only exception to this rule was the third battalion of the 45th Infantry, which happened to be garrisoned in Verona, the city used by Radetzky as his base of operations after the retreat from Milan. Of the Lombard regiments, the one spending the most time at home in the years before 1848 (the 44th) also suffered the most desertions, but the correlation does not hold true for the rest of the Lombards and there is no identifiable pattern of loyalty or disloyalty similar to the one for the Venetians.[27] While separation from home no doubt prompted a number of desertions, as a general rule excessive familiarity with home seems to have caused more.

The behavior of the army units in 1848–49 also debunks the old stereotype of the Lombards being more rebellious vis-à-vis Austrian rule and the Venetians somewhat "easier to handle."[28] On the contrary, the overall record of the troops from Lombardy was better than those from Venetia. But regardless of the precise origin of the loyal Italians, Radetzky held to his earlier belief that Austria "must not expect more of them than is reasonable." In the first weeks after the revolution he used his Italians with the utmost caution and called them "a great hindrance" to his overall efforts.[29] Nevertheless, he employed nine battalions of them at Santa Lucia, when his army was still weak and he had no alternative. At Custoza, however, when the situation was not so desperate, he used only three battalions and the following year at Novara, after ample reinforcements had arrived, only three saw action once again. The old field marshal's use of his loyal Italians in the campaigns of 1848 and 1849 set the tone for their future employment within the Habsburg army.

Radetzky's general pardon of 3 September 1848 paved the way for the return to the ranks of most of the men who had deserted the Habsburg colors the previous spring. But in his capacity as civil and military governor of Lombardy and Venetia, the field marshal made two critical mistakes that jeopardized his goal of winning the loyalty of the masses. His punitive measures against the aristocracy, whom he blamed for inciting and supporting the revolution, only hurt the peasants who depended upon landowners economically. More important for the future of the Italian regiments, his obsession with tracking down and accounting for every individual deserter only served to arouse suspicion that conscription would be renewed. The latter problem arose after Radetzky, having already promised that no new levy would occur, had lists compiled of all men between the ages of twenty and twenty-four in order to help account for all the deserters; because the army normally took this step in preparation for a fresh round of conscription, the populace reacted as if betrayed. Other promises, involving rewards for long-term loyalty—such as the granting of early furloughs—could not be kept for fear of leaving the ranks dominated by those who had deserted and returned under the amnesty. In May 1849, Radetzky was forced to admit that his measures had been misunderstood and had failed to inspire the intended good will. Because most of the deserters had been accounted for by then, he repealed the program of rewards and lifted the moratorium on conscription, effective 1 June 1849.[30]

Three and a half months later, Francis Joseph decreed a one-year reduction in the service term of all Italian soldiers who had remained loyal during the revolution.[31] It was a small consolation and prompted no outpouring of gratitude, especially because the return to peace brought the transfer of almost all of the Lombard and Venetian regiments, including their third battalions, to distant provinces of the monarchy. Before 1848 there was no systematic arrangement for stationing Italian troops outside of Italy and some units spent long periods of time in or near their home districts. At any rate, after 1830 over half of the Lombard and Venetian infantry battalions could be found at home in any given year, and even in 1848-49 Radetzky kept all of his loyal Italian units with him in Italy, passing up the opportunity to send them to Hungary.[32] But as soon as peace was restored the troops were ordered to march, the loyal regiments as well as those with disloyal records; most arrived at their new garrisons before the end of 1849. The 43rd (Lombard) Infantry, relocated from Cremona to Graz in September 1850, was the last line regiment to move.[33] Their departure left one grenadier and two garrison battalions as the only Italian units still stationed with the army in northern Italy.

The Austrian Empire's absolute government of the 1850s featured a military establishment under the "personal command" of the young emperor, free from the financial constraints of the years before 1848. The army was expanded and kept at an unprecedented peacetime strength, and after conscription resumed in Lombardy and Venetia it contained a larger number of Italians than ever before. In the fall of 1850 Francis Joseph ordered the creation of a fourth battalion in each of the Italian and Hungarian regiments, to bring them into line with a similar expansion of the rest of the army that had taken place in 1848.[34] Over the next two years, most of these units joined the rest of their regiment on garrison duty far from home.

In 1852, a series of reforms included the abolition of the old system of grenadier battalions, the reduction of the number of garrison battalions, the closing of the *Erziehungshäuser* for soldiers' children, and the implementation of a new two-year reserve obligation throughout the empire. Henceforth each regiment was to provide for four companies of grenadiers (double the previous number) which were to form a fifth battalion in wartime. This plus the merger of the two Italian garrison battalions (the 5th and the 6th) into one, designated the 1st Garrison, momentarily left only one battalion of Italian troops stationed in Lombardy–Venetia. After the closing of the two regimental schools at Bergamo and Cividale, the most promising of the older boys entered instructional battalions (*Lehrbataillone*) for training as future NCOs, a move that put still more Italians into the field. Meanwhile, the new reserve obligation, the first ever to apply in Lombardy and Venetia, meant that veterans no longer would be free from further military duty after completing their eight years of service. At the same time, the army instituted a system of "depots," providing for a cadre for yet another battalion to be garrisoned in the recruiting center of each regiment. The changes brought the Lombard and Venetian infantry to a strength of forty-four battalions (up from the pre–1848 figure of thirty–one), of which nine were stationed in northern Italy. A corresponding reform of the army's cavalry included the abolition of all regiments of chevaux–legers; the Italian 7th "Tsarevich" Chevaux–Legers were converted to lancers and designated the 11th "Tsarevich" Uhlans.[35]

The army high command soon increased the pressure on northern Italy still more by assigning another two cavalry regiments and a ninth infantry regiment to the region. In 1853, the 6th (Austrian) Uhlans became an Italian unit with recruiting rights in the Venetian districts;

the 11th Uhlans henceforth drew their manpower exclusively from Lombardy. In 1854, the 8th Dragoons were created as a new regiment, recruited from both Lombardy and Venetia. Meanwhile, at the end of 1852, the 63rd (Galician) Infantry, largely Ruthenian in composition, was redesignated the 55th Infantry and given a new recruiting center at Monza in Lombardy with conscription rights to the Alpine districts of Como and Sondrio. The two converted regiments were the first since 1817 to undergo the process, but contrary to the precedent of the immediate post–Napoleonic period, they were not sent to their new home districts for the transformation. Instead, both the 55th and the 6th Uhlans remained on their former stations in Hungary and received Italian recruits in a series of "transports" from Lombardy and Venetia; the new 8th Dragoons, also garrisoned in Hungary, filled its ranks the same way. The regiments received a number of Italian and Italian–speaking officers through transfers from other units.[36] In the 55th, however, the leadership consisted largely of veterans from the old 63rd Infantry.[37]

The need for armed force to back up Austrian diplomacy only increased the burden upon the people of northern Italy and the rest of the empire. The Austro–Prussian confrontation over Germany in the fall of 1850 occasioned a mobilization and the transfer of tens of thousands of men to Bohemia and other northern posts. The 13th Infantry was sent to the Saxon border during the height of the crisis,[38] while another Venetian regiment (the 16th) and two from Lombardy (the 23rd and 38th) were deployed elsewhere in Bohemia. The 44th (Lombard) Infantry, in Vorarlberg at the onset of the troop movements, ended up travelling the farthest: into Bavaria in November 1850, then on to Hesse–Cassel in January 1851, then via Brunswick to Lübeck in February. Perhaps the most troubled regiment in 1848, the 44th received praise for its good conduct while in Germany; its reward, however, was a new garrison assignment in Bohemia.[39]

After three years on a peace footing the army mobilized once again, in 1854, to support Austria's diplomatic maneuvering during the Crimean War. The course of armed mediation centered around the occupation of the Danubian Principalities (Moldavia and Wallachia) but also involved a buildup of forces in Galicia. Austrian troops saw no action during the war, but the mobilization drove the state debt to dangerous new heights and cost the army 40,000 dead from illness.[40] The first three battalions of the 45th (Venetian) and the new 55th (Lombard) regiment were sent into Moldavia on occupation duty. The latter, plagued by fever before it left its previous station in the Banat of Temesvar, had eight men die and another 1,200 incapacitated by illness on the long march to Jassy (Iasi). After being transferred southward to Braila on the Danube, the unit was riddled by cholera. The 23rd (Lombard) Infantry, sent to the Russian border in Galicia during the armed mediation, suffered from both cholera and typhus, and the 26th (Venetian) Infantry, which had already lost 2,000 men to cholera while stationed at Temesvar in 1849–50, lost another thousand during its frontier duty in Galicia. The 11th Uhlans, also assigned to Galicia, likewise succumbed to cholera and had to retire to Hungary in 1855.[41]

News of the epidemics no doubt reinforced the traditional fears of disease and could not have helped the morale of Italian conscripts. Still, desertions were not a great problem for the Italian regiments during the 1850s; indeed, there were even cases of Italians being sent out to hunt down deserters from other regiments.[42] Their record for the decade is remarkable, considering that for the most part they were kept away from home and moved to new stations far more frequently than in the years before 1848. While there is ample evidence that the former was not necessarily detrimental to the morale of a regiment, frequent moves historically had been a disruptive factor.[43]

In the summer of 1855 financial considerations prompted the army to disband all of its depot and garrison battalions; the fourth battalions of the regiments returned home to replace the depots. Notwithstanding the reductions, the number of Italians in the army stood at 74,900 in 1856.[44] The figure fell sharply during the demobilization that came with the end of the Crimean War, but the latest changes still left Lombardy and Venetia supporting nine of the army's sixty-two regiments of the line and three of its twenty-five Jäger battalions (a total of thirty-nine battalions of infantry) plus sixteen squadrons of lancers and six of dragoons in the three Italian cavalry regiments.

Radetzky's retirement in the spring of 1857—at the age of ninety—brought Francis Joseph's brother Ferdinand Max to Milan as governor-general of Lombardy and Venetia. The young archduke attempted to deal constructively with the rising discontent in the provinces and, after concluding that the army's demands for Italian manpower had been excessive, appealed to Vienna for a postponement of conscription in 1857. The emperor ignored his request and instead made matters worse by reassigning two cavalry regiments and two Jäger battalions from Bohemian to Italian recruiting grounds. The sixteen squadrons of the 7th and 9th Uhlans (lancers) joined the twenty-two already being manned by Italians, while the 6th and 18th Jägers raised to forty-one the number of infantry battalions supported by Lombardy and Venetia.[45] The following year, rumors of a new lighter conscription law raised hopes that the burden would be eased; however, the revised statute, which went into effect for the entire empire in the fall of 1858, merely clarified the old system of exemptions, retaining both the eight year term of service and two year reserve obligation. Finally, in December 1858, the government announced reductions in the size of the conscription classes for 1859—an 18 percent cut for Lombardy and 20 percent for Venetia—but the gesture came too late to soothe the public mood.[46] As Napoleon III and Count Cavour prepared to hatch their plans for 1859, Austria's hold on the populace of northern Italy was as shaky as it had been at any time since 1849.

The sequence of Franco-Sardinian machinations that led to the War of 1859 is well known. Through the secret treaty of Plombières (July 1858) France committed herself to intervene in an Austro-Sardinian conflict provided that Austria were the aggressor, and to pursue the war until Lombardy and Venetia were detached from the Habsburg Empire. The war scare started in January 1859, after Napoleon III's famous New Years' Day quip to the Austrian ambassador in Paris, Count Joseph von Hübner. Military preparations proceeded on both sides and as early as the third week of February, Adjutant General Count Karl Ludwig Grünne, *de facto* head of the army under Francis Joseph's "personal command," called for the withdrawal from Lombardy and Venetia of the fourth battalions of the nine regiments and of all soldiers on furlough from the Italian units.[47] Archduke Albrecht, commander of the army in Hungary, went so far as to warn against the deployment of Italian troops in his area for fear that they would join any Hungarian revolution that might occur.[48]

Both men were overreacting to the record of the Italian regiments in 1848–49, or at least to what they perceived that record to have been. Grünne took for granted that all Italian troops in Lombardy or Venetia would desert, even though less than half of those stationed there in 1848 had done so, and Albrecht assumed that Italians could not be trusted in Hungary either, even though relatively few had deserted there a decade earlier. In fact, the Italian units held up well enough during the weeks of prewar pressure. In January the fourth battalion of the 13th Infantry, stationed at home in Padua, even helped suppress anti-Austrian riots by university students. In March, when the regiment was placed on a war footing, all of its furloughed men reported for duty.[49]

Not everyone in the military hierarchy shared the prewar fears of Grünne and Albrecht. A plan promulgated in February called for the conversion of yet another cavalry regiment to Italian manpower, a decision which must be considered a vote of confidence in their reliability. After the mobilization began, Francis Joseph expressed his satisfaction at the speed and readiness "with which soldiers of the Italian nationality are rallying to the flag."[50] There were few problems in any of the Lombard or Venetian units during mobilization; once the fighting began, it would be a different story.

Istvan Deak's recent analysis of the role of the nationality question in the Austrian defeat of 1859 suggests that Lombard troops were markedly less reliable than Venetians:

> it was as if the Lombard regiments had had advance intelligence of their postwar cession to Sardinia-Italy, while the Venetians knew that they would have to wait until 1866.[51]

He goes on to demonstrate, however, that when desertions did occur the Venetian regiments also suffered their share.[52] In spite of the better Lombard record in 1848–49 and the absence of any diplomatic agreement conceding their province ahead of time (as would be the case with Venetia in 1866), Austrian war plans treated the troops from Lombardy with greater caution than the Venetians. For the Venetian regiments, there was a direct relationship between the number of decorations won by each of them in 1848–49 and their assignments in 1859. The two most distinguished units, the 45th and the 16th, went to the front in Lombardy; the third-most decorated, the 13th, was ordered to the Po opposite Modena; and the 26th, with the worst record a decade before, went to the northern corps that was expected to join Prussia and the German states in a second front against France on the Rhine. The Lombard units did not receive similar consideration. The 38th and 55th Infantry were ordered to the northern army while the 23rd and 43rd Infantry went to the Adriatic coastline to join the so-called *Küstenarmee*, which guarded against a French landing. The 44th, the most troubled Lombard regiment in 1848, was left on garrison duty in the Tyrol. As for the cavalry, the 11th Uhlans were assigned to the northern army while the other four regiments remained in garrisons far from the action.

The task of moving Italian units out of Lombardy and Venetia presented no difficulties, because hardly any of the line infantry field battalions (first through third) had set foot in northern Italy during the past decade[53] and none were there when the mobilization began. In March the nine fourth battalions all left to join their regiments, and depot battalions were formed to replace them in the home districts.[54] In May the army ordered a fifth battalion for each regiment, and in June these too left along with the depots to take up garrison duty in adjacent provinces. Much to the surprise of the Austrian high command, the troop movements were executed with no significant losses to desertion. When full mobilization brought the formation of regimental grenadier battalions, the nine regiments reached a peak strength of seven battalions and nearly 7,000 men apiece.[55]

After no Italian units participated in Austria's initial defeat at Montebello (20 May), the 45th Infantry went into action at Magenta on 4 June. Some of the men fought well against the French—45 were killed and 287 wounded—but after the battle the regiment listed a suspiciously high number—742—as "missing." The troops were kept in reserve during the battle of Solferino on 24 June, but the 16th Infantry was used there and fought with great distinction.[56] The news from the other regiments was far less encouraging. The 13th lost 110 men to desertion while en route to the Po from Hungary; it saw no action in Italy and, after Magenta, moved on to Innsbruck, ostensibly to join in the march to the Rhine if Prussia entered the war against France.[57] Meanwhile, the two Lombard regiments stationed on the Adriatic coast both started to disintegrate after word arrived of the defeat at Magenta and the Austrian retreat from Lombardy. Deserters from the 23rd and 43rd initially were hunted down by the 26th (Venetian) Infantry, which had been reassigned to the littoral at the last minute; the 26th, however, also had its share of problems and in late June was transferred to Vienna at the request of its commander.[58]

As for the remaining infantry regiments, the 55th suffered its most serious defections (42 men) when its fifth battalion was ordered to Hungary from Lower Austria in the middle of the summer.[59] The 38th (in Bohemia) and the 44th (in the Tyrol) lost few men to desertion. The five Italian Jäger battalions and five cavalry regiments likewise remained far from the fighting and experienced no serious problems. The only other Italians to see action in Italy were the field battalions and grenadiers of the 22nd (Trieste) Infantry, which enhanced their reputation as the *bastardi traditori* of the Risorgimento by fighting loyally, and with heavy losses, at both Magenta and Solferino.[60]

The armistice of Villafranca (11 July) disappointed the Sardinians, but the Austrians felt fortunate to have lost only Lombardy. Pending the definitive cession of the territory, however, the Lombard units of the Habsburg army remained in existence. To discourage further desertions and effect an orderly dissolution, those stationed in the littoral were transferred temporarily to the interior of the monarchy. The first step of their repatriation came in August, when Francis Joseph authorized the release of all who had completed their eight years of military service during the course of the war.[61] The demobilization of the rest of the men began in September, but delays in the peace negotiations kept them in Austrian uniforms for several more weeks and their release was not officially authorized until 3 November, one week before the Treaty of Zurich formally ended the war. Thereafter, the Lombard infantry regiments (the 23rd, 38th, 43rd, 44th, and 55th) lost the bulk of their common soldiers, as did three of the Italian cavalry regiments and two Jäger battalions.[62]

At the peak of mobilization in the summer of 1859, over 70,000 Italians from Lombardy and Venetia were serving in the Austrian army. Very few were trusted with roles in combat; however, those seeing action did not perform poorly in the losing cause. The men of the 45th Infantry received thirty-two silver medals for their bravery at Magenta, but the large number reported "missing" men in that battle, many of whom must have deserted, marred the regiment's record, as did the disappearance of dozens more after their transfer to the rear.[63] Following the impressive showing of the 16th Infantry at Solferino, its Italian commander, Colonel Giovanni Trentinaglia, was awarded the Order of Leopold. His men received one gold and sixty-six silver medals, making the regiment one of the most decorated of the entire war. The soldiers of Trieste and Istria also fared well, the 22nd Infantry winning nineteen silver medals for its service at Magenta and Solferino.[64]

Why did the Venetian troops fight as well as they did? For the 45th the good showing was nothing new, since it had been an exception to the general poor performance of Venetian regiments a decade earlier. The 16th had a far more impressive record in 1859 than in 1848–49, but it was also the only Italian regiment to have had Italian commanders throughout the 1850s.[65] Even though the 16th, like the rest of the Lombard and Venetian regiments, had only a small minority of Italian officers by 1859, there is good reason to believe that it enjoyed a healthier prewar spirit and rapport between officers and men than the other units. As was the case a decade earlier, a regiment relatively free from everyday internal discord could be expected to fight better once in battle.

Given the record of Lombard troops in 1848–49, why did they behave so poorly in 1859? Because no soldiers from Lombardy actually saw action, we may only speculate about how they would have performed in battle. One must assume that they would not have made a good showing, although in the case of the 38th Infantry (which spent the war in Bohemia), its past history of loyal service may well have held up. It is of some significance that the bulk of the desertions from the Lombard regiments did not come until after the men received word of the Austrian defeat at Magenta and the Franco–Sardinian occupation of Lombardy.

Austria's overall experience with Italian troops in 1859 was not negative enough to prompt a change in policy toward their future use. In the 1860s the army attempted to exploit to the fullest its pool of Venetian manpower, as it had in both Lombardy and Venetia during the 1850s. In February 1860 the infantry was reorganized from sixty-two regiments of four battalions each to eighty regiments of three battalions. Among the eighteen new regiments were two to be recruited in Venetia, the 79th and 80th. These and the 38th Infantry, converted from Lombard to Venetian, all received the former third and fourth battalions of the remaining Italian regiments as part of the reorganization.[66] The four recruiting districts in Venetia subsequently had to be divided into seven: the 79th Infantry received territory from the 26th and 16th and a recruiting center at Pordenone, while the 80th was given half of the western Venetian district of the 45th Infantry with a center at Vicenza. The transplanted 38th likewise took half of the southeastern district from the 13th Infantry and was headquartered at Rovigo. Other than leaving the 26th (Udine) with an even grater majority of Friulians than before, the redivision brought no significant changes to the character of the older units.

As for the rest of the old Lombard regiments, the 23rd, 43rd and 44th were assigned to new recruiting districts in Hungary over the winter of 1859–60, while the 55th became Galician once again. Two Jäger battalions, the 8th and 26th, remained Venetian, but the 8th

Dragoons were disbanded and the four regiments of Uhlans ordered to draw all future recruits from Galicia. Italian troopers with time still to serve were consolidated in the 11th Uhlans, where they constituted a majority for a few more years even though the unit was classified as Galician.[67]

The peace settlement of 1859 gave Lombards the option to remain in Austrian service. Of the common soldiers and NCOs only a few hundred decided to stay.[68] Among the officers, however, very few chose to leave. In 1859 between 15 and 20 percent of the officers in each Lombard and Venetian regiment were Italian; a redistribution of Italian officers after 1860 left each of the seven Venetian regiments with between 12 and 25 percent. Other than the 16th Infantry (Trentinaglia) and the 38th (Colonel Baron Carlo Cattanei di Momo), none of the regiments had Italian commanders.[69]

The postwar months were a tense time for Austria and for all of Europe. The unification of the Italian peninsula, except for Venetia and Rome, occurred without the blessing of the Great Powers and in contravention of the Treaty of Zurich. The Habsburg army remained mobilized and in the spring of 1860 still had almost half a million men under arms, of which 188,000 were in an "operative army" in Venetia under Feldzeugmeister Count August von Degenfeld, 43,000 on garrison duty in Venetia, and over 50,000 stationed in the Tyrol or along the Adriatic coast.[70] The 200 battalions of infantry on guard against another Franco–Italian or Italian attack included troops from everywhere in the empire except Venetia.[71] The two new regiments were kept in Vienna, where they had just been created; two others also made up part of the garrison in the imperial capital, another was stationed at Linz, and two in Bohemia. Though pleased with the good record of some of its Italian units in 1859, the army chose to follow Radetzky's maxim and not expect too much from them.

The Austrians were not so prudent in their conscription policies, imposing a new levy in Venetia as early as 1860. When almost one thousand conscripts fled rather than enter the service, the imperial government resolved to enforce to the letter existing laws which required cities, towns and villages to pay the price of a hired substitute for each missing man.[72] In small rural communities or impoverished areas, such payments were a great burden and must have resulted in local pressure against draft evasion. At any rate, the heavy-handed approach proved effective and in subsequent years almost all of the conscripts accepted their fate.

In the summer of 1861, after the kingdom of Italy was proclaimed and the war scare ended, the third battalions of the seven Venetian regiments returned to their home districts.[73] Late in the year Francis Joseph decreed the formation of a fourth battalion in every infantry regiment but postponed the order for those recruited in Venetia. The conscription problems of 1860 no doubt helped to motivate this decision, the army leadership deciding that it would be better not to squeeze Venetia too hard, at least for the present. When the fourth battalions were finally raised early in 1865, they remained at home while the third battalions joined their regiments in the field. After the expansion, Italians made up 10.7 percent of a total of 492,700 men either in the Habsburg army or on its muster rolls. Of all the nationalities of the monarchy, only the Germans and Czechs accounted for more.[74]

Once the postwar tension in the south subsided, other international developments kept the peacetime army busy. The Venetian units saw their share of activity in Germany, on the border of Russian Poland, and even in Denmark. In 1860 the proud 16th Infantry became part of the Austrian contingent in the garrison of the German federal fortress at Mainz. They were to remain in Mainz throughout Austria's last-ditch attempts to breathe new life into the German Confederation, an ironic symbol of the very reason why the Habsburg Empire could not take the lead in uniting Germany. In 1863, meanwhile, the 26th Jägers saw their first action ever in a brief firefight against Polish rebels on the Russian border. Early the following year the new 80th Infantry received its baptism of fire as part of the Austro-Prussian force that invaded Denmark to resolve the Schleswig-Holstein crisis. The regiment, accounting for over 20 percent of the Habsburg army's contribution to the campaign, distinguished itself in action at Fahrdorf-Lopstedt. The men received a total of nine silver medals and, while en route back to garrison duty in Vienna, were reviewed in Berlin by the king of Prussia, William I.[75]

In one respect, the peacetime stationing policies of the 1850s continued to prevail in the 1860s: none of the regiments was headquartered any closer to home than Vienna. But in a departure from the previous decade, the regiments did not move to new stations as frequently,[76] and their morale appears to have held up. Minor uprisings in Friuli and Belluno in the fall of 1864 did not disrupt conscription and had no effect on the units raised from those areas.[77]

When it became clear that the German question would not be resolved peacefully, Austria and Prussia prepared for war and the Venetian regiments were on the march again. On 8 April 1866, Count Bismarck raised the stakes by concluding a two-month alliance with Italy, designed to divide the Habsburg forces and deliver Venetia and possibly other Adriatic territories to the Italians. Fears of a war against a general European coalition prompted Austria, on 12 June, to agree to a postwar cession of Venetia to France in exchange for a pledge of neutrality from Napoleon III.

During the second half of April the Venetian units were placed on a war footing along with the rest of the army. The likelihood of a two-front war meant that Austria would need all the manpower she could muster; the army intended all along to make use of the Venetian troops, and the secret treaty with France brought no change of plans. Because the Jägers and all of the field battalions already were stationed in the northern provinces of the empire, logic as well as prudence dictated that they join Feldzeugmeister Ludwig August von Benedek's army in Bohemia rather than Archduke Albrecht's forces in the south. In Venetia itself, the fourth battalions were mobilized and preparations made for the creation of a fifth battalion in each recruiting district. In early May the seven fourth fattalions went north to join Benedek's army, and later the same month the fifth battalions were brought up to strength. Except for the depot of the Friulian 26th Infantry, which remained in Venetia, these units took up stations behind the lines in the north. Throughout their mobilization and transportation to the front, the Venetian battalions reported few incidents of desertion.[78]

By the time the war began, Benedek's field army included twenty battalions of Venetians—the field battalions of six of the regiments plus the two Jäger battalions. The seven fourth battalions were assigned to garrisons in Bohemia, most to either Prague or Olmütz. The onset of fighting found the three field battalions of the 16th Infantry still in Mainz, an exposed position that soon became untenable. Meanwhile, the only active Italian troops in Venetia were the *bastardi traditori* of Trieste, the 22nd Infantry, which left their peacetime garrison at Fiume to join Albrecht's army.[79]

The first major battle occurred in the south, where the Italian armies invaded western Venetia within days of the declaration of war. Expecting Albrecht to remain on the defensive in the Quadrilateral fortresses, they were caught by surprise when the archduke, though badly outnumbered, attacked on 24 June in and around Custoza. In a series of actions fought on the same fields where Radetzky had been victorious eighteen years before, the Austrians suffered greater casualties than the Italians but forced them to retreat back into Lombardy.[80] While the 22nd Infantry did not see action at Custoza, two battalions of the regiment later came under fire when defending the Tyrol against an Italian volunteer corps led by Garibaldi. The men of Trieste were involved on both sides in the Alpine campaign, the sons of many of the city's leading figures having fled to Lombardy before the start of the war to enlist in Garibaldi's legion.[81]

The war on the northern front took a few days longer to unfold, but the involvement of Venetian troops in the opening skirmishes indicates that the Austrian high command did not hesitate to assign them to front line duty. In a series of preliminary battles fought in northern Bohemia between 27–30 June, five of the Venetian regiments and the two Jäger battalions lost a total of over 300 men killed and more than a thousand wounded. The three battalions of the 13th Infantry alone suffered over 500 casualties in a costly Austrian victory at Trautenau, while the 45th lost 500 killed and wounded at Sobotka and Jičin.[82] These two regiments, each reduced by roughly one–sixth, were too battered to be of much use to Benedek when he engaged the Prussians in the decisive battle of Königgrätz on 3 July.

Königgrätz was the largest battle ever fought in Europe and the bloodiest one day encounter of the century. The Prussian armies, 220,000 strong, faced just under 200,000 Austrians and around 20,000 Saxons. Benedek's twenty Venetian battalions accounted for almost 10 percent of the allied forces. The Prussian attack, masterminded by General Helmut von Moltke, left Benedek outmaneuvered and defeated even though his troops for the most part fought well. The Venetians were no exception; in the heat of battle, their courage drew the praise of other regiments and shouts of "bravi italiani!" from officers riding by. As in the rest of the campaign, disloyalty or desertion in battle was not a serious problem. Indeed, when the Prussians attempted to form an Italian legion from among Venetian prisoners of war they met with such resistance that the project had to be abandoned.[83] Italians were still fighting and dying at Königgrätz even after the battle was lost. The 26th Jägers were one of the last units to leave the field and suffered heavy casualties in helping to cover the retreat.[84]

Altogether, the Italian units at Königgrätz suffered casualties of over 700 killed (more than the entire Italian army lost at Custoza) and 1,000 wounded, with more than 2,000 missing or taken prisoner. In proportion to the losses of the army as a whole, the Venetians accounted for more than their share of killed and wounded and substantially less than their share of the prisoners and missing.[85] Meanwhile, the 16th Infantry, the only Venetian regiment not with Benedek's army, withstood heavy losses on an impossible mission of its own. Stranded at Mainz when the war began, the three battalions joined forces with troops from Austria's German allies and attempted to fight their way eastward to Bohemia. They made it as far as the railway station at Aschaffenburg in northern Bavaria before Prussian troops blocked the way and forced them to surrender.[86] After the campaign, the Italian units were awarded dozens of decorations for their service. The men of the Jäger battalions led the way, the 26th winning twenty-eight silver medals and the 8th Jägers twenty-four. Of the infantry regiments the 13th received twenty silver medals, the 45th fifteen, the 26th ten, the 79th one gold and nine silver. The 16th and 80th won five silver medals apiece and the 38th received two. As for higher honors, Colonel Giulio Bagnalasta, commander of the 79th Infantry, was the only Italian among five officers awarded the Order of the Iron Crown. Twenty-seven officers from Venetian units received distinguished service medals, but only three were Italian.[87]

The defeat at Königgrätz forced Albrecht to evacuate Venetia and send the bulk of his troops to the Danube to help hold the line against a southward advance by the Prussians. He completed his retreat from Venetia on 20 July, taking with him the fifth battalion of the 26th Infantry, the last fresh Italian troops to leave the province in Austrian uniform. Thus, over five weeks after signing the secret agreement conceding Venetia, Austria was still exploiting Venetian manpower. The men were withdrawn without incident and sent to Vienna, where they replenished the regiment's other battalions.[88]

The preliminary Austro–Prussian Peace of Nikolsburg (26 July) enabled Albrecht, now commander-in-chief of the Habsburg army, to rush troops from the northern theater to the southern, where Italian forces had completed the occupation of Venetia and were threatening adjacent Austrian territory. By the time Austro–Italian armistice talks got underway at Cormons on 5 August, Albrecht had an army of 140,000 on the Isonzo, almost twice as many men as he had had at Custoza. Italy had to abandon all of her war aims except the acquisition of Venetia and, on 12 August, concluded an armistice on

Austria's terms. One of the most humiliating features of the agreement allowed the Austrians to station troops in Venetia to garrison Verona and other strategic points pending the conclusion of a definitive peace treaty.[89] Austria then added insult to injury by sending the 22nd (Trieste) Infantry to Verona to serve in the garrison there. The Veronese protested that they would rather have *croati*—the hated Croatian *Grenzer*—than the *bastardi traditori*, but to no avail. After Austria and Italy concluded the Treaty of Vienna on 3 October, formally ending the war, the citizens of Verona grew impatient and clashed with the 22nd and other Austrian units before the occupation finally ended two weeks later.[90]

The Venetian regiments were not among those sent back to the southern theater after the Peace of Nikolsburg. Instead, they remained in and around Vienna or in Hungary pending their demobilization and repatriation. Their behavior during the peace negotiations stood in sharp contrast to the impatience shown by some of the Lombard troops in 1859, but they had little choice in the matter because they were stationed too far from Venetia to take matters into their own hands. Many also feared that if they returned home, the Italian government would punish them for having fought against its Prussian ally. These concerns were so widespread that in late September the Italian plenipotentiary at the Vienna peace talks, General Luigi Menabrea, had to give assurances that the soldiers would not be prosecuted by Italian authorities.[91] After the conclusion of the treaty the two parties had to agree to a timetable for the repatriation, but this too became a problem. Austria wanted to send the men home over a ten-day period but so many were involved—some 48,000—that Italy argued for a timetable of three weeks or more. An outbreak of cholera in eastern Venetia suspended the question temporarily, but on 3 November the process finally began. Thereafter, the repatriation proceeded at a rate of 4,000 men per day and was completed in two weeks.[92]

The demobilization of the seven regiments and two Jäger battalions came amid emotional scenes, as officers and men temporarily laid aside differences of nationality. Prior to leaving Vienna the men of the 80th Infantry passed in review before Francis Joseph, shouting "Evviva Imperatore!" for the final time. When the 38th Infantry disbanded, "the men were escorted to the train by their officers and the regimental band" for a "tumultuous departure from their former commanders."[93] Since there was only one Italian-speaking regiment left in the Habsburg army (the 22nd), few of the men opted to remain in the service. For the same reason, more officers of Italian nationality left the army in 1866 than in 1859 or 1848–49. Under the terms of the peace settlement, they were eligible for commissions in the Italian army, at their old Austrian rank, provided that they filed an application by March 1867.[94] In some regiments as many as a dozen officers accepted the offer, but the majority chose to remain in Habsburg service. There were even cases of officers deciding first to enter the Italian army, then wanting to go back to the Austrian; upon petition, they were allowed to return.[95]

Four of the Venetian regiments (the 16th, 26th, 38th, and 45th) were assigned new recruiting districts in Hungary while three (the 13th, 79th, and 80th) became Galician; the 8th Jägers were converted to Styrian manpower and the 26th Jägers became Austrian. Aside from the Trieste infantry regiment and the Italian minority in the Tyrolese Kaiser–Jägers, Austria's experience with Italian soldiers had come to a close. The relationship had always been a stormy one and, with varying degrees of justification, the army leadership on several occasions had been wary of their reliability. In 1848–49 the men of Lombardy made their best showing, but in 1859 and especially in 1866 the Venetians also acquitted themselves in action. The problems with the Italian units were not unique; the Hungarians had caused their share of concern in 1848–49 and again in 1859, and troops of other nationalties—in particular the Czechs—were to present problems for the army later in the century.

All things considered, the record of Austria's Italian troops was not markedly worse than those from other parts of the empire. Either because of the army's discipline or their own ignorance, the common soldiers for the most part served well; in any event, the performance of the Venetians against Prussia helped balance the ledger of the previous decades. In the wake of a sharp action in Bohemia early in the war of 1866, a dying Jäger of the 26th battalion was overheard mumbling to his German commander "Lei sara contento di noi, abbiam fatto il nostro dovere."[96] The officer no doubt was contented that they, indeed, had done their duty, and his approval would have found an echo throughout much of the leadership of the Habsburg army.

Chapter 4

AUSTRIA'S ITALIAN NAVY

Austria's defeat in 1805 deprived her of the Venetian navy she had inherited just eight years earlier, and the subsequent lost war of 1809 left her completely landlocked, without even the tiny "Trieste navy." As with the army, the bulk of the Italians in the Habsburg navy after 1814 were veterans of Napoleonic Italian service, brought into the fold following Austria's postwar occupation of Lombardy and Venetia. The similarities ended there. Whereas the new Italian units made up only a small part of the Habsburg army, the new Austrian navy consisted overwhelmingly of personnel and ships from the Franco–Italian Adriatic fleet of the war years.[1]

While Eugene de Beauharnais and the Italian army battled the invading forces in the campaign of 1813–14, the Italian fleet remained in port in Venice, its French commander unwilling to challenge a squadron the British had deployed in the Adriatic. Upon occupying the city in April 1814, the Austrians took possession of a fleet roughly the same size as the one the Venetian Republic had left them in 1797: ten ships of the line and eight frigates, many of them still under construction, plus countless smaller vessels. The personnel were not so impressive. The crews, showing the effects of the recent months of inactivity, still included a handful of seamen from France and the other former Napoleonic satellite states. Several failed to remove the red–white–green Italian cockade from their caps before taking their oath to the Austrian emperor.[2]

The process of conversion was not as simple for the Italian officers. Like the seamen, many of them had served Austria once before, in the years 1797-1805 when Venetia belonged to the Habsburgs. But while the crews of the new Austrian navy were organized almost exclusively from Napoleonic Italian veterans, the officers corps was to be an amalgamation of their commanders and the officers of the old "Trieste navy," most of whom had transferred to the Austrian army after the war of 1809. In adjusting the *Rangliste*, the Hofkriegsrat in Vienna automatically awarded the "Trieste" men seniority at every rank. This decision created awkward situations in which Venetians who had served Austria through 1805, then passed into the Italian navy from 1806 to 1814, returned to Habsburg service as subordinates to men they had once commanded.

The most glaring manifestation of the seniority problem came at the highest level of the corps. In July 1814, the Hofkriegsrat appointed August de Conninck commander of the navy (Marine-Kommandant). Born in the Austrian Netherlands, Conninck was among the original officers of the "Trieste navy" and had served in the fleet from 1786 to 1809 before taking command of the army's *Pontonierbataillon* from 1810 to 1814. As of 1805 he held captain's rank, along with former Venetian navy officer Sylvestro Dandolo, but stood behind him on a seniority list formulated after the initial Austrian annexation of Venetia in 1797. During the war of 1805 Dandolo advanced to the role of commander of the navy, but the Treaty of Pressburg forced the Austrians to discharge him along with the rest of their Venetian personnel. After returning to Habsburg service in 1814, Dandolo was offered a captain's commission with seniority inferior to Conninck, whose appointment as commander carried with it the rank of major general.[3]

Dandolo and other officers in similar situations called for a restoration of the *Rangliste* of 1805, arguing that the Treaty of Pressburg had required their discharge from the Austrian navy; between 1806 and 1814, they had had the choice of the Italian navy or no navy at all. Dandolo, charged by the French with "conduite susceptible" during his years in Napoleon's Adriatic fleet, was among those with a strong argument that his Italian service had been neither voluntary nor enthusiastic.[4] But Vienna rejected his solution on the grounds that it would be tantamount to granting credit for service in an enemy fleet. In the years that followed, Conninck's inability to deal with Dandolo and the Venetians kept their wounds from healing, and his favoritism toward fellow "Trieste navy" veterans created a serious rift within the officer corps.

If nationality alone had been the issue, the conflict in the postwar corps would have been no contest: in 1817 73 percent of the active sea officers had Italian surnames. But roughly one-fourth of the officers—the "Trieste" veterans—had never been in the Venetian or Italian navies, while another 25 percent (including Dandolo) had been through the full range of changes in loyalty, from Venetian service to Austrian, then Italian, then again to Austrian. A smaller faction were veterans of Italian service whose initial commissions had been with Austria between 1797 and 1805; a much larger group of younger men receiving their first commissions from the Italian navy had never served the Habsburgs before.[5] The rift between the veterans of the Venetian navy and "Trieste navy" remained the primary source of trouble within the officer corps until the 1830s, when retirements and deaths eliminated most of the antagonists.

Amid the early differences within the naval command, no one questioned the thoroughly Italian character of the new Austrian fleet. The Venice Arsenal became the shipyard of the navy and the Venice lagoon its primary anchorage. The Royal Italian naval academy, established in 1810 by French authorities in the abandoned convent of Sant'Anna, was taken over virtually intact by the Austrians, who retained both the faculty and the curriculum. Conninck introduced German as the official written language of the navy but did not enforce its use. Reports to Vienna frequently were written in Italian and many older Italian officers, most notably Dandolo, never learned German. Italian remained the language of instruction at the naval academy and, in the first sessions after 1814, German was not even offered as an elective course.[6]

In the immediate postwar years, Austrian leaders showed a marked lack of interest in developing the empire's maritime interests. Emperor Francis, foreign minister Count Metternich, and finance minister Count Stadion all agreed that the exercise of sea power should be left to the other major states of Europe. Their main concern was the disposal of the "surplus" ships that had been inherited at Venice; schemes to sell the various ships of the line and frigates all eventually fell through, but this did not mean that the vessels were saved for the Austrian navy. Of the ten ships of the line only two ever entered service, and then, only after being remodeled for use as large frigates. The "customary" navy budget became fixed at 1.5 million gulden per year, in an overall military budget that never dipped lower than 38 million in any year before 1848.[7] Reluctance to spend money on the navy affected every aspect of its operation. Because new programs and pay increases would require a larger budget, such measures were rare. Investigations and reforms came only when Vienna had reason to believe that further savings would result.

The first such initiative came in 1819, when the Hofkriegsrat sent Marquis Amilcare Paulucci delle Roncole to Venice to study the Arsenal, prison hulks and naval education. A veteran of the Neapolitan, French, and Italian navies, Paulucci had finished the Napoleonic wars in the Italian army and, in 1814, received a major general's commission from the Austrians.[8] The navy requested his services, but he was assigned instead to the army and served as a brigadier in Bohemia until receiving a post in the Marine Department of the Hofkriegsrat in 1818. His naval experience and status as an "outsider" placed him in a good position to investigate the navy; though Italian, his non-Venetian (Modenese) birth precluded any overly cordial relations with the Venetian faction in the service.

Paulucci's mission brought improvements in the administration of the shipyard and prison hulks, but the greatest changes came at the naval academy. The school the marquis visited suffered from bad management, its students were undisciplined and poorly supervised, and expenditure, though modest, was out of line with the current results. Enrollment had fallen from fifty-eight in the last non-Austrian term (1813–14) to twelve in 1819–20. Paulucci proposed sweeping reforms of the administration and curriculum that would bring the school into some degree of conformity with the Austrian military academy at Wiener Neustadt and military engineering academy in Vienna. After entertaining thoughts of closing the school altogether, the Hofkriegsrat followed his suggestions and, in the fall of 1820, reopened it as the "kaiserliche königliche Marine-Cadetten-Collegium." The course of study was increased to five years from three, with the third year to be spent at sea. History, German, religion, and the law of the sea joined the traditional mathematics and navigation classes. To stimulate attendance, Vienna offered twenty scholarships for the sons of Habsburg officers and bureaucrats.[9]

But amid the changes, the new academy retained the Italian character of the old. The staff still included no German Austrians, and Italian remained the language of all courses of instruction, to the extent that even German was taught in Italian. To reduce the operating deficit and help pay for the scholarship students, the school allowed the enrollment of anyone whose family could afford the tuition and required only the scholarship students to enter the navy upon graduation. Thus, the academy could be used to educate young men for careers as merchant captains or as a preparatory school for other studies. This policy was a financial success, and the student body, after reaching a low of five in 1821, grew to average fifty per session by the 1830s. But the perennial presence of a number of students with no intention of ever serving in the Austrian navy kept the naval academy from developing into a purely military school. The imperial government's continued insistence on limiting expenditure also meant that most students spent their third year "at sea" on cruises in the lagoon or the Gulf of Venice. The first genuine training cruise in the Adriatic came only years later, in 1827.[10]

The next great investigation came in 1822, when the Hofkriegsrat commissioned Feldmarschalleutnant Count Louis Folliot de Crenneville to study the material condition of the fleet. A former adjutant to Archduke Charles, Crenneville had experience in the pre–1789 French fleet and in Habsburg naval administration. After making his tour of Venice, he called for a dramatic expansion in the size of the Austrian navy and in the scope of its operations. The count also commented on personnel and other matters extraneous to his official mission, arguing in the strongest terms that it was in no way dangerous for Austria to have a navy so completely Italian in character. The Venetians, he concluded, were a maritime people, natural seamen, for whom the navy provided a vital outlet.[11]

The Hofkriegsrat rejected Crenneville's call for a larger fleet but certainly did not challenge his remarks on personnel. While a number of Italians in the Austrian army were suspected, justly or unjustly, of Carbonari activity, the navy thus far had remained free from any sign of liberal or revolutionary sympathy. Venetians young and old appeared to be perfectly trustworthy, and there was no reason to question their loyalty to the emperor. Though the Flemish Conninck remained in command, retirements of other "Trieste navy" veterans left the officer corps dominated by Venetian navy veterans and younger Venetians first commissioned by the Napoleonic kingdom of Italy. From the 1820s onward, non–Italians entered the corps in increasing numbers, but their growing presence brought no change in the Italian character of the service. A German Austrian boy aspiring to a career at sea had to learn Italian before matriculating at the naval academy, usually between the ages of twelve and fifteen. Once there, pressure from peers combined with the charms of Venice to "italianize" all but the most stubborn youth. Those not assimilated were ostracized, as were non-Italian officers entering the navy via transfer from the Austrian army.[12]

Meanwhile, the common manpower of the fleet remained overwhelmingly Venetian Italian and largely volunteer. For men from Venice and the adjacent littoral, enlistment in the Italian-speaking navy was an attractive alternative to conscription into the army, which could result in years of service far from home in non-Italian garrisons. Dalmatia was the only province reserved for naval conscription; the regiments of northern Italy and the Küstenland were supposed to turn over all *seekundige* conscripts to the navy but often hesitated to do so.[13] This combination of policy and preference left the crews of the fleet with a Venetian majority, followed by Italians from Istria and the ports of Dalmatia and a contingent of italianized Dalmatian Croats, in all, a congenial mixture which the Italian officer corps sought to preserve. In the 1820s, when the Hofkriegsrat sent several dozen German Austrian artillerymen to Venice for naval service, their Italian officers dismissed almost all of them as being unfit for sea duty.[14] Of all the sailors, the best ironically came from the cities of Trieste and Fiume, which traditionally were exempt from all conscription. Without the Venetian incentive of avoiding service in the army, the veteran merchant seamen of these ports had to be lured with good salaries for their six year volunteer enlistments.[15]

Much to the detriment of the overall morale of the navy, high pay was not a common feature. Officers not from wealthy families had difficulty making ends meet on their meager salaries, and many turned to illegal activities to supplement their incomes. The deployment of the fleet during the 1820s put Austrian commanders in a perfect position to engage in the smuggling of Levantine goods. Starting in the summer of 1821, the Greek War of Independence disrupted the peace in the Eastern Mediterranean, and Austria, with substantial commercial interests in the region, maintained a squadron there to guard her merchant ships against attacks from Greek pirates. As the war dragged on through the rest of the decade, the Habsburg naval presence took on a more permanent character, based in the Turkish port of Smyrna (Izmir), and Austrian naval vessels regularly plied the route between the Levant and their home ports in the Adriatic. The full extent of their smuggling cannot be ascertained, but one celebrated incident in 1827 called the practice to the attention of the naval command. That year a customs cutter intercepted the brig *Orione* off Venice and found it to be carrying a cargo of salt. The lenient treatment of the commander and his crew would appear to indicate that such incidents were relatively common. The *Orione* case did not come to trial until 1831, when all charges were dropped. Far from being ruined by the affair, the commander of the ship, Lieutenant Giovanni Alberti, received a promotion while the case was still pending.[16]

The handling of the *Orione* incident reflected the style of Connick's successor as naval commander, the Marquis Paulucci. The year after he completed his investigation of the navy, the Hofkriegsrat chose Paulucci to command the squadron supporting the Austrian invasion of Naples; in 1824, when Conninck retired, the marquis succeeded him with the elevated title of Marine–Ober–Kommandant. From Vienna's point of view he was the perfect navy commander, an Italian but not a Venetian. The higher officers in the corps, however, did not appreciate being superseded by an outsider for the command of the Naples mission in 1821 or the overall command three years later. Dandolo, next in line on both occasions, did not take the setbacks well. On the contrary, he became Paulucci's chief nemesis in the years that followed.

The two men clashed often over the navy's disciplinary policies. Paulucci's actions in cases such as the *Orione's* smuggling reflected his genuine sympathy for the plight of the junior officers and their crews. Salaries and general working conditions were poor, and because the marquis, being a good politician, had no intention of undercutting his own position with Vienna by campaigning actively for a larger budget, they would continue to be poor. In his view, it was only fair to look the other way when the pressures of life in the service caused seemingly minor problems. Dandolo, the Venetian aristocrat, took the opposite view. Already thirty when the republic fell, he had been virtually reared in the old Venetian navy. He lived by the values of a bygone age and had nothing but contempt for those whose standards of honor and duty were any less stringent than his own. Paulucci, of course, fell into this category, frustrating Dandolo with his apparent inability to see that lax discipline ultimately would lead to a general deterioration of morale.[17]

Dandolo also took it upon himself, under both Conninck and Paulucci, to speak on behalf of all Venetian officers whenever he felt that their dignity or that of their city had been offended. One of his loudest and most nonsensical protests came in 1830, after Paulucci had the unseaworthy frigate *Bellona* scrapped in Trieste rather than in Venice. Dandolo, incensed, complained to the Hofkriegsrat that the decision was an insult to the city of Venice and to all Venetians.[18] Fortunately for Paulucci, Dandolo did not have much of a personal following within the corps; younger officers, even those from Venice, considered him an arrogant relic from the past. Vienna learned to handle him with care, placating him with active commands in the Levant. After he became too old to go to sea, he was officially designated as Paulucci's second-in-command. When the Hofkriegsrat finally introduced admiral's ranks, it made a point of elevating Dandolo to rear admiral, the same designation given to Paulucci, before promoting the commander to vice admiral a year later.[19]

As an army officer in the immediate postwar years, Paulucci had missed the initial eruption of the conflict between the "Trieste navy" veterans and the former Venetian navy officers. Having never served in either force, he was able to stand above the lingering feud in his first years as commander. With time, both factions grew smaller and less significant, and a younger generation came to dominate the corps. By the 1830s, most of the captains were from the group of officers whose first commissions or ship commands had been with the Napoleonic Italian navy; the brightest star among them was the Venetian Francesco Bandiera, leader of a mission against Moroccan pirates in 1828-30 and of a cruise to North America in 1833-34. Below them, the generation born during or immediately after the Napoleonic wars now provided the junior officers and cadets. Maturing in the aftermath of the revolutions of 1830, they were far more receptive to Italian nationalism than their elders. In the loose atmosphere of Paulucci's navy, many of these subalterns sympathized quite openly with Giuseppe Mazzini and the Young Italy movement.

During the decade of the 1830s, Mazzinian revolutionary literature became popular with younger Italian officers and even circulated at the naval academy in Venice. The faculty there, still predominantly Italian, did nothing to stop the flow of subversive ideas, and some instructors actually encouraged nationalism among their students. History professor Emilio Tipaldo, an internationally known scholar and the only Ph.D. on the staff, lectured on the glories of Rome and the Renaissance, as well as the more recent exploits of Italians fighting in the Napoleonic wars. Carlo Alberto Radaelli, a student at the school from 1831 to 1836, later recalled that Tipaldo's depictions of the great Italian past "aroused in us a sense of shame" at the plight of a modern Italy "divided by foreigners and slave to so many tyrants." He described himself and his classmates as "patriotic, hating the foreign domination, and ready to make any sacrifice for *la patria*." At the naval academy, literally under the noses of the Austrians, the future officers received the "most liberal" education available anywhere in Italy.[20]

This remarkable state of affairs evolved because of the general attitude Vienna had had toward the navy since 1814 and the spirit that prevailed under Paulucci's command. The marquis, though deferential toward his superiors, cooperated with the army command in Venice only rarely and tried to avoid all contact with the Austrian police.[21] He treated the navy as his personal domain and would not tolerate the interference of outsiders. The officer corps and naval academy thus were insulated from the watchful eye of the army and police, while among the officers and cadets themselves, an increasing social cohesion offered further protection for the young radicals. Whereas Dandolo and those of his background maintained barriers between themselves and all non-Venetian, non-aristocratic officers, Venetians among the younger generations were far more likely to embrace any non-Venetian (or even non-Italian) receptive to assimilation. The small size of the corps—between 100 and 150 sea officers, and never more than fifty cadets—made it almost as close-knit as a regiment, and ties between father and son or uncle and nephew were reinforced by frequent intermarriage among navy families. In addition to the nascent bonds of nationalism among the younger men, the broader ties of family and friendship were to make it all the more difficult for the Austrian authorities to investigate and reform the navy once its disloyalty became apparent.

The initial spread of Mazzini's ideas within the fleet was aided tremendously by the fact that two of his greatest sympathizers were sons of the highly esteemed Captain (later Rear Admiral) Francesco Bandiera. Attilio Bandiera, academy class of 1828, had his first direct exposure to Italian revolutionaries while on a voyage from Trieste to New York in 1835, one of the number of cruises the navy made in the 1830s to deport political prisoners and internees (most of them Polish) to the United States. The Italians among these emigrants included the famed Federico Confalonieri, but Attilio's contact was Pietro Maroncelli, with whom he corresponded as early as April 1836. That same spring his younger brother Emilio, a classmate of Radaelli, finished his course of study at the naval academy; his subversive activity dated from 1834 when, as a fifteen year-old student, he began to distribute patriotic leaflets to his friends. Radaelli later recalled Emilio's fascination with the Italian revolution of 1831 and his admiration for the Polish patriot Kosciuszko.[22]

In light of the sentiments and activities of the younger Bandieras, it is no small irony that their father, Francesco, played a part in suppressing the Italian revolution of 1831. After Austrian troops crushed the rebel army in the Romagna in the spring of that year, its leader, General Carlo Zucchi, attempted to escape by sea from Ancona with 100 of his followers, only to be intercepted in the Adriatic by Captain Bandiera and the corvette *Abbondanza*. This feat earned the captain the personal thanks of Metternich and the title of hereditary baron of the Austrian Empire.[23] The capture of Zucchi was only one highlight of a distinguished career which, by the late 1830s, made Bandiera the premier sea officer in the corps. When the Near Eastern crisis flared up again in 1839, the Hofkriegsrat naturally insisted that the aging Paulucci place the baron in charge of Austria's Levant squadron, an honor soon accompanied by promotion to rear admiral. Bandiera's new rank and clout within the fleet enabled him to take along both of his sons on the campaign. Ironically, it was while they were in the Levant in 1839–40 that their political activity assumed a more organized form.

At the beginning of 1840, Attilio Bandiera asked Radaelli to join "a new secret society with the goal of freeing Italy from foreign domination."[24] Their group, called Esperia after the ancient Greek name for Italy, had at least a dozen members at its founding; it continued to meet aboard the ships of the squadron even as they went into action against the Egyptians in the fall of 1840. In league with a larger British fleet, the Austrian ships intervened in the Turco-Egyptian war and dislodged the forces of Mehemet Ali from Beirut, Acre, Sidon, and other coastal strongholds. The Bandiera brothers did not distinguish themselves in the fighting, although Attilio received a commendation for his participation in the shelling of Acre. Other Esperia members won greater laurels. Cadet Domenico Chinca, one of the founders, served as standard bearer for the young Archduke Frederick in a daring assault on the citadel at Sidon, and his climb to plant the imperial flag on the highest parapet won him a medal for bravery. Ensign Domenico Moro, another Esperia leader, also received a decoration in the campaign.[25]

Isolation from Italy and other Mazzinian sects was Esperia's biggest problem in its first years of existence. Its members were all aboard ships of the Austrian Levant squadron, which spent their time either cruising the Eastern Mediterranean or anchored in the harbor of Smyrna. The Bandieras longed to communicate with Mazzini, who was unaware of their existence. In 1842, the Austrian government unwittingly provided the opportunity for Esperia's first, and only, direct contact with the leader of Young Italy.

The occasion was a special cruise by Archduke Frederick, a Habsburg prince being groomed as Paulucci's successor. He was scheduled to take the new frigate *Bellona* to England, where he would have a reunion with British officers from the Levant campaign, meet with Queen Victoria and Prince Albert, and receive the Order of the Bath. His crew, hand-picked from among those decorated in 1840, included Esperia member Domenico Moro. Mazzini had been living in exile in London since 1837, and Attilio Bandiera pinned his hopes on Moro's ability to find him and deliver a letter telling of his group's activity. Frederick's three and a half month stay in Britain provided the young ensign with more than enough time to visit the revolutionary leader and convey Esperia's greetings. In his letter Attilio outlined his personal philosophy and emphasized his value to the Italian cause: he was "not an exile" like most Young Italy members, but rather an officer in the navy of one of the governments standing in the way of Italian independence and unity. If it continued to gain support within the fleet, Esperia could grow to become a tremendous asset in the fight against Austria.[26]

After the *Bellona* returned home in early 1843, it proceeded without Frederick to the Levant, where it became the flagship of Rear Admiral Bandiera. In the months that followed, correspondence continued between the Bandieras and Mazzini, and Esperia finally established contact with other Young Italy sects in the Mediterranean. Their most significant connection was Nicola Fabrizi's Legione Italica, a group of émigrés based on Malta. Meanwhile, within the squadron, the brothers continued to proselytize and gain more converts for Esperia. In late August 1843 Emilio informed Fabrizi that they had "120 men of the most firm resolution" who were prepared to seize the entire squadron: Attilio was to lead the mutiny aboard the *Bellona*, Emilio on the corvette *Clemenza*, Moro on the corvette *Adria*, and Ensign Ippolito Mazzuchelli on the brig *Tritone*. Radaelli, transferred home to Venice later in the year, estimated that two-thirds of the officers in the navy were in sympathy with the secret society.[27]

The brothers apparently made no attempt to keep their views

secret from their father. Fellow officers later revealed that Attilio turned mealtime in the stateroom of the *Bellona* into a forum for his revolutionary ideas, and that such talk "bey der Tafel des Contre-Admiral Bandiera" was not uncommon. Given his own past record, the elder Bandiera no doubt would not have countenanced similar diatribes from other junior officers; coming from his own sons, however, the outbursts presented him with a serious dilemma. His own bitterness over being robbed of the opportunity to command the navy may have been the key to his decision to tolerate their behavior: next in seniority after the aging Paulucci and Dandolo, he was the one most hurt by the Hofkriegsrat's decision to designate the young Archduke Frederick as the next Marine-Ober-Kommandant. There is no evidence, however, that the rear admiral ever sympathized with his sons' views. Attilio's subsequent plotting to seize the *Bellona* by force indicates that his father had no intention of ever willingly placing his ship at the disposal of the Italian cause.[28]

During the second half of 1843, Fabrizi urged the Bandieras to put their plans in motion and take over the squadron. After the ships were flying the Italian tricolor, they could be used to attack the Sardinian, Papal or Neapolitan coast, supporting a blow by the Legione Italica. Mazzini had to intervene to persuade Esperia to delay the mutiny, arguing that the naval effort would be futile unless it were accompanied by a truly formidable uprising on land.[29] Late in the year the society was dealt a further blow when the navy transferred two of its leaders to Venice: Emilio Bandiera to the post of personal adjutant to Paulucci, and Mazzuchelli to a teaching position at the naval academy. The brothers parted pledging to maintain contact; over the winter of 1843–44, they coordinated plans to desert and rendezvous at either Corfu or Malta.

On 17 February 1844, Emilio Bandiera received two days' leave from Paulucci to attend a Carnival ball in Trieste. Once there, he contacted former officer Giulio Canal, one of the founders of Esperia, who helped him obtain civilian clothes and a false passport. On the 20th he sent word to Paulucci that illness would delay his return to Venice; three days later he boarded a merchant steamer for Corfu. On 28 February, Attilio Bandiera went ashore in Smyrna with Paolo Mariani, a gunner's mate who had been acting as his personal servant. They headed west aboard a Greek merchant ship, but only after staying in the city for several days. During this time, Attilio informed his father by letter that he had deserted in order to foment revolution at home. The rear admiral then shared the news with his second-in-command, Captain Luigi Matticola, but neither of them informed any higher authority.[30]

Traditional Italian accounts contend that Emilio Bandiera deserted after seeing an order for his arrest among Paulucci's incoming correspondence; most attribute this letter to Field Marshal Radetzky. The same sources contend that Attilio's timing was dictated by the treachery of an aide Mazzini had sent to Turkey to act as a liaison between Esperia and Young Italy; the agent supposedly betrayed him to the Austrian ambassador in Constantinople, Count Bartholomäus von Stürmer, who informed the imperial authorities of his treasonous schemes. The correspondence of Radetzky and Stürmer provides no evidence for either scenario.[31] The Austrians were aware of plans for a general uprising in Italy in the spring of 1844[32] but had no knowledge that a revolutionary group within their own navy planned to be involved. The brothers may have left their posts to participate in this revolt, or to remain together as they continued their plotting. February 1844 most likely was the earliest that they were able to coordinate their desertions. In any event, they considered their status as revolutionaries to be strengthened by their own break with the past. Far from relinquishing their role in Esperia or their plans for a general mutiny, they expected other officers and men to follow their lead.

After learning of the desertions, the Hofkriegsrat noted that the flight of "the sons of a man so highly placed as Rear Admiral Bandiera" must raise suspicions of the loyalty of other officers. Paulucci flatly rejected this assertion, but the manner in which he and other navy officials handled the Bandiera case ended up being far more damaging to the reputation of the service than the desertions themselves. In the Levant, eleven days passed before Captain Alexander Bujacovich, one of Admiral Bandiera's captains, sent word to Paulucci of Attilio's desertion. In Venice, the commander himself refused to treat Emilio's disappearance as a desertion until mid-March, when Captain Leone Graziani, Attilio Bandiera's father-in-law, gave him letters that the younger brother had written from Corfu to his mother, Baroness Anna Marsich Bandiera, and sister-in-law, Maria Graziani Bandiera.

The letters confirmed that the two desertions were coordinated and that the brothers planned to join forces for a "holy war" to liberate and unite Italy. But Paulucci still refused to acknowledge the seriousness of the affair, instead choosing to treat the Bandieras (aged thirty-four and twenty-five) as a pair of wayward youths. Along with the viceroy of Lombardy–Venetia, Archduke Rainer, he supported a plan which sent Baroness Bandiera to Corfu to plead with her sons to give themselves up. She reached the island in late April, around the time Attilio finally arrived, but returned to Venice disappointed after the brothers rejected the viceroy's offer of a pardon in exchange for surrender. After the failure of her mission, the navy finally charged the Bandieras with high treason.

While waiting for his older brother to join him, Emilio Bandiera travelled from Corfu to Malta to consult with Fabrizi and members of the Legione Italica, who provided him with money to purchase a boat for an expedition to the Italian mainland. Much to the dismay of the Austrian consular officials monitoring his activity, the British refused to cooperate in apprehending him on the grounds that he had broken no law in their territories.[33] The Austrians responded by sending the corvettes *Adria* and *Veloce* to Malta to increase their own surveillance.

Ironically, the assignment of the two warships only worked to the advantage of the Bandieras. On 7 May, after the *Adria* arrived at Malta, Ensign Domenico Moro deserted the ship to join the "honorable patriots," as he characterized the brothers in a letter to his commander, Captain Antonio Morari. The captain of the *Veloce*, Giorgio Bua, advised Morari to burn Moro's letter, but after a few days he had second thoughts and took the initiative in reporting the desertion to Paulucci. The marquis, however, did not report the incident to Vienna. He had spent the past two months trying to persuade the Hofkriegsrat that the Bandieras had acted alone and that no broader conspiracy existed in the fleet. Moro's desertion wrecked his attempts to limit the crisis and assured that outsiders would intervene to conduct an investigation.

It took almost a month for the navy to inform Vienna of Moro's desertion. After he left the *Adria*, the ship joined the Levant squadron at Smyrna, where Morari told Admiral Bandiera the distressing news. The elder Bandiera, taking some solace in the fact that the scandal no longer involved his sons alone, hastened to report it to Vienna by way of Venice. His version reached Metternich only after the chancellor had heard the story from Count Ferdinand Zichy, the army commandant in Venice, and through his own espionage network: Austrian spies reported from Paris that Mazzini already had sent a letter there from London, informing the local Italian exiles of Moro's defection. The stock of Paulucci's navy, higher than ever after the Near Eastern campaign of 1840, fell to an all time low.

In late May, before word of Moro's action reached the imperial capital, the president of the Hofkriegsrat, Count Hardegg, formally recommended that Paulucci be replaced as Marine–Ober–Kommandant. Archduke Frederick, currently training to take over the job, simply would do so ahead of schedule, as soon as the present crisis came to an end. With the new leadership in place, Austria would finally do what it should have done in 1814—make the navy an integral part of the imperial armed forces and eliminate its anomalous Italian character.[34] As a first step, Admiral Bandiera was relieved of his command effective immediately and ordered to return home with the *Bellona*.

In the meantime, Moro joined the Bandieras and helped lay the plans for their expedition. On 12 June, they finally left Corfu aboard a small fishing boat, accompanied by the deserting seaman Mariani and sixteen other émigrés. Their destination, the Calabrian coast of the kingdom of Naples, was chosen because an uprising had occurred there recently and because it was within easy sailing distance of their leaky vessel. After landing near Crotone on the 16th, they found the local population indifferent to their cause. The Austrian consul in Corfu sent word of their departure to Neapolitan authorities, and the defection of one of the rebels, the Corsican Pietro Boccheciampe, further compromised the operation. On 19 June, Neapolitan forces killed two of the group and captured the rest, wounding Moro and Emilio Bandiera in the process.[35]

Count Zichy, placed in charge of the investigation of the navy, was among the army leaders calling for an Austrian trial of the deserting officers; only then could the full extent of the conspiracy within the fleet be uncovered. But Metternich recognized that if Habsburg authorities tried and executed the Bandieras and Moro, it would increase their stature as Italian martyrs and cause Austria more trouble in Lombardy and Venetia. He waived all claims to their extradition, allowing the Neapolitans to try them before a special court at Cosenza. There, on 25 July, the brothers and Moro were executed along with six of their fellow rebels. Seaman Mariani and seven others received prison terms.[36]

In August 1844, Archduke Frederick took over as commander and the process of building a more loyal navy finally got underway.

When the *Bellona* arrived in Venice the following month, Admiral Bandiera was forced to join Paulucci in retirement. Captain Morari also lost his commission for failing to report his receipt of Moro's letter in Malta. Ironically, the man who advised him to burn the letter, Captain Giorgio Bua, was sent to the Levant with the *Veloce* to replace Bandiera and the *Bellona*. After Bua admitted to his earlier knowledge of Moro's desertion, the navy transferred him to a post on land in Trieste and assigned Captain Giuseppe Marsich to the Levant instead. Marsich's loyal record overrode the fact that he was the uncle of the late Bandiera brothers, but his appointment reflected the dilemma the Austrians faced in the wake of the crisis: most of the senior officers of the navy either had failed to tell all they knew about the desertions, or else were connected by blood or marriage to the Bandiera family. More cause for alarm came from the testimony at Cosenza, where the Corsican Boccheciampe revealed that during their weeks at Corfu, the Bandieras had corresponded with a number of other naval officers in an attempt to incite further desertions; Moro, as it turned out, was the only one to take the bait in time. Count Zichy resolved to uncover the would-be accomplices, and had the officers and crew of the *Bellona* detained for questioning.

The naval officers refused to reveal anything about Attilio Bandiera or Esperia, forcing Zichy to rely on the testimony of two army officers who had been on temporary assignment aboard the *Bellona*: captains Adolf Kübeck and Count Ladislaus Karolyi. They confirmed that both Admiral Bandiera and his subordinate, Captain Matticola, had known of Attilio's desertion from the start. Karolyi eventually became Zichy's leading witness but proved to be more disturbed by the homosexual behavior of some of *Bellona's* officers than by their revolutionary plotting. The investigation ended with a sodomy trial of Ensign Francesco Baldiserotto, a close friend of the Bandieras and founding member of Esperia. The proceedings shed no new light on the revolutionary conspiracy within the fleet and ended in Baldiserotto's acquittal on the sex charges.[37] The affair officially came to an end in January 1845, when plans to charge Admiral Bandiera with treason were dropped. Other officers suspected of revolutionary sympathies were returned to duty, while the crew of the *Bellona* was dispersed among other warships.[38]

According to Radaelli, one of the only Esperia members to quit the service in 1844, an Austrian official later told him that "four-fifths of the officers in the navy" could have been condemned for their action, or lack of action, before and during the Bandiera affair.[39] When it came to those already holding commissions, Archduke Frederick's new administration could do little other than rearrange the lineup to put the least compromised men in the most sensitive positions; anything bolder would have risked a full scale mutiny. When it became apparent that there were not enough trustworthy officers to go around, the navy simply scaled down its operations. After showing the Austrian flag in the Eastern Mediterranean for most of the preceding twenty years, the Levant squadron was recalled and merged with the Adriatic squadron.

When it came to the future officer corps, there were fewer impediments to decisive action. At the naval academy, much maligned during the course of Zichy's investigation, a rigorous purge of the faculty and student body brought an immediate change of atmosphere. Captain Andrea Bordini, director of the school for the past ten years, was exiled to a post in Dalmatia. Mazzuchelli and other unreliable service faculty went back to sea, and civilian instructors, including the famous Dr. Tipaldo, were fired. The navy retained Italian as the language of instruction but intensified the teaching of German, even adding German literature to the course of study. In an effort to disentangle the bonds of family and class that formed such a vital component of the navy's Italian character, the number of scholarship positions was increased and officers' sons, automatically accepted in the past, were subjected to the same standards of admission as other students. Frederick, however, handicapped the recovery by appointing the disgraced Captain Matticola to serve as interim director of the academy for the 1844–45 term. Thereafter, a non-Italian director, Captain Ludwig Kudriaffsky, stayed with the job for only two years.[40]

The reform of the naval academy, though far from perfect, served the purpose of making it less attractive to Italians. Within four years the proportion of Italians in the cadet corps fell from 68 percent to 34 percent, while the German Austrian contingent grew from 14 percent to become the largest, at 38 percent. At the same time, the decision not to attempt a purge of the sea officers left their ranks virtually unchanged: 59 percent Italian and 17 percent German in 1844, 60 percent Italian and 16 percent German at the beginning of 1848.[41] As for the common manpower of the fleet, the Bandiera affair inspired a shift of recruiting efforts away from Venetia and also Lombardy, after it was discovered that Attilio's companion, the seaman

Paolo Mariani, was a native Lombard. Investigators learned that men from the districts around Lake Maggiore and Como had been passing themselves off as *seekundig* for years, avoiding army service in favor of the navy. The Hofkriegsrat called a halt to all enlistment of inland Italians, and Frederick stepped up recruiting on the eastern shore of the Adriatic. This brought more Croatians and Dalmatian Italians into the service, but budget cuts caused most of them to be discharged after only a short time.[42] The archduke also set plans in motion for the future transfer of the navy's headquarters across the Adriatic to Pola, site of an ancient Roman naval base. Though predominantly Italian, this sleepy Istrian fishing village was considered a safe haven from the corrupting influence of Venice.

At the end of 1846, Pola became the center of operations for the Adriatic squadron, now commanded by a Croatian captain, Johann von Buratovich. The following autumn, Frederick ordered a redeployment of the larger Austrian warships away from Venice, ensuring that none of the navy's frigates would be there in the event of trouble. The archduke's sudden death in October 1847, at the age of twenty-six, forced the Hofkriegsrat to look for a successor at a time when the rising tensions in Lombardy and Venetia were starting to show within the navy as well. Dandolo, at eighty-one, became Marine-Ober-Kommandant but died a month after Frederick. Vienna then appointed Feldmarschalleutnant Anton von Martini to take over the navy.

The son of a fortress commander of Lombard descent, Martini did not consider himself Italian. He was touted as the most intelligent Austrian general and, at the time of his promotion, was serving as director of the Wiener Neustadt Military Academy. A cavalryman with no maritime experience, he took the new job reluctantly, only after being assured that Frederick's adjutant, Captain Johann Marinovich, would serve him in the same capacity. Unfortunately, Marinovich was universally hated within the navy, by Italians and non-Italians alike.[43] In the six weeks between Dandolo's death and Martini's arrival in Venice, the Croatian captain served as interim head of the fleet and, together with the army's Count Zichy, reopened the investigations of Matticola, Baldiserotto, and other officers implicated in the Bandiera affair. By the time Martini assumed command at the end of December 1847, the navy was on the verge of rebellion.

The city of Venice as a whole was restless during the winter of 1847–48. The anti-Austrian party, led by lawyer Daniele Manin and liberal scholar Niccolo Tommaseo, espoused a mixture of Venetian particularism and Italian nationalism attractive to the tastes of the traditionally moderate Venetian public. While Mazzini still had his share of secret followers within the navy, the radicalism of Young Italy had never been popular in the city and claimed even fewer adherents after the Bandiera fiasco.[44] But Austrian authorities played into the hands of the extremists by arresting Manin and Tommaseo in January 1848. Outraged Venetians responded by striking out at the various symbols of Habsburg rule, including naval officers, who had to be permitted to dress in civilian clothes while off duty. As tensions rose, Martini received orders from Vienna to warn all naval personnel that disloyalty would be punished "with all force of the law."[45]

The revolution of 1848 came to Vienna on 13 March, and when the news reached Venice four days later, Austrian authorities quickly lost control of the city. The civil governor freed Manin and Tommaseo and allowed the creation of a civic guard. The latter soon had their own cannon courtesy of the chief of naval artillery, Major Antonio Paulucci, son of the former commander. Zichy lost his nerve in the midst of the crisis and Martini, still new to his job, was of little use to the cause of law and order. Nevertheless, the navy commander took it upon himself to see that calm was maintained in the Arsenal, where convicts provided most of the labor. On the 22nd, he made a personal visit to the shipyard in an effort to defuse tensions; Marinovich went along, though, and his appearance promptly touched off a riot. After the Arsenal workers murdered Marinovich, the naval infantry was called in to restore order. But with cries of "Viva l'Italia! Viva la Repubblica!" and "Viva San Marco!" filling the air, the marines deserted rather than disperse the rioters. The naval artillery followed suit, and the civic guard occupied the Arsenal. The three Italian army battalions in Venice (the 6th Garrison, the Venetian Grenadiers, and the third battalion of the 13th Infantry) also deserted, enabling Manin to take control of the city. Later the same day, he formed a provisional government and proclaimed the restoration of the Venetian Republic.[46]

Antonio Paulucci became navy minister in the rebel cabinet, while Captain Graziani, the highest-ranking active Italian officer, was named commander of the Venetian navy. Zichy, the civil governor, and their non-Italian subordinates were allowed to leave the city on the night of 22 March aboard a merchant steamer bound for Trieste. Graziani ordered its captain to go first to Pola to inform the fleet of the revolution; a packet of instructions included letters recalling all Austrian warships to Venice. But the captain subsequently revealed the orders to the Austrians and agreed to sail directly to Trieste. The army commander there, Feldmarshalleutnant Count Franz Gyulai, alerted the head of the squadron, Captain Buratovich, and ordered him to remain at Pola. By the narrowest of margins, the Venetian rebels were denied control of the Austrian fleet.[47]

The orders recalling the fleet to Venice should not be viewed as a presumptuous attempt at a coup, for the political and naval leaders of the provisional regime clearly did not see it in that light. On the contrary, the instructions were given as a matter of course, evidence that the Venetians considered it *their* navy, not Austria's. For the past thirty-four years they had been allowed to dominate the service but never to command it. Now, with the Austrian hierarchy removed by the revolution, the aberration, in their view, had ended and they were once again in complete control. All along, the Italian majority in the officer corps had taken some solace in the past: in 1847, when Archduke Frederick died, the officers' formal expression of sympathy even made a point of referring to the Austrian navy as the "successor to the Venetian."[48] After March 1848, the "restored" Venetian navy commenced operations with an air of business-as-usual; seniority earned under the Austrian flag was respected, from Graziani down to the lowest cadet, but with everyone promoted at least one rank.

The difference was that just over one-third of the officers decided to remain in Habsburg service. Their rump of an Austrian navy, setting up shop at Pola and Trieste, also controlled most of the seaworthy ships. The resulting stalemate marked the beginning of a new era for the fleet. In the next eighteen years, until the Austrians permanently lost both Lombardy and Venetia, a majority of their navy's common seamen would still be Italian. But in this era of tension and intermittent war, a "de-italianized" hierarchy would command the navy and take decisive measures to erase all memory of its disloyal Italian past. In the years 1814–48, Austria distrusted her Italian soldiers when she had little reason to; at the same time, her Italian sailors were trusted when they, or at least their officers, should not have been. The navy endured a traumatic experience in 1848, but it left no doubt as to what the future role of Italians in the fleet would have to be.

Chapter 5

DENOUEMENT AT SEA

The Lombard and Venetian revolutions of 1848–49 were crushed largely through the efforts of Radetzky and the Austrian army, whose victories at Custoza (July 1848) and Novara (March 1849) guaranteed that the provinces would remain under Habsburg control. But the old field marshal's soldiers could not walk on water, and despite their best efforts they were not able to subdue the rebels of Venice until August 1849, twelve months after the city's last links to the *terra firma* were severed. The Austrian navy, after recovering from the revolution in the safer harbors of Trieste and Pola, ultimately contributed to the fall of Venice by blockading it from the open sea while the army shelled it from the shores of the lagoon.[1]

Before then, the war in the Adriatic went through several phases. In April 1848 the new commander of the Austrian squadron, Captain Kudriaffsky, imposed a blockade on Venice, but the following month a joint Sardinian–Neapolitan squadron, with Venetian support, intervened to blockade Trieste. The Italian fleet kept the Habsburg warships in port even after the Neapolitans withdrew their support in June, but in August, following Radetzky's victory at Custoza, the terms of the armistice required the Sardinians to break off their blockade. The Venetians lacked the resources to sustain it on their own, and in September, Kudriaffsky again blockaded Venice. This time, however, a French squadron—in a gesture of support for the rebels—shadowed his forces and helped keep the port open. The following month, after the second revolution in Vienna raised Italian hopes once again, the Sardinians reappeared in the upper Adriatic to join the French in their passive obstruction of Kudriaffsky's efforts. The Austrian navy then spent most of the winter of 1848–49 in port, but foul weather in the Adriatic compelled the Sardinians and Venetians to do likewise. In February 1849 the Habsburg government hired a Danish commodore, Hans Birch von Dahlerup, to fill the posts of Marine-Ober-Kommandant and squadron commander; by the time he reached Pola, the armistice following the battle of Novara had brought a definitive end to the Sardinian campaign in the Adriatic. Dahlerup reinstituted the blockade of Venice and maintained it until August 1849. He was challenged only by a few desperate sorties of the rebel navy in the last days before the city surrendered.

When the revolution of 1848 divided the navy between the Venetians and the Austrian loyalists, the latter retained all three of its frigates, two of six corvettes, six of eleven brigs, and one of two steamships. Whereas the Austrian ships were all ready for sea, having been on duty at the time of the revolution, the Venetian share of the fleet consisted of older reserve vessels and those undergoing repair in the Venice Arsenal. The Venetian advantage came in personnel, especially officers: of the 157 sea officers active at the start of 1848, 101 left Habsburg service after the revolution. Of these, ninety-two served in the rebel navy at one time or another.[2]

For the Italian sea officers, the decision to go over to the Venetians was by no means unanimous. Of ninety-four Italian surnamed officers on the pre-revolutionary roll, sixty-seven joined the Venetian navy, eight quit the Austrian navy but did not join the Venetian, and nineteen stayed with the Austrian. The South Slav contingent, which included a number of italianized Dalmatian Croats, sent eighteen of twenty-seven officers into Venetian service; seven others remained with the Habsburg fleet, one retired, and one—Marinovich—did not live to see the division. Twenty of the twenty-three German surnamed sea officers remained with the navy, but the others (ensigns Hafner, Frischholz, and Hochkofler) went over to the Venetians. In addition to crossing lines of nationality, the division of the corps also occurred at all ranks and stations, and every ship of the active squadron had at least one officer or cadet in each camp. Year of graduation from the naval academy was as much a determining factor as any other: over 70 percent of the officers completing the course of study within the past twenty years left the service, compared with less than 60 percent among pre-1828 graduates or those who had never attended the school. All former classmates of Emilio Bandiera (class of 1836) and Domenico Moro (1838) still on active duty in 1848 left the navy. When the dust settled, the Germans finally could claim to be the largest group within the Austrian sea officer corps, but only by the narrowest of margins—twenty to nineteen—over the Italians, who accounted for 35 percent of the officers remaining.

This physical division of the navy proved to be a tedious process. Even after the Venetian orders of 22 March failed to reach Pola, the Austrian position was far from secure. News of the revolution could not be kept from the fleet; some greeted it with great enthusiasm while even more grew anxious simply to return home. Buratovich was faced with the strong possibility that Italian officers and seamen would take matters into their own hands, seize their ships and sail them to Venice. Because four of the seven warships in the Adriatic squadron were commanded by Italians and all had predominantly Venetian crews, there would be no shortage of sentiment for such a solution.

But Count Gyulai acted decisively to head off further mutinies. After unilaterally assuming responsibility for the navy, he arrested the Venetian-born commander of its small contingent at Trieste. Then, on 26 March, he offered all officers and men born in Lombardy or Venetia a discharge with three months' pay. In Trieste, those eligible for the bargain queued up to be processed and repatriated to Venice. At Pola, however, the Italian officers formulated a demand of their own, conveyed to Buratovich the following morning by Lieutenant Giovanni Sagredo, commander of the brig *Venezia*: in addition to Gyulai's terms, they wanted an unconditional release from their oath of loyalty to the emperor. Even in the midst of a revolution, they still took seriously their honor as officers; Buratovich was moved and, in the conciliatory spirit of the moment, agreed to the demand. With the lone obstacle removed, their repatriation began the following day. Native Venetians and Lombards were joined by a number of non-Italians, mostly Dalmatian Croats, with some claim of family ties in Venice. By 6 April twenty-two officers and 600 men had been disarmed, formally discharged, and sent to Venice on rented merchant vessels, all without incident and, more important, without the loss of an Austrian warship.[3]

For Italian personnel not at Trieste or Pola, the road back to Venice was not so smooth. The frigate *Guerriera* and steamer *Vulcano* were in Naples at the time of the repatriation, having been sent there after the Neapolitan revolution of January 1848 to show the Austrian flag and, if necessary, evacuate the embassy or the Bourbon royal family. The ships reached their destination in late March, to be greeted with the news of the recent upheavals in Vienna, Milan and Venice. After small harbor craft surrounded the warships, their crews hoisted the Italian tricolor and echoed the revolutionary songs of the local seamen. *Guerriera* cadet Giovanni Moro, brother of the martyred Domenico, received a rousing reception, but the other Italian officer aboard the frigate, Lieutenant Sebastiano Delucca, worked with the rest of the staff to salvage what appeared to be a lost situation. After several days of celebration, discipline was restored, the Austrian flag replaced the Italian, and the *Guerriera* sailed for home. The *Vulcano* left later, evacuating the personnel of the Austrian embassy, and almost succumbed to a mutiny en route to the Adriatic. The ambassador, Prince Felix zu Schwarzenberg, was able to restore order aboard the steamship and returned safely to Austria to become the political strongman of the counter-revolution.[4]

By the time the two ships arrived from Naples, however, it was clear that a state of war existed between Austria and Venice. The rebels, angry over their failure to recall the fleet, had continued to hold Admiral Martini and a handful of non-Italian naval officers who survived the Arsenal riot of 22 March. Vienna responded by detaining all Venetian officers not yet repatriated, in order to force a release of these hostages. When the *Guerriera* and *Vulcano* reached Pola, the officers wishing to leave Habsburg service were sent to Ljubljana to await a general exchange of prisoners. The same fate befell those aboard a corvette returning from Greek waters and a schooner from Constantinople, as well as all others making a late decision in favor of the Venetians. In late July, after months of acrimonious negotiations, two dozen men finally were exchanged for Martini and five subalterns being held in Venice.[5]

For the navy, the war in the Adriatic was a civil war. The division left former classmates and friends on opposite sides in the conflict, and only the more pragmatic element in the Austrian fleet recognized the great opportunity that recent events had created. A thorough reform of the service had been impossible after the Bandiera affair, but now, with the revolutionary element gone, nothing stood in the way of a move toward a new, loyal, non-Italian navy. Caught in the middle were Italian officers seeking to remain in Habsburg service. The navy leadership had to view their past loyalty in light of their future utility, and the latter consideration carried far more weight.

While the navy proceeded to fill the vacancies in its officer corps by bringing non-Italian officers out of retirement, calling in others from the merchant marine, and promoting young cadets and ensigns, it used age and infirmity as a pretext to pension off four of the five highest-ranking Italians still in the service. In some cases, such as that of Captain Andrea Bordini, former director of the naval academy, the retirements were not challenged, but other verdicts generated bitter appeals from the officers involved. Lieutenant Matteo Higgia, popular commander of the harbor watch at Zara, was let go over the objections of the governor of Dalmatia, who feared that the "great injustice" of his forced retirement would arouse the Italian community of the city against Austrian rule. Higgia himself pleaded that he was "the father of a large family" which could not be supported on a pension, but the navy refused to reverse its decision.[6] Lieutenant Luigi Sandri, "although a Venetian," rejected the republican cause and refused to be repatriated. After the war ministry's ruling of 4 April he was sent to Ljubljana with the other Italian officers, protesting all the way that he wanted to remain on active duty. Five months passed before he finally acquiesced in retirement, at captain's rank and pension and with an imperial resolution acknowledging his "high character."[7] Another native of Venice, Lieutenant Delucca, met a sadder fate. After returning from Naples with the *Guerriera* he refused an offer to return home, only to have an illness compromise his plans to stay in Austrian service. He subsequently offered to renounce his claim to a pension in return for permission to join his family in Venice. Delucca's wish was granted but with a dishonorable discharge; the navy did not take into account a decoration for bravery, earned earlier in his career, or his recent role in saving the *Guerriera* from mutiny.[8]

The most curious case of an Italian being retained despite his past record was that of young Count Carlo Michieli, whose name appears on a number of lists of men suspected of revolutionary activity during the years 1844–48. After Michieli's death, Radaelli identified him as the only member of Esperia to betray the Italian cause in 1848.[9] In the days following the revolution, Michieli provided valuable service to the navy as a courier between Trieste and Pola, a position in which his own treason could have meant the loss of the fleet. His unshakeable loyalty to Austria brought him two promotions during the war; by 1850 he held lieutenant's rank and was on his way to a successful career.

As for the common manpower of the Austrian fleet, the repatriations of March and early April 1848 left the active squadron with less than 1,000 sailors. Men from the third and Landwehr battalions of the 22nd (Trieste) Infantry, which provided the garrison for Pola, had to be pressed into service aboard ship to help make up the difference. Conscription sweeps of the Dalmatian islands and coastline netted hundreds more seamen, Italian as well as Croatian. But the need to put more ships to sea made the shortage of personnel still worse; when steamers from the Trieste-based Austrian Lloyd were requisitioned to serve as auxiliary warships, they had to be manned by their regular crews of Italian merchant seamen. The Italian character of the fleet remained strong and, even as the officer corps was being "de-italianized," there could be no question of changing the language of the service. After the Danish Dahlerup succeeded Martini as Marine-Ober-Kommandant early in 1849, his poor command of Italian made a difficult transition that much harder.[10]

After the surrender of Venice, Dahlerup was able to set about the task of rebuilding the navy for the future. In a symbolic gesture, the ships for the first time were given German names: the *Venere* was rebaptized *Venus*, the *Vulcano* became *Vulkan*, and so forth. As "punishment" for Venetian infidelity, the brigs *Veneto* and *Venezia* were renamed *Pola* and *Triest*, respectively. The loyal city of Trieste also became the site of a new naval academy, which from the start suffered from a shortage of German-speaking instructors and German-language textbooks. Some courses were offered in Italian, with teachers from the *Scuola reale di commercio e navigazione*, the local merchant marine academy, providing much of the instruction, but conditions did not permit the regularization of naval education until the 1852-53 school year.[11] In the meantime, temporary measures had to be taken to satisfy the navy's need for non-Italian sea officers. Dahlerup brought in a number of foreigners from the Low Countries and Scandinavia, and the collapse of a project to create a German federal navy brought the Austrian navy over a dozen officers from northern Germany.[12] Slovenes from nearby Carinthia, Carniola and Styria entered the navy for the first time, and Croatian officers were taken in from the merchant marine. The land-based branches of the service—naval infantry, artillery, and engineering—traditionally had been even more Italian than the corps of sea officers; all were completely decimated by defections in 1848 and had to be rebuilt from scratch. While transfers from the army sufficed in the case of the infantry and artillery, Scandinavians and other foreigners accounted for most of the new engineers.

Adhering to a policy formulated shortly after the revolution of

1848, the navy refused to readmit officers who had served the Venetian rebel government. The first test case came while the war was still in progress. Naval artillery captain Antonio Fumanelli appeared in Trieste in September 1848, asking to have his Austrian commission restored. Instead, he was court-martialled, convicted of treason and imprisoned at Brünn in Bohemia.[13] Seven other Venetian officers eventually applied for readmission to the corps, but all were rejected. Many more veterans of the rebel navy found their way into Sardinian service.[14] As with deserting army officers, those from the navy wishing to return to the Austrian Empire to live as civilians had to apply for a pardon from the emperor. Many simply sought a retroactive release from their oath, to clear their name of any dishonor. Francis Joseph handled a number of these cases throughout the 1850s, following no standard criteria for their evaluation.[15]

In dealing with the common sailors, the navy followed the army's example of welcoming its deserting soldiers back into the fold. A thorough investigation of the Arsenal riot of 22 March 1848 led to the acquittal of all present defendants except two shipyard workers, who were hanged for the murder of Captain Marinovich.[16] But the returning Venetian seamen came back to a very different Habsburg navy, one in which some of the officers (the north Germans and Scandinavians) spoke no Italian. To make matters worse, their intermediaries, the non-commissioned (petty) officers, were less likely than before to be native Italians.[17]

After Dahlerup's resignation in 1851, an interim commander, Feldmarschalleutnant Count Franz Wimpffen, continued to fight the navy's traditional Italian character. He was backed by a new Navy Law, promulgated in 1850, which committed Austria to a program of naval expansion over the upcoming decade; in addition to increasing expenditure on the fleet, it called for the enforcement of the existing regulations (dating from 1814) that prescribed German as the language of command and correspondence. As a dispassionate outsider, Wimpffen was in a perfect position to implement the new guidelines. Under his direction, officers and naval academy instructors unable to read, write and speak German were pensioned off, regardless of their past service or other merits. The casualties included Captain Matteo Salvini, the highest-ranking Italian sea officer. A native of Fiume, Salvini had risen to second in seniority among captains after having entered the navy as a common seaman back in 1814. He was revered by the Italians in the fleet, especially the junior officers, who were woefully short of role models after 1848–49. But unfortunately, he could speak only Italian and could not be spared from the purge. Aside from the circumstances of his retirement, he was well treated by the Austrians, receiving a rear admiral's pension and the title "Ritter Salvini von Meeresburg."[18]

In spite of their efforts, however, Dahlerup and Wimpffen could not change the fact that Italian was still the language of the bulk of the common seamen and, as such, the *de facto* language of command aboard ship. Attempts after 1849 to draw men from the mountainous interior of Dalmatia had to be abandoned because too many of these conscripts knew neither German nor Italian and, notwithstanding their relative proximity to the sea, made terrible sailors.[19] The navy finally tried to turn to the Italians of Trieste—Italians it felt it could trust—but the introduction of conscription within the city limits in 1852, after more than a century of immunity, caused such an uproar that Francis Joseph had to restore the traditional privilege; naval conscription finally began in Trieste only with the war of 1859. The army, ever eager for new sources of manpower, complicated matters by insisting that a share of any Trieste city conscripts go to the 22nd Infantry. The controversy touched off a battle between the two services over recruiting rights in the Adriatic littoral that lasted for two decades. The navy placated the army somewhat in the late 1850s by conceding the inland districts of Dalmatia to two new Jäger battalions, but only after determining that the men in this region were of little use as sailors.[20] Meanwhile, the navy had to content itself with demonstrations that, at least under some circumstances, it could operate without Italians. In 1853 the brig *Hussar* made a much publicized cruise with an all German-speaking crew, but the vessel was small enough to be manned by 100 seamen. The navy did not attempt to repeat the experiment with a larger warship.

In the fall of 1854 the appointment of Archduke Ferdinand Max to the post of Marine-Ober-Kommandant ushered in a new era for Austrian seapower. Better known for his later, and briefer, reign as Emperor Maximilian of Mexico, Francis Joseph's talented younger brother spent a decade as naval commander and was responsible for the construction of Austria's modern ironclad battle fleet. When the archduke first entered the navy in 1851, at the age of nineteen, the emperor made a surprising choice for his personal adjutant: Lieutenant Count Carlo Michieli. There are no clues as to why the former Esperia member won this coveted position, but in the long run it did little for him personally, because Ferdinand Max, as commander, was not one to allow his subordinates a great deal of power or influence. But Michieli no doubt was responsible, at least in part, for the archduke's conciliatory attitude toward Italians. It became a constant feature of his tenure as head of the fleet and also of his concurrent service, from 1857 to 1859, as governor general of Lombardy and Venetia.

After taking over the navy, Ferdinand Max quickly recognized that the personnel reforms of the past five years were leading to a tense future in which a predominantly German officer corps would be in command of predominantly Italian seamen.[21] By "de-italianizing" the command structure without being able to do the same for the common manpower, the navy was solving its problems with a formula that had led to disaster for many army units in the revolution of 1848. The archduke, while sticking with the general policy of movement toward a German-speaking navy, followed an open door policy with regard to the officer corps. Any qualified candidate fluent in German could pursue a naval career, and mastery of Italian, native or otherwise, was considered a further asset.

The material expansion of the fleet during Ferdinand Max's decade as commander naturally required an expansion of personnel, and the need for sheer numbers of officers and seamen left even less reason for discrimination against Italians or any other nationality. Two members of the Paulucci family were even able to enter the navy, despite the fact that three Pauluccis had left Austrian service to fight on the Venetian side in 1848–49. The sons of Matteo Salvini and other loyal officers recently cashiered for their inability to speak German were welcomed into the fold, as were children of Trieste businessmen and merchants. With the collapse of the Bourbon monarchy in Naples, sons of displaced Neapolitan aristocrats also found a home in the corps. In all cases, reliability and competence carried more weight than national origin. The number of Italian sea officers rose from seventeen in 1850 to thirty-five in 1862, a deceptive figure, though, because the overall size of the corps increased from ninety-three to 248 during the same period. Still, the decline of the immediate postwar years was arrested and Italians were able to hold on to second place among the nationalities of the officer corps, trailing only the Germans. Until 1866 they consistently accounted for between 10 and 15 percent of all sea officers.[22]

The concurrent expansion of the navy's common manpower did nothing to displace Italian as the language of a majority among the crews. In the summer of 1858 Ferdinand Max ordered the recruiting of men "aus den deutschen Provinzen," but only as a supplement to efforts in the littoral.[23] In 1860, when the expansion of the army brought the creation of new regiments for Venetia, the navy reiterated its traditional right to all *seekundige* conscripts; the war ministry eventually agreed to transfer men in this category from the new 80th Infantry to the navy.[24] In the wake of the unification of Italy, the creation of a united Italian army generated a number of deserters, a handful of whom sought to enter the Austrian navy. The archduke at first welcomed these men, by the same logic that permitted Neapolitan aristocrats to enter the officer corps, but subsequent problems forced him to change his mind. In the spring of 1862 the navy finally stopped its practice of taking in "questionable Italian refugees," on the grounds that it compromised the long term aim of decreasing the "Italian element" within the service.[25] Still, Ferdinand Max fought hard to maintain Austria's monopoly on the best Italian seamen, those from the Adriatic littoral. After the new united Italian navy was caught recruiting covertly in Venetia, Trieste, Fiume, and on the island of Lussin (Lošinj), the active squadron was ordered to watch for suspicious vessels possibly engaged in transporting these men back to Italy.[26]

Under the archduke's command, the navy budget soared to unprecedented heights. The imperial government appropriated money for frequent peacetime cruises, and sailors spent relatively little time ashore in comparison to the typical pre-1848 routine. This activity, along with an iron discipline unknown in the old navy, left Ferdinand Max with few personnel problems. The fleet saw little action during the lost war of 1859 but the men remained calm, largely because the two groups most troublesome to the army in that year, Hungarians and Lombard Italians, were not represented in the navy. But Garibaldi's successful operations against Sicily and Naples during 1860 sparked fears of a similar landing in Venetia, Istria or Dalmatia; the latter two (despite their predominantly Slavic populations) also were claimed by many Italians as part of *Italia irredenta*.[27] The navy spent the last part of 1860 and most of 1861 on alert against seaborne invaders, and in this atmosphere some commanders of navy shore installations grew suspicious of their own Italian personnel. In January 1861 the district commander of Venice, by then only a minor base for the navy, requested the transfer of all of his Italian seamen. Ferdinand Max refused to sanction such a discriminatory action but agreed that those guilty of "bad conduct" should be moved to the main base at Pola.[28] All things considered, the Italian common sailor must have continued to receive fair treatment even during these difficult times. Otherwise, the navy certainly would not have attracted deserters from the Royal Italian army.

The Italian minority in the officer corps likewise caused little concern, but its post–revolutionary record was not spotless. Lieutenant Alberto Spigliatti of Trieste, son of a Habsburg bureaucrat, began passing information to an Italian spy in 1861, while stationed at Pola; he had to flee to Italy the following year, however, after his activity was uncovered.[29] During the summer of 1862 the army arrested Ensign Cesare Pozzo for his "suspicious conduct" while commanding a gunboat on the River Mincio near Mantua. After being turned over to the navy for interrogation, Pozzo was released on his own recognizance and returned to duty. The naval command in Pola agreed to keep him under surveillance, but the allegations against him must have been unfounded. He remained with the service well into the 1880s and rose to the rank of captain.[30]

Italians played an important part in Austria's successful naval wars in 1864 and 1866, but only rarely in leadership roles. Captain Wilhelm von Tegetthoff's small squadron went into action against the Danes in the North Sea in 1864 with no Italian officers in positions of responsibility. The crews of his warships, however, were predominantly Italian. At the Battle of Helgoland (9 May 1864) German Austrian officers shouted encouragement to their men in Italian and were answered with cheers of "Evviva Imperatore!"[31] Two years later, when Austria went to war with Italy, Italians commanded four of the thirty ships in the Habsburg fleet, a share conforming almost exactly to the total proportion of Italians in the sea officer corps.[32] Tegetthoff, by then a rear admiral and, with the departure for Mexico of Ferdinand Max, the leading figure within the navy, chose an officer of Neapolitan Italian descent, Lieutenant Baron Francesco Minutillo, to serve as his personal adjutant during the campaign. Trust had its limits, though, and at the Battle of Lissa (20 July 1866) there were no Italians among the commanders of Austria's seven armored warships, the core of the battle fleet. Captain Marco Florio had the best assignment, the wooden steam frigate *Erzherzog Friedrich*; Captain Guglielmo Calafati commanded the gunboat *Seehund* and Lieutenant Gustavo Masotti the gunboat *Kerka*. Captain Biagio Adrario's paddle steamer *Santa Lucia* stood watch at Pola while the rest of the fleet was away.³³

Italian naval historians have made much of the fact that Austria won the Battle of Lissa with an Italian-speaking fleet, and it is true that the decisive confrontation for control of the Adriatic was, to some extent, a battle between a pair of Italian navies. But in attempting to find a historical continuity between the maritime traditions of the Venetian Republic, Austria's Venetian navy of 1814–48, and the victory of the Habsburg fleet in 1866, the traditional Italian literature has grossly overestimated the Venetian role at Lissa. In the most recent work of this genre, Franco Micali Baratelli claims Lissa as "the last victory of the Lions of San Marco" and, as evidence, cites the generally accepted figure of 600 Venetian sailors serving on the Austrian side in the battle.³⁴ Such contentions appear preposterous, however, when one considers that there were some 8,000 seamen aboard the Habsburg warships at Lissa, and that the Venetian contingent represented less than 10 percent of the whole. The Croatian share of the Austrian manpower at Lissa has been estimated at one-third, and since all of the ships were steam-powered and machinists' mates were most likely to be German or Czech, a minority was neither Italian nor Croatian. But the remainder of the men—roughly 60 percent—were Italian and, given the relatively small number of Venetians, just over half must have been non-Venetian Italians, from Trieste, Istria, Fiume, and the ports of the Dalmatian coast. The Austrian triumph at Lissa was not a "Venetian" victory but a victory of the post-1848 multinational navy, in which Italian manpower still played a very important part.

Those searching for a Venetian connection in the Battle of Lissa would be well served to look on the Italian side, where a number of prominent figures had connections to the Austrian navy and naval academy from the years before 1848. Lieutenant Domenico Chinca, Esperia member and contemporary of Domenico Moro at the academy (class of 1838), served as detail officer at Lissa aboard Admiral Persano's flagship *Affondatore*, while Captain Tommaso Bucchia (1841) was chief of staff to Admiral Vacca and Captain Guglielmo Paulucci (1840), son of the former Austrian naval commander, served in the same capacity under a third Italian admiral, Albini. Meanwhile, Luigi Fincati, academy classmate of Emilio Bandiera (1836), captained the armored gunboat *Varese*, and a number of other former Austrian officers commanded wooden ships that saw no action in the battle: Captain Antonio Gogola (1829) on the paddle steamer *Governolo*, Esperia ringleader Francesco Baldiserotto (1833) on the paddle steamer *Ettore Fieramosca*, Captain Antonio Sandri (1843) aboard the gunboat *Montebello*, Captain Vincenzo Foscolo (1843) aboard the gunboat *Vinzaglio*, Lieutenant Giovanni Moro (1847), brother of the late Esperia leader Domenico, on the paddle steamer *Flavio Gioja*, and Lieutenant Dionisio Liparachi on the transport *Indipendenza*.[35] Like the conflict of 1848–49, the Austro–Italian war of 1866 pitted former classmates, friends and even relatives against one another. The years had dulled the emotions, though, and with the postwar cession of Venetia to Italy, the active conflict between Italians and Austrians entered a half–century hiatus.

The repatriation of Venetian–born naval personnel involved well under a thousand men, a simple operation compared with the tens of thousands of Venetian soldiers the Austrian army sent home in 1866. The loss of Venetia also cost the navy fewer officers than the army. While the release of an overwhelming majority of the Italian soldiers caused many army officers of Italian descent to ponder their future in Austrian service, their counterparts in the navy were faced with no similar doubts, because even without the Venetian seamen, Italians still accounted for a bare majority of the fleet's common manpower. Only five sea officers and one cadet resigned their commissions after the war; four more Italian officers left the land–based branches of the navy. All Italian sea officers above the rank of ensign chose to remain in Habsburg service.[36]

Through almost two decades of political tension and periodic warfare, a time in which Austria stood as the primary enemy of Italian nationalism, the Habsburg navy managed to retain significant elements of its Italian character. But the years after 1848 were a calm denouement to the more dramatic action of the pre–revolutionary era. As the haughty former Venetian republican officers and the younger generation of Mazzanian idealists became a more distant memory, a different sort of Italian carried the mantle of his nationality within the service. The Habsburg fleet gradually phased out its operations in Venice and, as soon as new facilities at Pola were ready, the former center of Austrian naval activity became a minor base of little strategic value. Likewise, the traditional dependence upon Venetian manpower gave way to a new reliance upon the navy's former secondary sources of seamen: Trieste, Fiume, Istria, and Dalmatia. For the Italians in most of these lands, Habsburg domination was centuries old. Their own history, and life at close quarters with other nationalities, gave them an important common denominator with the rest of the Habsburg Empire that Lombardy and Venetia never had. *Italia irredenta* was to produce its share of Italian patriots in the years after 1866, but a silent majority acquiesced in the continuation of Austrian rule, and the loyalty of Italians within the armed forces ceased to be a matter of great concern.

Chapter 6

UNDER THE DUAL MONARCHY

Venetia adjusted quickly to life without the Austrians. In June 1867, amid great fanfare, the remains of Attilio and Emilio Bandiera and Domenico Moro were transported from Naples to a new resting place in Venice. The eighty–one year old widow of Admiral Bandiera presided over the emotional ceremony. The dignitaries included former Esperia members whose lives had not ended so abruptly; many now wore the uniform of the Italian navy.[1] Meanwhile, in the hinterland of the former Habsburg provinces, the Italian army's first attempts at conscription brought the same sort of pleasant surprise that the Austrians had experienced time and again: resistance averaged less than 3 percent, compared with over 50 percent in Naples and the southern regions of the kingdom.[2] In the north, as in the south, old habits were hard to break.

After the loss of Venetia, the Habsburg army had no units in which the manpower was exclusively Italian. The 22nd (Trieste) Infantry still had an Italian majority, but over half of the army's Italians—natives of the southern Tyrol (Trentino)—were scattered among the battalions of the Tyrolese Kaiser–Jäger Regiment. As before, these Alpine units were conscripted on an at–large basis throughout the provinces of Tyrol and Vorarlberg, a practice which ensured that each battalion would have a German–speaking majority. In 1868, new conscription regulations changed the terms of army service from eight years of active duty and two of reserve to three active years, seven of reserve, and two with the Landwehr, an institution dormant in recent times. In every levy the Landwehr received around one–fourth of the conscripts, a luckier group that discharged its obligation in two years. Initially the Landwehr of the Austrian half of the monarchy remained disorganized and at a lower level of readiness than its Hungarian counterpart, the *Honvéd*. A third line of defense, the Landsturm, existed only on paper in both halves of the monarchy. Italians were the smallest of the ten major nationalities in this postwar army; their 0.9 percent share in 1872 was a far cry from the 10.7 percent recorded just seven years earlier.[3]

Even after the loss of Venetia, Italians still provided roughly half of the common manpower for the fleet and were by far its largest national group; Croatians, accounting for one-third, were second. Over the next twenty years, though, these figures gradually became reversed: in 1885, the first year for which official statistics were compiled, 44.9 percent of the seamen were Croatian and 32 percent Italian.[4] From 1866 onward, the navy recognized the importance of these peoples and their languages in the curriculum of the naval academy. When the school reopened at Fiume for the 1866-67 term—the first since before the war of 1859—both Italian and "Illyrisch" were required of all students. But by the 1869-70 term, the schedule already showed a marked emphasis on Croatian over Italian. The four years of study included 148 semester hours of course work (if characterized in modern American units), seven devoted to "Illyrisch" and only four to Italian. In comparison, twelve hours were spent on German and five each on French and English.[5]

The array of languages to be mastered by the prospective naval officer grew as a consequence of the Austro-Hungarian Compromise (*Ausgleich*) of 1867. Hungarian was offered as an elective at the academy starting in 1869, and from the 1882-83 term onward, it was required of all students from the Hungarian half of the monarchy. Thus an Italian from Fiume, the only substantial Italian community not in the Austrian half, had the opportunity to add German and Hungarian to his native Italian while also studying Croatian, French, and English. A Trieste Italian, not having to take Hungarian, would study only five languages. Necessity made linguists out of a number of naval officers; the average one mastered between 3.5 and four languages, against an average of 2.5 to three for army officers.[6]

The decline of the Italian contingent among the seamen after 1866 was not mirrored in the officer corps. In 1868 there were twenty-nine Italians among 308 sea officers, and in 1885, forty-eight among 496, 9 percent in both years. But in the intervening period, Hungarians and Czechs entered the corps in sufficient numbers to become the second and third nationalities among sea officers, while the Croatians rebounded from their earlier decline to surpass the Italians as well.[7] Italian officers of this era had no built-in handicaps to their advancement; unlike the holdovers from the years before 1848, they certainly were not limited by poor language skills. But evidence of discrimination could be found at the highest levels of the naval hierarchy. In the first quarter-century after 1866, as during the period from 1848–66, no officer of Italian origin was promoted past the rank of captain. The navy eventually had Hungarians, Poles, and even one Ruthenian officer reach admiral's rank, but no Italians. Domenico Adriano Morelli (academy class of 1841) made it to the top of the captain's list in the late 1860s but rose no higher. Gustavo Zaccaria, a volunteer in the spring of 1848, met the same roadblock in the early 1880s. Marco Florio, another volunteer cadet from 1848, commanded a ship at the Battle of Lissa and reached the highest grade of captain in 1871, at age 43, only to be denied further promotion.[8] But the absence of Italians at the top of the naval hierarchy did not mean that there were no Italian influences. The most prominent officers in the service between 1866 and the turn of the century all were educated in the pre-1848 Venetian naval academy: Tegetthoff (class of 1845) commanded the navy from 1868 until his death in 1871, Friedrich von Pöck (1843) succeeded him until 1883, and Max von Sterneck (1847) held the post until 1897. Their Italian secondary education and Venetian experience continued to influence them long after the navy had been "de-italianized." Tegetthoff frequently used the Venetian dialect when chatting with old friends, and years later, the editor of Sterneck's memoirs discovered idiosyncracies in his writing of German that could be traced to Italian. All three men spoke fluent Italian, as did the rest of the officer corps for years after 1866. As late as 1887, 100 percent of the sea officers listed Italian among their languages.[9]

The advancement of Italian-born officers to high rank posed no problem in the army, where Count Carlo di Lilia and Giovanni Bordolo di Boreo both reached the grade of Feldmarschalleutnant; Bordolo also served as a corps commander and eventually, governor of Transylvania.[10] But Italians had accounted for only a small minority of the army officer corps after the initial post-1814 period and, except for the Carbonari scare, their position was never tinged with the controversy that dogged their counterparts in the navy. After 1866 their share of the corps fell to around 1 percent, a figure consistent with the representation of Italians in the ranks.

Notwithstanding their small numbers, the Italians managed to participate in the army's first campaign after 1866. During 1869 the three field battalions of the 22nd Infantry were transferred to southern Dalmatia from Buda in Hungary, where they had been since the end of the war; that fall, they stood on the front line in the suppression of a rebellion in the Bocche di Cattaro. Two companies of the regiment saw extensive action against the rebels, and five men received silver medals for bravery.[11] The three battalions remained in Dalmatia on garrison duty after the fighting ended, an assignment that guaranteed the regiment a role in the Austrian occupation of Bosnia and Herzegovina eight years later.

The Habsburg monarchy's invasion of Bosnia occasioned an outpouring of irredentist propaganda in Italy. As the diplomats of Europe met at the Congress of Berlin during the summer of 1878, Garibaldi, the aging revolutionary, issued a manifesto to the Italians of the Trentino, Trieste, and Istria, urging them to resist the Austrian mobilization. He promised that after fleeing to Italy they would be welcomed into the ranks of the Italian army, which would soon be fighting in alliance with the Bosnians against the hated Habsburgs. Guglielmo Oberdan of Trieste, just conscripted into the 22nd Infantry, heeded the call and embarked upon an adventure that would make him a martyr to the Italian cause.[12]

Oberdan was an unlikely hero. The illegitimate son of a Slovenian housekeeper and a former Habsburg soldier,[13] he was in his first year at the Technische Hochschule in Vienna when, upon reaching his twentieth birthday earlier in 1878, he received his army induction notice. Taking the customary route of a promising student, he chose to discharge his military obligation through one year of volunteer service, which was deferred until 1880-81. But in early July 1878, the 22nd Infantry was assigned an active role in the Bosnian campaign and the subsequent full mobilization orders called all men of the "class of 1858" to its colors. Oberdan returned to Trieste and was inducted, but deserted after only four days in uniform. Garibaldi's manifesto began with the stirring appeal "Ai monti!", but Oberdan and his companions, a pair of Istrian Italian corporals, preferred to flee by boat. When they reached Ancona on the opposite shore of the Adriatic, Oberdan volunteered for service in the Italian army.

He soon found that Garibaldi's patriotic appeals had no connection to the policies of the Italian government, which was isolated diplomatically and had no intention of going to war during the summer of 1878. After the army refused his application, Oberdan went to Rome and began a checkered career as a university student and amateur revolutionary. Much to his frustration, however, sentiment within Trieste for union with Italy had reached its nadir, and the warming of Austro–Italian relations made a war for *Italia irredenta* even less likely than before. In 1881 came a pair of harsh blows, the death of Garibaldi and a cordial visit to Vienna by King Umberto. The following spring, Austria–Hungary and Italy formalized their friendship in the Triple Alliance.

Oberdan and the radical irredentists recognized that their cause needed a dramatic spark to prevent it from dying altogether. Within months of the Austro–Italian alliance, they had their occasion: in September 1882, Emperor Francis Joseph was to visit Trieste for ceremonies commemorating the city's 500th anniversary under Habsburg rule. Plans were hatched to assassinate the monarch, with Oberdan to deliver the coup de main. But the day before Francis Joseph's arrival, Oberdan was arrested at the town of Ronchi, half-way between Trieste and the Italian border, in possession of a handgun and two primitive bombs. One month later, he was tried before a military court on charges of desertion and high treason.

Since it was a foregone conclusion that Oberdan would be sentenced to death, it became a question of whether the emperor would pardon him. The governor of Trieste, Baron Sisino de Pretis–Cagnodo, warned against executing the prisoner on the grounds that it would only work to the favor of the irredentists and upset the relative calm that prevailed in the city. Minister–President Count Eduard Taaffe and other high officials disagreed and persuaded the emperor to let justice take its course. The wheels turned slowly, however, and the case attracted unwanted international attention; French writer Victor Hugo even appealed to Francis Joseph to spare Oberdan from the gallows. But the Italian government, anxious not to upset its new allies, made no entreaties on his behalf. Oberdan himself was eager for martyrdom, and in the end he got his wish. On a morning in December 1882, in the locked courtyard of the Trieste barracks, he was hanged.

Though he was only a soldier for four days in 1878, Oberdan's notoriety must earn him a place among the most famous (or infamous) of Austrian deserters. In the years after 1882, patriotic Italians everywhere commemorated the anniversary of his death. Even though he failed to come close to his goal of assassinating the emperor, he provided the irredentist cause with the new life it needed. Oberdan's execution called attention to the irreconcilable differences between Austria-Hungary and Italy, and his memory would cast a long shadow over the Triple Alliance. Fortunately for the Habsburg army and navy, few of their Italians followed his example in the summer of 1878 and none sought involvement in high political murder. Oberdan and his two companions were among only fourteen men to desert the 22nd Infantry as it mobilized for the Bosnian invasion. Four of the regiment's five battalions saw action in the campaign, and a total of twenty-two officers and fifty-eight men received decorations.[14]

But rosters of medal recipients and casualties reveal the extent to which the 22nd had ceased to be an "Italian" regiment by 1878. Lieutenants Emerico de Sarracca and Count Luigi Marchesi were the only Italian officers decorated; most of their peers were non-Italians and almost all of the common soldiers named were South Slavs.[15] The regiment always had had a mixture of Italians, Slovenes, and Istrian Croats, but its internal balance shifted in favor of the Croatians after 1874, when the main recruiting base was moved from Trieste to Split (Spalato) in Dalmatia. Thereafter, the 22nd conscripted heavily in the interior of Dalmatia, taking the mountain Croats the navy had long ago deemed unfit for sea duty. Although the regiment maintained a reserve battalion and an induction center in Trieste after 1874, its Italian faction quickly became a minority; by the time of the Bosnian campaign, even the regimental songs were being sung in Croatian.[16] The transformation of the 22nd Infantry left the Habsburg army without a single predominantly-Italian regiment for the first time since 1813.

On New Year's Day 1883, less than two weeks after the hanging of Oberdan, an expansion of the Habsburg army brought a new infantry regiment to Trieste. The 97th Infantry was one of twenty-two regiments added in 1883, raising the total from eighty to 102. In the redistribution of recruiting grounds the city of Trieste and the predominantly Italian coastal fringe of Istria, along with the Dalmatian coastline and "Hungarian" city of Fiume, became the exclusive preserve of the navy. The 97th had its recruiting headquarters in Trieste but took its manpower from the inland districts of the Küstenland province, including Gorizia and the Isonzo valley along the border with Italy, and a district in Western Carniola around Adelsburg (Postojna).[17] This guaranteed the regiment a Slovene majority, with an Italian minority that fluctuated between 30 percent and the 20 percent minimum required to maintain Italian as one of the languages of command. The 97th also had a Croatian minority which, at first, remained below the 20 percent barrier.

The army reforms of 1883 included a division of the empire into sixteen command districts or *Wehrkreise*. In peacetime, regiments were to be deployed within their *Wehrkreis*, if not at home, whenever possible. The stationing of the 97th Infantry during the remainder of the century demonstrated the effect of the new policy: from 1883–86 in Pola, 1886–87 in Gorizia, 1887–97 in Pola once more, then home to Trieste after 1897.[18] In another innovation, the Reichsrat in Vienna voted to increase the strength of the reserve formations for the Austrian half of the empire. The Landwehr was grouped into independent regiments, each drawing manpower from the veterans and a share of the conscripts in an area usually larger than a regimental recruiting district. In the Küstenland, the new 5th Landwehr Regiment filled its ranks from the grounds of the 97th and, when fully mobilized, would have a national mixture similar to that of the regular infantry unit. In 1886, further changes brought the recruiting center of the 20th (Styrian) Field–Jäger battalion to Trieste. In subsequent years, it too had a Slovene majority and an Italian minority in proportions similar to those of the 97th Infantry.[19]

The reforms of the 1880s were followed in the 1890s by a restructuring of the Tyrolese Kaiser–Jägers. To account for population growth in the Tyrol, the Kaiser–Jäger regiment had added more battalions over the years until it reached a strength of twelve, three times the size of a normal infantry regiment. In 1895, the number of battalions was raised again, to sixteen, but these were divided into four regiments, designated the "1st Kaiser–Jägers," the "2nd Kaiser–Jägers," and so forth. The result was a more efficient exploitation of Tyrolese manpower, drafted into regiments the same size as those of the rest of the regular line infantry. But the Italians of the Trentino still were not permitted to form a majority in any of the battalions: the army conscripted for the four Jäger regiments on the traditional at–large basis throughout the Tyrol and Vorarlberg, preserving the German Tyrolese domination.[20]

Before the creation of the 97th Infantry, the Italian contingent within the army had fallen to a mere 0.7 percent of the whole. By 1895, however, the combined effects of the 97th, the relocation of the 20th Field–Jägers, and the expansion of the Kaiser–Jägers almost doubled the figure to 1.3 percent, close to the Italian share of the overall population of the Habsburg monarchy. Meanwhile, the navy continued to have a far more significant Italian faction than the army, but the number of Italian seamen also continued to decline from the levels of 1866. In 1896 they accounted for just 27.7 percent of the common manpower, and in 1907 a mere 24.4 percent, still second only to the Croatians but barely ahead of a growing German Austrian contingent. In the corps of sea officers the Italians actually rebounded from fifth place among the nationalities in 1893 (7.6 percent) to third in 1907 (10.6 percent).[21]

This modest Italian recovery within the naval officer corps coincided with the end of the unofficial "policy" that had long denied them access to the highest ranks. Count Oscare Cassini, a native of Trieste, was promoted to rear admiral in 1892 and joined at that grade two years later by Baron Francesco Minutillo, Tegetthoff's personal adjutant at the Battle of Lissa. Cassini retired in 1897 with the rank of vice admiral, Minutillo in 1905 as a full admiral. A handful of other Italians were to reach similar heights by 1918, but the most significant was Count Rudolf Montecuccoli, commander of the navy from 1904 to 1913.

Serving the Habsburgs as soldiers or statesmen had been a tradition for the Montecuccoli family ever since the seventeenth century, when Raimondo Montecuccoli organized and commanded the imperial army. The Modenese-born Count Rudolf was a worthy heir to this legacy. A young ensign at the Battle of Lissa, he rose through the officers' ranks over the next three decades to become rear admiral in 1897. After commanding the Habsburg squadron off China during the Boxer Rebellion, he advanced to vice admiral and second-in-command in 1903, to Marine-Kommandant the following year, and to full admiral in 1905. Montecuccoli was sixty-one when he assumed command and was hardly the sort of charismatic leader that younger officers preferred. Nevertheless, he showed remarkable energy where it counted, in pushing for a modernization and expansion of the fleet. His tact and persistence helped secure funding from the Austrian and Hungarian parliaments for expensive battleships of the *Dreadnought* type, which the other powers all were building on the eve of the First World War. When he retired in 1913, the Habsburg fleet, relative to the other navies of Europe, was stronger than it had been at any time since 1866.[22]

Montecuccoli achieved his material goals for the fleet largely because of renewed tensions between Austria-Hungary and the kingdom of Italy. Approval of his plans for the *Dreadnought* battleships came only after Italy started to build vessels of this type; the Italians then retaliated by building more of the battleships, and as 1914 approached, the two "allies" were engaged in a heated naval arms race. The new rivalry helped inspire a final effort to decrease the Italian contingent among the common manpower of the Habsburg fleet. As late as 1899, 36 percent of all new recruits were Italian; this figure fell to 28 percent in 1905, 16.8 percent in 1908, and just 14.4 percent in 1913.[23] Ironically Montecuccoli, the only Italian to command the navy after 1848, presided over the last attempts at "de-italianization."

The outbreak of the First World War found the Habsburg monarchy with a small but still significant Italian population. The last imperial census, in 1910, recorded just under 800,000 Italians, or 1.5 percent of the whole. Between five and ten thousand lived in the interior of the monarchy, most of them in Vienna and other industrial cities, while the rest—over three quarters of a million people—were divided almost evenly between the Tyrol and the Adriatic hinterland. In 1914 Italians still provided 1.3 percent of the army's manpower, concentrated in a handful of units: in the Tyrol they accounted for 41 percent of the 2nd Kaiser-Jägers and 38 percent of each of the other three Alpine regiments; in the littoral, 31 percent of the 20th Field-Jägers and 20 percent of the 97th Infantry. Italians provided only 0.7 percent of the officers for the army but 9.8 percent for the navy, to which they also contributed 18.3 percent of the manpower.[24]

Italy's failure to enter the war on the side of her allies in the summer of 1914 placed the Italians of the empire in an unenviable position. Cesare Battisti, representative of the Trentino in the Austrian Reichsrat and Tyrolese Landtag, led the exodus of prominent figures to Italy, where the irredentists were already clamoring for intervention on the side of the Entente. While Italy negotiated the secret Treaty of London, which promised to deliver *Italia irredenta* and more, the Austrians grew increasingly suspicious of their Italian population. In some cases the feelings were justified: by the time Italy declared war on Austria–Hungary in May 1915, hundreds had fled the Habsburg monarchy to enter Italian service. Trieste was home to 1,000 of these volunteers, while 1,000 more came from other parts of the Adriatic littoral and hinterland. The Tyrol provided another 700.[25]

The traditional Italian historiography naturally has highlighted the exploits of those serving Italy, but their overall significance appears in a more accurate light when one considers that tens of thousands of Habsburg Italians dutifully served in the Austro–Hungarian army and navy. With the start of hostilities in August 1914 against Russia and Serbia, the Italians of the Trentino were drafted into the Kaiser–Jäger regiments and four reserve formations of *Landesschützen*; over the next four years, some 60,000 served in these units alongside the German Tyrolese.[26] The Adriatic Italians also provided in excess of 50,000 men for the Habsburg war effort between 1914 and 1918, divided among the navy, the regular army formations, and the reserve 5th Landwehr or *Schützenregiment*. The Italian minorities in the urban melting pots of the empire likewise contributed a scattering of men to the local regiments.

The field battalions of the 97th Infantry received their baptism of fire at the onset of the campaign in the east. The troops reached Galicia from their prewar Croatian garrisons just in time to be completely overrun by the Russians on 26 August, only three days after the fighting began in earnest. Much of the regiment ended up behind Russian lines at Kniaze, where many of the wounded died before their transport to a prisoner of war camp at Tambov, ultimately the home to most Italians captured on the Russian front. The battered remnant of the 97th was pulled from the line at the end of August and sent to Lemberg (Lvov) to be reorganized. Meanwhile, the 5th Landwehr spent the first round of the Russian war far from the action, as garrison of the main naval base at Pola. The need for manpower in the east soon brought an end to this comfortable situation, though, and by December 1914 two battalions of the regiment were en route to northern Hungary, where they were deployed to guard strategic rail lines behind the front.[27]

While all of the belligerents suffered staggering casualties in the initial months of the First World War, Austria–Hungary never recovered from the losses of men and materiel. In the words of one historian, the Habsburg army after the winter of 1914–15 was "essentially a skeleton, fleshed out with hastily mustered and trained conscripts."[28] To make matters worse, in the spring of 1915 the nationality problem finally reared its ugly head: on the day before Easter, in the battle for the strategic Dukla Pass in the Carpathians, the 28th (Prague) Infantry surrendered to the Russians without offering resistance. The lack of zeal of these Czech soldiers for a fight against their Slavic brethren was not forgotten by the imperial authorities. Six weeks later, when Italy entered the war, Austria took decisive measures against her own Italian citizens to ensure that they would not compromise the war effort on the new southern front.

On both land and sea, the war zones of the Austro–Italian conflict bordered the cities and villages that were home to the Habsburg Italian populations. Some 114,000 residents of the Trentino—almost one-third of the Italians in the entire Tyrol—were evacuated during or shortly after the spring of 1915, to spend the war in internment camps in the interior of the monarchy. The Adriatic Italians, most of whom lived farther from the front on land, did not share this fate. They also had fewer of their number interned on political grounds— less than 1,000, compared to some 1,700 for the Italian Tyrolese–even though the men of the littoral had accounted for an overwhelming majority of those fleeing to Italy in 1914–15. The Italian invasion of these borderlands ironically brought no relief for the population; the "redeemers" interned 30,000 civilians from the Trentino in camps in Lombardy and remained suspicious of the loyalties of all former Habsburg Italians.[29]

With the manpower shortage already at a crisis stage even before Italy's declaration of war, it was clear from the outset that the Habsburg army would have to remain on the defensive in the south and cover the front with whatever units it could muster. In spite of ever stronger overtones of distrust, the Italians were among those answering the new call to arms. 3,400 Italian Tyrolese were enrolled during the mobilization of the provincial Home Guard (*Standschützen*), in which they accounted for almost 15 percent of the manpower. Meanwhile, in Trieste, the teenaged sons of *kaisertreue* families formed the *Triester Jungschützbataillon* to defend their endangered city.[30] Other units were transferred from the eastern front to fend off the Italian advance, including the 20th Field–Jägers and some Kaiser–Jägers and *Landesschützen*, which had seen action in the Carpathians. In the winter of 1915–16, the Italian minorities in these regiments were joined on the southern front by a battalion of the 5th Landwehr Regiment, part of which was still serving in the garrison at Pola.[31] At the same time, other Italian formations were moved farther away from Italy. In May 1915, the reserve or *Ersatz* battalions of the 97th Infantry and 5th Landwehr were transferred inland to Styria, where they could better discharge their functions as quartermaster corps for their regiments, channeling supplies and recruits to the front. As the war went on, the *Ersatz* battalions increasingly assumed a policing function behind the lines, giving the army all the more reason to keep most of them in areas where their troops were not of the same nationality as the populace.³²

The most sensational war stories about Italians from the Habsburg Empire typically did not involve the many thousands fighting on the Austrian side, but men from among the hundreds that had fled to Italy in the summer of 1914. On the first anniversary of the Italian declaration of war, the Austrians captured artillery lieutenant Damiano Chiesa during the course of a battle in the Alps. The son of an Italian member of the Tyrolese Landtag, Chiesa had been at home on vacation from studies at the polytechnic institute in Turin when Austria went to war with Russia; he fled to Italy to avoid conscription by the Habsburg army and subsequently volunteered for Italian service. Rather than treat him as they would any other prisoner of war, the Austrians charged Chiesa with high treason. He was executed in Trento only three days after his capture.³³

The summer of 1916 provided the irredentist cause with still more celebrated martyrs. In early July, Habsburg forces in the Alps captured an Italian Alpine company led by Cesare Battisti, the most prominent of the émigrés of 1914. Like Chiesa, the former Reichsrat member was arraigned before a military court for high treason; the same charges were brought against one of his subalterns, Fabio Filzi, a native of Istria. They were hanged on 12 July, in Battisti's home town of Trento, but the story did not end there. Exhibiting the gruesome humor of war, Habsburg officers and their men took turns having their pictures taken next to the dangling corpse of the traitor Battisti. Copies of the photographs appeared in the press in Austria and even on postcards, prompting Italy and the Entente powers to protest the brutality of the execution. The sight of Austrian soldiers mugging for the camera next to Battisti's lifeless body also helped inspire the famous Viennese author and critic, Karl Kraus, to write his epic antiwar play *Die letzten Tage der Menschheit* [*The Last Days of Mankind*].³⁴ Only a month after the hanging of Battisti and Falzi, the Austrian navy gave the irredentists yet another hero by capturing Italian navy lieutenant Nazario Sauro. An Istrian merchant captain by trade, Sauro had fled to Venice in the summer of 1914 and, the following spring, volunteered for Italian naval service. His knowledge of the Dalmatian coastline made him a valuable commander for sabotage missions, and he was leading one in August 1916 when the Austrians captured his surfaced submarine off Fiume. Sauro was brought before a military court at Pola and, like his more famous predecessors, executed for high treason.

While the patriotic conscience of these men led them to fight and die against Austria, hundreds of other Italians from the Trentino and the Adriatic littoral continued to fall on the southern and eastern fronts. In the German and Austrian counterattack against Russia in the summer of 1915, the battalions of the 5th Landwehr saw as much action as the 97th Infantry, even though they were supposed to be reserve formations. The killed and wounded of the two regiments were among some 700,000 casualties the Habsburg army suffered in driving the Russians from Galicia. Their losses were even higher the following summer, when Romania joined the Entente powers and supplemented the Russian counterattack of General Alexei Brusilov, which drove deep into Habsburg territory before finally fizzling out.[35] The political collapse of the tsarist government followed early in 1917, but the Habsburg army had to endure yet another assault after Alexander Kerensky and the leaders of the new Russian provisional regime decided to keep their country in the war. The so-called "Kerensky offensive" of July 1917 could not be sustained, however, and the Russian army started to disintegrate. As Habsburg and German units advanced virtually unopposed all along the front, the 97th Infantry ended up in the Ukraine and the 5th Landwehr in Romania, which was overrun following the Russian collapse.

Victory in the east was of little consolation to the new Emperor Charles, who had succeeded Francis Joseph in November 1916. His efforts to save his war-weary empire from political breakdown included a secret peace initiative to the Entente and, at home, the reconvening of the Austrian Reichsrat. In June 1917, in one of the first sessions of the parliament, Trentino representative Alcide de Gasperi, a colleague of the late Battisti, spoke out bitterly against the Austrian policy of transporting Italian civilians to the interior of the monarchy.[36] His protests in Vienna fell on deaf ears; in the imperial capital, and on the southern front itself, suspicion of and discrimination against Habsburg Italians continued to increase unabated. With the exception of an estimated 500 Tyrolese Kaiser–Jägers and *Landesschützen* who served in the Russian army after being captured on the eastern front, there had been no significant instances of desertion or mutiny by Italians.[37] Nevertheless, after the bulk of these Alpine forces were redeployed on the southern front against Italy, the army gradually purged them of their Italian personnel. By the spring of 1918 only 6 percent of the 2nd Kaiser–Jäger Regiment was still Italian, and the figures were even worse for the other units: only 4 percent of the 2nd *Landesschützen* Regiment, just 3 percent of the 1st and 3rd *Landesschützen*, and only 2 percent of the 1st and 3rd Kaiser–Jägers. The 4th Kaiser–Jägers and the 20th Field–Jägers had no Italians at all.[38]

After being excluded from their customary units, the Italian Tyrolese were forced to serve in eight new formations tactfully named "Southwest battalions" (*Südwestbataillone*) but commonly referred to as *Italienerbataillone*. These were among a growing number of "P.U. units (*PU-Einheiten*)," so designated because of the real or imagined "political unreliability (*politische Unzuverlässigkeit*)" of their soldiers. During 1917–18, the army used these troops to patrol areas where they would be more of an asset to the public order than a liability. By the summer of 1918, three "Southwest" battalions were on cordon duty between Galicia and the Ukraine, which was still occupied by German and Habsburg forces, while another three served a similar function in Romanian Wallachia.[39]

Thus, the southern Habsburg army had few Italians in its ranks when it finally broke the stalemate in the war against Italy. While the eastern front remained relatively fluid throughout the war, the fighting in the south bore a closer resemblance to the western front in France. But the front lines finally strayed from the prewar Austro–Italian border in October 1917, after a German-assisted Habsburg offensive breached the Italian lines at Caporetto and advanced to the Piave River in Venetia. The Italian army formed a new front with British and French support, which held until the internal collapse of the Habsburg monarchy a year later.

As the war entered its final year, the multinational Habsburg army became even more of a melting pot than it had been in peacetime. The frequent decimation of front line regiments and the cost, in time and money, of replenishing them from their home districts led to a series of makeshift arrangements. Troops were transferred from one unit to another, from line infantry to Landwehr and back again, and regiments often simply filled their ranks with local men from wherever they or their reserve battalions happened to be stationed. Most of the Italians not sent to "P. U. units" ultimately were concentrated in the 5th Landwehr, which had its reserve (*Ersatz*) battalion in Voitsberg, Styria, for most of the war. Its Italian contingent swelled to 61 percent by May 1918, more than three times as large as the one in the 97th Infantry. The latter regiment, which had its *Ersatz* formation in the Styrian–Hungarian border town of Radkersburg, ended up with an even greater Slovene majority than it had had in the prewar years, in part because Radkersburg was adjacent to the Slovene region of southern Styria.[40] By the same date, a number of traditionally non-Italian units had significant minorities of Italians within their ranks: the 84th (Vienna) Infantry reported 20 percent, the 4th (Vienna) Infantry 18.5 percent, and the 40th (Galician) Infantry 3 percent. The 110th Infantry—one of thirty-nine new regiments created in the field in 1917—also was 3 percent Italian. The Habsburg army's last Italian cavalry regiment had been disbanded in 1859, but the figures for May 1918 show that the 13th (Galician) Uhlans were 14 percent and the 6th Mounted Landwehr 3 percent Italian. As for light infantry, the 4th (Galician) Field–Jägers and the 10th (Austrian) Field–Jägers each reported an Italian contingent of 11 percent. Another eleven infantry regiments, two Landwehr regiments, two battalions of Field–Jägers, one regiment of dragoons and three of mounted Landwehr registered Italian minorities of as much as 2 percent, and still more Italians were scattered among the Landsturm and other formations that constituted the last line of defense.[41] These units, the 97th Infantry, the 5th Landwehr, and the eight "Southwest" battalions were home to the tens of thousands of Italians still in Habsburg uniforms in the last months of the war.

The ranks of the army's Italian contingent swelled anew after the Peace of Brest–Litovsk (March 1918). With the official end of the war on the eastern front, the new Bolshevik government began to repatriate the Habsburg prisoners the Russian army had taken between 1914 and 1917. Conservative estimates placed their number at a staggering 1.6 million, of which thousands were Italian. While many Habsburg and German army prisoners were sent deep into Central Asia or Siberia, the Italians were more fortunate: their main camp, at Tambov, was a mere 200 miles southeast of Moscow.[42] As the flood of men crossed into Galicia, the Habsburg army attempted to weed out those infected by Bolshevism before sending the rest on to the *Ersatz* battalions of their former regiments. Some were to remain with these units and help police the interior of the empire, while the most fit were slated for a return to active duty on the Italian front.

A minority among the former prisoners wanted to spread the revolution they had seen triumph in Russia, but most simply wanted to go home; certainly, none wanted to go to the Italian front. Resistance to the army's plans took many forms. Some of the repatriated men deserted upon reaching Habsburg soil, either before or after their official processing, while others took advantage of the army's transportation as far as their *Ersatz* battalion, then deserted. Still others stayed with the reserve formations, which were filled with teenaged recruits bound for the front, in order to proselytize for revolution in the name of some class or national cause. The latter group clearly were the most dangerous to the army and to the empire as a whole. Their numbers remained relatively small in the *Ersatz* unit of the 5th Landwehr at Voitsberg, but the same was not true at Radkersburg. In May 1918, the reserve battalion of the 97th Infantry staged one of the more serious of the war's behind-the-lines mutinies.

For the past three years, the strength of the garrison at Radkersburg had fluctuated between four and five thousand men, a number almost double the size of the normal population of the town. As the war went on, the soldiers heading to and from the Russian front via the battalion tended to be more disenchanted and harder to discipline. They terrorized the German townspeople on a regular basis, and the attacks grew more brutal after the general shortage of food caused their rations to be reduced. The situation only became worse after the first of the former prisoners arrived. By April the walls of the barracks latrine were filled with various forbidden phrases; next to the Slovenian "Živjo Jugoslavija!" the Italians scrawled "Viva la rivoluzione russa!" and "Soldati disertate," along with the more ominous "Al primo maggio aspettiamo l'ora della rivoluzione."[43]

The first of May passed without incident, but a week later a soldier of the regiment killed a postman for the money in a registered letter, and in the middle of the month a group of soldiers exchanged shots with Hungarian gendarmes while foraging eastward for food. Then, on the night of the 23rd, 1,600 veterans in the battalion, mostly Slovenes, staged a mutiny. German officers had to suppress their rampage with the raw recruits on hand, some of whom were Italian. As luck would have it, the loyal youths had machine guns, the mutineers only rifles, and the barracks were retaken by the following morning. A total of four men were killed and six seriously wounded, while dozens sustained lesser injuries; within a week, eight ringleaders of the mutiny had been executed. The record shows that the condemned men went to their deaths shouting "Živjo Jugoslavija!," with an occasional "Viva l'Italia!" indicating the involvement of at least some Italians. In the summer of 1918 the battalion was transferred from Radkersburg to Székesfehérvár (Stühlweißenburg) in Hungary, supposedly a "safer" post, but the soldiers responded by deserting in droves. By mid-August over 2,000 of them were unaccounted for, as were over 400 of the regiment's repatriated prisoners of war. They joined the growing mass of armed and unarmed men wandering the countryside as the Austro-Hungarian army started to disintegrate.[44]

During the last months of the war, the Italian troops in the east were in only slightly better order than these reserves. In August 1918 the 43d Landwehr Division, which included the 5th Landwehr Regiment, was withdrawn from Romania to Bukovina and slated for transport by rail to the Italian front. But at the last minute, the predominantly-Italian regiment was transferred to the 54th Landwehr Division, which belonged to the German and Habsburg army of occupation in the Ukraine. The morale of the 5th Landwehr plummeted, and when November finally came they were running amuck in the streets of Odessa, participating in a general mutiny of the 54th Division. Meanwhile, the field battalions of the 97th Infantry, which were already on the Ukrainian-Bessarabian border when the Treaty of Brest-Litovsk was signed, advanced deep into the Ukraine as part of the occupying force. Apparently no one considered transporting them westward to fight against Italy.[45]

Compared to the lot of Austria's Italian soldiers, the Italians serving in the fleet experienced a secure and relatively uneventful four years of war. With the major Mediterranean naval powers all on the side of the Entente, the Austro-Hungarian navy was as inactive as its German counterpart in the North Sea. As a "fleet in being" it attracted an inordinate amount of attention from enemy navies, tying up warships that the Entente powers could have made better use of elsewhere, but the monotony and strain of life at anchor eventually had the same demoralizing effects in Pola and Cattaro as it had for the German navy in Kiel and Wilhelmshaven.

By the time the Habsburg fleet started to experience its worst problems, the Italian contingent within it had been reduced to an unprecedented low. The trend toward "de-italianization" in the immediate prewar years continued after 1914, and by the beginning of 1918 only 14.4 percent of the common manpower was Italian, down from 18.3 percent in 1910.[46] The first sign of open discontent came in July 1917, when demonstrations involving men of all nationalities occurred aboard the ships of the main fleet at Pola. The unrest was widespread but, fortunately for the navy, also easily suppressed. Italians did not participate at all in the first actual mutiny, in October

1917 aboard Torpedoboat 11. This small vessel was on a routine patrol in the Adriatic when a Czech machinist and a Slovene boatswain's mate led the crew in overpowering their two officers. After seizing control of the boat, they ran up a white flag, motored across the sea, and surrendered to the Italians.[47]

In January 1918, a wave of strikes that swept the empire included one by the 10,000 Italians and South Slavs employed in the Arsenal at Pola. Their demonstration soon found sympathy within the fleet, and representatives from among the 15,000 sailors of the naval base tried to make common cause with the workers.[48] Negotiators ultimately persuaded the Pola strikers to go back to work, but their success came too late to spare the navy from further infection. The broader revolutionary influences drove the common seamen to protest the unfairness of the social division with the navy: they complained that the officers had easy access to social life ashore while they spent most of their time confined aboard ship, and that the officers' mess remained well stocked with fine food and drink while they were told of food shortages and given reduced rations. Tensions grew especially serious in Cattaro at the southern tip of Dalmatia, the relatively isolated base of the navy's Fifth Fleet. There, over 2,700 sailors manned the largest six ships, while hundreds more served on smaller vessels and submarines. The fleet included the cruiser *Kaiser Karl VI*, which had been in Pola during the unrest of the previous summer.

During the first weeks of 1918, the news of the latest trouble in Pola combined with word of Woodrow Wilson's Fourteen Points to create the backdrop for an uprising at Cattaro. The officers of the Fifth Fleet did not help matters by antagonizing their men on a number of occasions during the course of the month. In one celebrated incident aboard the cruiser *Novara*, a third-generation Habsburg naval officer, Lieutenant Osvaldo Salvini, armed himself with a bottle of champagne after an officers' party and went about bellowing toasts "to ten more years of war."[49] To sailors longing for peace, it seemed the height of insanity. The eruption finally came on the morning of 1 February, and by noon, the mutineers controlled almost all of the ships.

Seamen of all nationalities joined in hoisting the red flag of revolution. It was a wondrous sight to the bored and ill-fed crews of the fleet. "La bandiera rossa trionfera!" shouted seaman Giovanni Vascotto, observing the spectacle from the deck of one of the torpedo boats.[50] But the navy retained control of the shore installations overlooking the bay, and the local command quickly called for help. Three battleships from Pola came to block the entrance of the harbor, and troops from Bosnia cordoned off the area by land. When one of the mutinous ships defied an order from shore and attempted to move, the batteries opened fire. The rebellion fizzled out, and by 3 February the officers once again were in command of the fleet.

The Cattaro mutiny divided the fleet along lines of class rather than nationality.[51] Italians were well represented among the officers risking their own lives to foil the plans of the rebels. Decisive actions by Captain Gaetano Afan de Rivera of the auxiliary ship *Cyclop*, Captain Riccardo Florio of the harbor-watch ship *Erzherzog Rudolph*, Lieutenant Count Gastone degli Alberti of the cruiser *Helgoland*, Lieutenant Carlo Cerri of Torpedoboat 15, and reserve lieutenant Oreste Cheracci of the tug *Büffel*, all helped to contain the uprising. On the other hand, Italian seamen were not prominent among the leaders of the mutiny. After the restoration of order, some 800 of the mutineers were ordered ashore and, after an initial investigation, charges were brought against 392 of them: 167 South Slavs, eighty-one Italians, and smaller numbers from every other nationality.[52] A further select group of forty men, identified as leaders of the uprising, included only five Italians: Marcello Calligaris, Rafaele Turina, Giovanni Chibò Paroi, Paolo Ubaldini, and Renato Berti. At their trial, Berti gave the most energetic denial of wrongdoing, on his own behalf and for other Italian seamen: "I have not incited or agitated" he testified, ". . . there were only fourteen Italians aboard [his vessel, the auxiliary ship *Gäa*]. We promised to stand loyally alongside the officers."[53] There must have been some truth to what he said, for neither he nor any of the other Italians was condemned to death. Only four men were executed in the wake of the mutiny, three South Slavs and one Czech.

During the last months of the war, the focus of unrest shifted northward. In May, navy officials uncovered a plot to seize the port of Sebenico (Šibenik) and executed its leaders, a Czech and a Dalmatian Croat. Again, no Italians were involved; the would-be mutineers were found to have connections with South Slav nationalists at Zagreb.[54] Over the summer of 1918 tensions rose once more at the main naval base in Pola, this time with nationalism rather than class conflict as the primary theme. By the fall, the substantial Croatian contingent within the fleet had its own political organization, and the Czechs, out of Slavic sympathy, supported their cause. Italians apparently accounted for a smaller percentage of the naval personnel at the main base than at Cattaro, and in the final days of Habsburg rule, outbursts of Italian nationalism in Pola were limited to the residents of the town.

In the last week of October, as the Italian army launched its final assault along the southern front, the naval command at Pola informed Vienna that the fleet could not be counted upon to resist an enemy attack. In the interest of an orderly transition, Emperor Charles on 30 October decreed that the fleet should be turned over to representatives of the Yugoslav national committee. The transfer occurred the next day at all naval installations on the Adriatic coast. South Slav personnel were left in control of the ships, and all other officers and men were free to go home.[55] It was perhaps fitting that the navy's last Venetian admiral, Alfredo Cicoli, relinquished the main body of warships. Born in Venice during the last weeks of Austrian rule in 1866, Cicoli was promoted to rear admiral in 1917 and named harbor commandant of Pola early in 1918; in this capacity, it became his responsibility to surrender the fleet. With these ceremonies, held a few days before the formal end of the war, the Italian experience in the Habsburg navy came to a close.

In contrast, many of the Italians in the Habsburg army remained in uniform until long after the action stopped. By the time the soldiers of Trieste and the Küstenland were shipped home, Austria–Hungary had ceased to exist. The empire had some 4.6 million men in uniform in the fall of 1918, but less than 900,000 were considered reliable enough to be stationed on the southern front. When the final Italian offensive began on 24 October, there were far too few Habsburg troops to hold the line of the Piave River. Their retreat soon became a rout, and the Italian army took over 350,000 prisoners before an armistice, on 4 November, brought an end to the war. The captives included 7,000 Italian soldiers, evidence that at least some were trusted to serve on the southern front in the last months of fighting.[56] Emperor Charles never issued a formal order to demobilize what remained of the army and subsequently left Austria without abdicating the throne. The soldiers still on the southern front and in the interior of the former empire either went home or joined the armed forces of the various successor states. The army in the east finally abandoned the Ukraine and, ironically, an Italian oversaw its repatriation. Major General Count Lelio Spannocchi, the Habsburg army's last plenipotentiary at Kiev, coordinated the evacuation by rail of the former occupation forces, including the 97th Infantry and the 5th Landwehr. He finally left his post in January 1919.[57]

There were no Bandieras in the Austrian navy or army during the First World War. Even as the empire underwent its final disintegration, Italians were noticeably absent among the leaders of mutinies or mass desertions in the armed forces. The soldiers and sailors of nationalities that were forming or attempting to form new national states—the Croatians, Slovenes, and Serbs in the south, the Czechs and Slovaks in the north, and the Ukrainians and Poles in the east—were the ones most likely to be involved in such activities. The Italians, however, were in a position similar to that of the Romanians: the patriotic sympathizers among them awaited the arrival of liberators from an adjacent state of their own nationality. The Romanian government, forced to surrender to the Germans and Austrians in 1917, was in no shape to act on behalf of the Romanians of Transylvania,[58] and the Italian army, still on its own territory along the Piave with just a week to go in October 1918, likewise did not seem to be a threat to liberate the Italians of the Trentino and Adriatic littoral anytime soon. The Italians in the Habsburg armed forces thus joined the Germans, Magyars, and Romanians in a slightly more stable group of nationalities that generally chose to await events rather than make them happen.

In the end, of course, it did not matter. The Dual Monarchy was going to collapse anyway, and few Italians were sad to see it go. The loyalty of the Habsburg Italian population, hardly an issue after 1866, had become one again during the pre-1914 deterioration of Austro-Italian relations. Vienna's concerns intensified during the period of Italy's neutrality and erupted into full scale paranoia after the Italian declaration of war. Whereas the navy's recruiting policies brought a dramatic reduction in its Italian personnel before the outbreak of war, the "de-italianization" of army units such as the Kaiser-Jägers had had to wait until after the fighting was underway. The majority of Adriatic and Tyrolese Italians had been indifferent toward the irredentists for almost half a century, largely because nationalism and national identity were complicated issues in these regions. But during the war years, widespread mistrust in the littoral and the internment of civilians from the Trentino were enough to leave a bad taste in the mouth of even the most austrophile and *kaisertreu* Italian. In November 1918 the advancing forces of the Italian army were greeted warmly in Trento, Gorizia, Trieste, and Pola. The second thoughts would come later.

EPILOGUE

At the Paris Peace Conference in 1919, the victorious powers made good on most of their promises of the Treaty of London of 1915, under which Italy had entered the war against her former allies. Instead of the ethnic border in the Alps, she received everything south of a line that roughly followed the watershed between the Mediterranean and Black Sea basins. The Italian flag was planted at the Brenner Pass and, in the northeast, on the crest of the Julian Alps. In addition to "redeeming" their own countrymen of the Trentino and Adriatic littoral, the Italians became the new masters of hundreds of thousands of Slovenes, Istrian Croats, and German Tyrolese; the latter still live under Italian rule today.

From the Italian nationalist perspective, the road to this triumph had been paved with the blood of countless patriots, all of them suffering or dying at the hands of the Austrians. The Carbonarist General Carlo Zucchi, the Mazzinian naval officers of the 1840s, and the irrendentist Guglielmo Oberdan all had some experience within the Habsburg armed forces, ranging from the years of service of the Bandieras and Domenico Moro to the few days of Oberdan. The irredentist martyrs of the First World War—Battisti, Filzi, Chiesa, and Sauro—never wore Austrian uniforms but fled to Italy, in part, to avoid serving, and all ultimately were executed as a consequence.

But the evidence shows that their stories were in no way typical of the Italian record in Habsburg military service. If even a bare majority of Austria's Italian subjects really had considered the Habsburg uniform to be a symbol of slavery and repression, the Austrians would not have been able to make such extensive use of Italian soldiers and sailors over the course of so many years. The story of Italians in the Austrian armed forces thus becomes one of gauging and explaining the success of the exploitation of Italian manpower, through times of war, peace, and revolution. The reconstruction of this record provides at least some indication of the attitude, the relative defiance or malleability, of the common man, the "silent majority" of Habsburg Italians not inspired to risk their lives in dramatic acts of patriotism.

There are few common threads between the Austrian policies in Lombardy and Trieste prior to the Napoleonic wars and what was to come later, after 1814. In the eighteenth century the Habsburg army never made Lombardy contribute a share of men in proportion to its overall population, and the various attempts to develop Austrian seapower culminated only in the "Trieste navy," which was more a flotilla than a fleet. Only with the postwar establishment of Habsburg rule in Lombardy and Venetia did the employment of Italians in the Habsburg armed forces finally assume significant proportions.

The creation of an Austrian navy from the defunct Franco–Italian Adriatic fleet, the assimilation of troops from the former Napoleonic Italian army, and the conversion of existing Habsburg regiments to Italian manpower combined to put around 2 percent of the male population of Lombardy and Venetia into Austrian uniforms. But the burden of conscription was not a major public issue in the relatively peaceful years between 1814 and 1848; even though the population of the two provinces rose by roughly 25 percent, the demands of the army and navy remained the same.[1] The nature of service, however, differed from that which the Lombard regiments of the 1700s had experienced. After 1814, the northern Italian units in the Habsburg army had few Italian officers and NCOs, and some were stationed far from home for long periods of garrison duty. The common soldier apparently did not mind the non-Italian officers, since Italian commanders frequently were tougher on them, but the shortage of Italian NCOs was a crucial factor against the development of a healthier atmosphere within the regiments. As for the posting in distant provinces, it was unpopular with the men but also made them less likely to desert, the evidence coming in the revolutions of 1848.

The experience in the navy, which had an Italian (though not Venetian) commander for most of the period between 1814 and 1848, further smashes the theory that leadership by non-Italians promoted disloyalty by the men. To the contrary, in the 1840s it was the Italian naval officers, inspired by ideals and concepts often beyond the grasp of the common sailor, who led the rest of the service astray. Traditional Venetian conservatism, promoted by Silvestro Dandolo and other aristocratic holdovers from the old Venetian navy, kept the Austrian fleet virtually untouched by the Carbonari scandal of the immediate post-Napoleonic years. By the 1830s, however, the

Italian character of the navy combined with the idiosyncracies of its command and social structures to provide a unique, insulated atmosphere in which Mazzinian ideas were able to gain currency among younger officers. The Italian army regiments, in contrast, were practically immune from this second wave of revolutionary activity. By that time, the number of Italians among their officers had been reduced by the crackdown of the Carbonari era and, even more so, by the negative atmosphere it had generated for the entry of the next generation of Italians into the army officer corps. It is no small irony that Austria's confidence in her Italian navy for most of the period before 1848 was just as unwarranted as her equally firm suspicions of the Italian units in the Habsburg army.

In 1848-49 the men of Lombardy made a more loyal showing in the Habsburg army than the Venetians; the latter, of course, also took the lead in bringing the navy to the brink of collapse. It has been demonstrated, at some length, that the stationing and internal chemistry of individual army units were the greatest determining factors in their behavior during the revolution. Another influence, especially in the navy, was the Venetian revolution's mixture of traditional particularism and Italian nationalism, an ideological blend that appealed to all generations and classes. The deep divisions between urban and rural Italy, a vexing problem for Italian patriots throughout the Risorgimento, also played to the Austrian advantage. The bulk of Italian manpower, especially for the army, came from the *contadini*, whose national consciousness tended to be either primitive or nonexistent.

During the 1850s, Austria's exploitation and employment of Italian manpower took on a harsher tone. It became a matter of policy to station Lombard and Venetian troops away from home, while for the first time ever under Habsburg rule, conscription assumed proportions sufficient to make it a public issue. By 1857, there were one-third more Italians in the infantry and almost five times more in the cavalry than in 1848, even though the population of Lombardy and Venetia rose only 3 percent during these years.[2] At the same time, the navy already was making its shift away from Venetian manpower, although much of the change was simply to other Italian sources in the Adriatic littoral. Venetian soldiers fought well enough in 1859, even if their Lombard brethren, in their last appearance under Austrian colors, did not. In this war, as in the revolutions a decade earlier, the problems that crippled some Italian units were not unique; the

Hungarians caused similar concerns in 1848–49 and again in 1859. During the war of 1866, roughly 4 percent of the male population of Venetia was in the Habsburg armed forces, mostly in the army, on the northern front.[3] From the Austrian point of view, the performance of the Venetians in the campaign against Prussia helped atone for their earlier record.

Under the Dual Monachy of Austria–Hungary, Italians accounted for less than 2 percent of the overall population. Their small numbers, plus the Habsburg Empire's alliance with the kingdom of Italy, left little reason for concern over the loyalty of Italians in the armed forces. Only with the increase in Austro–Italian tensions in the years before 1914 did the navy finally take steps to reduce its Italian manpower; the army chose to avoid discriminatory measures until the war years. Between the summer of 1914 and Italy's entry into the war in the spring of 1915, the number of young Italians fleeing Habsburg conscription reached measurable levels for the first time in over half a century. Previous instances of great resistance and flight had come in times of similar duress for Austria's Italian subjects, in Lombardy and Venetia prior to the revolutions of 1848 and in Venetia in 1860, during the unification of the rest of the peninsula.

During the First World War, Austria again was able to exploit its Italian population for military manpower. Even though nationalism had begun to affect the Italians of the Trentino and Trieste long before 1900, relatively few of them were inspired to challenge the political status quo, and fortunately for the Austrians, this continued to be the case after 1914. For most Italians still living under Habsburg rule, *italianità* was something that set them apart from their German or Slavic neighbors without necessarily bringing them closer to the people of the kingdom of Italy. Even for irredentist leaders, it was hard not to think of other Italians as foreigners. Wartime service in the Italian army was a disenchanting experience for many of them, including Cesare Battisti, who even remarked that his southern Italian soldiers "resembled Muslims."[4]

Vienna's treatment of Habsburg Italians during the war helped bridge this gap, leading most to celebrate their annexation to the kingdom, but the bitterness eventually faded. As recently as the 1960s, researchers still could find old men in the Trentino willing to speak with pride of their service in the Kaiser–Jägers; they considered themselves "Tyrolese of Italian speech" rather than Italians.[5] Over the years, a nostalgic attitude toward the Habsburg monarchy also emerged in Trieste. No doubt the excesses of Italian fascism made the period of Austrian rule appear in a somewhat different light.

NOTES

Notes to Preface

1. See Gunther E. Rothenberg, "The Austrian Army in the Age of Metternich," *Journal of Modern History* 40 (1968): 155-65, and *The Army of Francis Joseph* (West Lafayette, Ind.: Purdue University Press, 1976).
2. Alan Sked, *The Survival of the Habsburg Empire: Radetzky, the Imperial Army and the Class War, 1848* (London: Longman, 1979).
3. See Raimondo Luraghi, "Italians in the Habsburg Armed Forces, 1815-1849," in Béla K. Király, (ed.), *War and Society in East Central Europe*, vol. 4: *East Central European Society and War in the Era of Revolutions, 1775-1856* (New York: Social Science Monographs, Brooklyn College Press, 1984), pp. 219-229.
4. These works are listed separately in section IV of the bibliography.
5. Moriz von Angeli, *Altes Eisen: Intimes aus Kriegs- und Friedensjahren* (Stuttgart: J. G. Cotta'sche Buchhandlung Nachfolger, 1900); Carlo Alberto Radaelli, *Storio dello Assedio di Venezia negli anni 1848-1849* (Venice: Tipografia Antonelli, 1875).

Notes to Chapter 1

1. Luraghi, "Italians in the Habsburg Armed Forces," 219-20.
2. *Ibid.*, 220.
3. Alphons von Wrede, *Geschichte der k.u.k. Wehrmacht: Die Regimenter, Corps, Branchen und Anstalten von 1618 bis Ende des XIX. Jahrhunderts*, 7 vols. (Vienna: L. W. Seidel & Sohn, 1893-1900), 3/2:473, 2:42-114 passim.
4. Thomas M. Barker, *Army, Aristocracy, Monarchy: Essays on War, Society, and Government in Austria, 1618-1780* (Boulder,

Colo.: East European Monographs, 1982), pp. 61–111, provides an account of Piccolomini's life and career.

5 *Ibid.*, pp. 1–21 and passim. See also Thomas M. Barker, *The Military Intellectual and Battle: Raimondo Montecuccoli and the Thirty Years' War* (Albany, N.Y.: State University Press of New York, 1975).

6 The most recent comprehensive biography of Eugene of Savoy is Max Braubach's *Prinz Eugen von Savoyen: Eine Biographie*, 5 vols. (Munich: R. Oldenbourg, 1963–65). Because of his Savoyard descent and French upbringing, there is a strong case for classifying Eugene as "French" rather than "Italian." In this regard the author will follow the lead of Italian historians, who consistently claim Eugene as one of their countrymen.

7 A pair of Italian regiments served briefly in the Imperial armies during the 1660s and 1670s. See Wrede, *Geschichte der k.u.k. Wehrmacht*, 2:147–55.

8 Khevenhüller quoted in *ibid.*, 1:97–98.

9 *Ibid.*, 2:182–200 passim, 221–23. Four former Spanish–Italian regiments had fought the Turks earlier, in 1716–17, under the command of Eugene of Savoy.

10 See Josef Rechberger von Rechkron, *Geschichte der k.k. Kriegsmarine*, part I: *Österreichs Seewesen in dem Zietraume von 1500–1797* (Vienna: Verlag des k.k. Reichs–Kriegs–Ministeriums, Marine–Section, 1882), pp. 25–33; on the marine infantry see Wrede, *Geschichte der k.u.k. Wehrmacht*, 2:200. Two more regiments were raised in Naples in the 1730s but likewise disbanded after the Bourbon conquest. See *ibid.*, 2:202.

11 *Ibid.*, 2:221–23.

12 Christopher Duffy, *The Army of Maria Theresa: The Armed Forces of Imperial Austria, 1740–1780* (London: David & Charles, 1977), p. 66; Heinrich Benedikt, *Kaiseradler über dem Apennin: Die Österreicher in Italien 1700 bis 1866* (Vienna: Verlag Herold, 1964), p. 64, refers to the first recruits of the Clerici as "deserters, bandits and unemployed men." He incorrectly calls them "Austria's first Italian regiment."

13 Wrede, *Geschichte der k.u.k. Wehrmacht*, 2:221. The system of proprietary colonels survived until the end of the nineteenth century and regiments usually were still known by the name of their proprietor rather than their official number. To simplify matters, the numbers will be used throughout the present text.

14 *Ibid.*, 1:430-31, 2:222-23.
15 *Ibid.*, 1:428, 2:222. From 1770 until the disbanding of the 48th in 1795, the two Lombard regiments in turn contributed men toward a common grenadier battalion. See *ibid.*, 2:313.
16 Population figures from Benedikt, *Kaiseradler über dem Apennin*, p. 71.
17 Barker, *Army, Aristocracy, Monarchy*, p. 234.
18 Wrede, *Geschichte der k.u.k. Wehrmacht*, 1:429-30, 2:221, 223.
19 *Ibid.*, 4:431. A German Austrian ensign of the 44th resisted capture and was the lone officer to survive the courtmartial with his commission intact.
20 Benedikt, *Kaiseradler über dem Apeppin*, p. 121.
21 Wrede, *Geschichte der k.u.k. Wehrmacht*, 1:429.
22 The privileged classes of Lombardy were offended by Joseph's encroachments on their traditional autonomy, a part of his overall drive to centralize the Habsburg domains. For the best recent work on Habsburg rule in Lombardy see Domenico Sella and Carlo Capra, *Il ducato di Milano dal 1535 al 1796* (Turin: U.T.E.T., 1984), most of which concerns the era of Austrian domination.
23 Wrede, *Geschichte der k.u.k. Wehrmacht*, 1:431, 433, 2:223.
24 *Ibid.*, 1:431, 2:223.
25 *Ibid.*, 1,431.
26 *Ibid.*, 1:431-32.
27 *Ibid.*, 1:103, 429-33.
28 *Ibid.*, 2:526.
29 On Lamberti's career and influence on Francis see Manfried Rauchensteiner, *Kaiser Franz und Erzherzog Carl: Dynastie und Heerwesen in Österreich, 1796-1809* (Vienna: Verlag für Geschichte und Politik, 1972), pp. 12-13, 22, 49, 70-78 passim. Born as sons of Grand Duke Leopold of Tuscany, the brothers Francis and Charles spent their formative years in Florence and spoke Italian as fluently as German or French.
30 See Franz Szabo, "Unwanted Navy: Habsburg Naval Armaments under Maria Theresa," *Austrian History Yearbook* 17-18 (1981-82): 29-53.
31 Theodor Braun, *Geschichte der k.u.k. Kriegsmarine*, part I: *Österreichs Seewesen in dem Zeitraume von 1500-1797* (MS, Vienna, 1944), Vienna, Kriegsarchiv (hereafter cited as KA), Ms/Ma 1, pp. 294-303.

[32] For an exhaustive official Austrian history of this period see Josef von Lehnert's *Geschichte der k.u.k. Kriegsmarine*, part II: *Die k.k. österreichische Kriegsmarine in dem Zeitraume von 1797 bis 1848*, vol. 1: *Geschichte der österreichisch-venetianischen Kriegsmarine während der Jahre 1797 bis 1802* (Vienna: Gerold & comp., 1891), a chronicle continued in Artur von Khuepach's vol. 2: *Geschichte der k.k. Kriegsmarine während der Jahre 1802 bis 1814* (Vienna: Staatsdruckerei Wien, 1942). Figures on officers compiled from Khuepach, pp. 294-317, and KA, Nachlass Folliot de Crenneville, B/216, no. 3, fol. 118-21.

[33] Khuepach, *Geschichte der k.k. Kriegsmarine* II/2, pp. 242-43; statistics compiled from appendix of same, pp. 406-25.

[34] Population figures from Benedikt, *Kaiseradler über dem Apennin*, p. 71.

Notes to Chapter 2

[1] Wrede, *Geschichte der k.u.k. Wehrmacht*, 2:469, 531.

[2] Francis, decree, Paris, 26 Apr. 1814, quoted in Wilhelm Buschek et al., *Geschichte des k.u.k. Infanterieregiments Markgraf von Baden No. 23*, 2 vols. (Budapest: Im Selbstverlag des Regiments, 1911), 2:4. Artillery units were not formed from old Napoleonic Italian personnel. See also *ibid.*, 2:4-5.

[3] *Ibid.*; see also [Moriz von Joelson], *Geschichte des k.k. Feldmarschalleutnant Eugen Graf Haugwitz 38sten Linien-Infanterie-Regimentes seit seiner Errichtung im Jahre 1814 bis zu Gegenwart* (Leitmeritz: C. W. Medau, 1865), p. 7. The life-long term of service had been universal in the Habsburg army until 1802, when a ten-year term (later raised to fourteen) became the rule everywhere but in Hungary. Alan Sked, *Survival of the Habsburg Empire*, p. 176, quite erroneously characterizes the liquidation of the Italian army as a ruthless process which was the source of great enmity between Italians and Austrians. Vienna even assumed the burden of paying pensions to retired veterans of the Napoleonic Italian army and to their widows, an undertaking that would still be costing the imperial government thousands of gulden at mid-century.

[4] Joelson, *Haugwitz 38sten Regiment*, p. 4.

[5] Buschek, *Markgraf von Baden No. 23*, 2:5. For the Napoleonic-army origin of various Italian units, see Table I in Appendix.

6 *Ibid.*, 2:6. At this point, Sommariva (born in Lodi in 1755) was appointed governor of Milan; he later retired to Vienna, where he died in 1829.

7 Friedrich Mandel, *Geschichte des k.u.k. Infanterie-Regiments Guidobald Graf von Starhemberg Nr. 13*, 2 vols. (Cracow: W. L. Anczyc & Comp., 1893), 2:202; Joelson, *Haugwitz 38sten Regiment*, p. 4.

8 Buschek, *Markgraf von Baden No. 23*, 2:7-8.

9 Wrede, *Geschichte der k.u.k. Wehrmacht*, 2:469; Buschek, *Markgraf von Baden No. 23*, 2:6.

10 Wrede, *Geschichte der k.u.k. Wehrmacht*, 1:206, 277, 390, 425-26. Even though the wartime reforms of Archduke Charles had greatly curtailed the privileges of the regimental *Inhaber* (proprietary colonel), the institution survived long after the Napoleonic era. For the sake of simplicity, the post-1814 Italian regiments will be referred to by their numbers.

11 Buschek, *Markgraf von Baden No. 23*, 2:7.

12 *Ibid.*, 2:11.

13 The cavalry, posted to Hungary in November 1814, made it as far as Melk in Lower Austria before being ordered back to Hungary in August 1815. See Hugo von Komers-Lindenbach, *Geschichte des k.k. Uhlanen-Regimentes Alexander II., Kaiser von Russland Nr. 11 (vormals 7. Chevauxlegers Regiment) von seiner Errichtung 1814 bis Ende 1877* (Vienna: Ludwig Mayer, 1878), pp. 3-5.

14 Benedikt, *Kaiseradler über dem Apennin*, pp. 116, 140; Hans Kramer, *Österreich und das Risorgimento* (Vienna: Bergland Verlag, 1963), pp. 198-99. Benedikt reports that 444 ex-Napoleonic officers took the oath during the Hundred Days but gives no source for this figure.

15 Carlo Zucchi, *Memorie del generale Carlo Zucchi*, Nicodeme Biachi (ed.) (Milan : M. Guigoni, 1861), p. 87, refers to colonels named Moretti and Olini as being tried and acquitted in 1815; both had accepted Habsburg commissions in 1814.

16 Buschek, *Markgraf von Baden No. 23*, 2:9. For an account of the declining number of Italian officers in the regiments, see Table III in Appendix.

17 Buschek, *Margraf von Baden No. 23*, 2:9-10.

18 *Ibid.*, 2:6. Lt. Col. Joseph von Young of the 1st (Bohemian) Infantry was transferred to Milan to become the first commandant

of the regimental school.
19 *Ibid.*, 2:10, 14.
20 Komers-Lindenbach, *Kaiser von Russland Nr. 11*, pp. 1-2, 308f.
21 Alfons Dragoni von Rabenhorst, *Geschichte des k.u.k. Infanterie-Regimentes Prinz Friedrich August Herzog zu Sachsen Nr. 45 von der Errichtung bis zur Gegenwart* (Brünn: Rudolf M. Rohrer, 1897), p. 243; Wrede, *Geschichte der k.u.k. Wehrmacht*, 1:224, 299, 428.
22 Buschek, *Markgraf von Baden No. 23*, 2:14. For a complete account of the movement and stationing of the Italian units after 1814, see Table II in Appendix.
23 E. g., Count Ferdinand Bubna (cmdr. in Lombardy) to Metternich, Milan, 21 Jan. 1821, Vienna, Haus- Hof- und Staatarchiv, Staatskanzlei, Provinzen, Lombardo-Venezien (hereafter cited as HHSA, StK., Prov., L-V), Carton 22: Korrespondenz mit den kommandierenden Generäle (Korr. kom. Gen.), Berichte 1821, fol. 39-40. Initially these regiments were not even "half-Italian." For example, the 44th Infantry, which arrived from Galicia in October 1817, had to wait until July 1819 for its first Italian recruits. See Franz von Branko, *Geschichte des k.k. Infanterie-Regimentes Nr. 44 Feldmarschall Erzherzog Albrecht, von seiner Errichtung 1744 bis. 1875* (Vienna: k.k. Hof- und Staatsdruckerei, 1875), p. 227.
24 Wrede, *Geschichte der k.u.k. Wehrmacht*, 1:107. According to Sked, *Survival of the Habsburg Empire*, p. 35, by the 1830s it cost three times as much (around 1,500 gulden) to hire a substitute in northern Italy as in the Austrian or Hungarian provinces. The difference most likely was caused by the lack of exemptions for the aristocracy of Lombardy and Venetia, which clogged the local market for substitutes with a clientele much wealthier than the middle-class one common in the rest of the empire.
25 Bubna to Metternich, Milan, 24 Apr. 1819, HHSA, StK., Prov., L-V, Carton 21: Korr. kom. Gen., Berichte 1818-19, fol. 418-25 passim.
26 Metternich to Bubna, Rome, 8 June 1819, *ibid.*, Weisungen 1818-19, fol. 69-72.
27 Bubna to Metternich, Milan, 1 Sept. 1819, *ibid.*, Berichte 1818-19, fol. 467-86 passim.
28 Kent Roberts Greenfield, *Economics and Liberalism in the Risorgimento: A Study of Nationalism in Lombardy, 1814-1848* (Bal-

timore: Md.: The Johns Hopkins Press, 1934, rev. ed. 1965), p. 30.
29 See Sked, *Survival of the Habsburg Empire*, and Chapter 3 below.
30 Bubna to Metternich, Milan, 1 Sept. 1819, HHSA, StK., Prov. L-V, Carton 21: Korr. kom. Gen., Berichte 1818-19, fol. 467-86 passim.
31 Buschek, *Markgraf von Baden No. 23*, 2:15.
32 Komers-Lindenbach, *Kaiser von Russland Nr. 11*, p. 8.
33 Bubna to Metternich, Milan, 21 Jan. 1821, HHSA, StK., Prov., L-V, Carton 22: Korr. kom. Gen., Berichte 1821, fol. 39-40.
34 *Ibid.*
35 Joszef M. Borus, "Hungarian Regiments, Officers, and Soldiers of the Habsburg Army during the French Revolutionary and Napoleonic Wars," in Béla K. Király, (ed.), *War and Society in East Central Europe*, vol. 4: *East Central European Society and War in the Era of Revolutions, 1775-1856* (New York: Social Science Monographs, Brooklyn College Press, 1984), p. 37, reports that Frimont "spoke Hungarian flawlessly, without an accent."
36 Giuseppe Antinori, the Duke of Brindisi, brought this to the attention of Habsburg officials in 1820. The matter is discussed at length in Bubna to Metternich, Milan, 20 Oct. 1820, HHSA, StK., Prov., L-V, Carton 21: Korr. kom. Gen., Berichte 1820, fol. 363; Bubna to Count Heinrich Bellegarde (HKR president), Milan, 1 Sept. 1820, Vienna, Kriegsarchiv, Hofkriegsrat Akten, Präsidialreihe (hereafter cited as KA, HKR Akten, Präs.), 1820/713-714-715, fol. 18, 21; and in other correspondence involving Frimont, Bellegarde, Francis, and imperial police chief Count Joseph Sedlnitzky. Carlo Tivaroni, *Storia critica del Risorgimento Italiano*, 9 vols. (Turin: Le Roux, 1888-97), 3/1:361-62, discusses the cases of various Napoleonic Italian veterans implicated following the arrest in October 1820 of Carbonari activist Pietro Maroncelli, whose incriminating personal papers also led to the trial and conviction of Federico Confalonieri.
37 The infantry included 14 battalions from Bohemia and Moravia (Czechs and Germans), 12 from German Austria, 12 Hungarian, 8 South Slav (from the Croatian Military Border and Slavic provinces of Hungary), 4 "Illyrian" (German and Slovene), and 2 Romanian from Transylvania. The cavalry included 14 squadrons from Bohemia and Moravia, 12 from German Austria, and 12

from Hungary. See Alberto Dallolio, (ed.), *I moti del 1820 e del 1821 nelle carte Bolognesi* (Bologna: Nicola Zanichelli, 1923), pp. 215–29.

[38] Branko, *Erzherzog Albrecht Nr. 44*, pp. 232–34.

[39] Dragoni, *Herzog zu Sachsen Nr. 45*, p. 249. The 45th was praised for its good discipline on the 44-day march from Verona to Pressburg.

[40] Mandel, *Graf von Starhemberg Nr. 13*, 2:203.

[41] Quoted from a report by the Graz Generalkommando, 1848, in Sked, *Survival of the Habsburg Empire*, p. 60.

[42] From 1817–25, at least three (and as many as four) of the eight regiments had been in Lombardy–Venetia at any given time. The 16th and 26th, both converted from non-Italian regiments starting in 1817, were to remain in Venetia until 1839 and 1838, respectively.

[43] Buschek, *Markgraf von Baden No. 23*, pp. 19–21.

[44] Alphons von Wrede, *Geschichte des k.u.k. Infanterie-regimentes Michael Grossfürst von Russland Nr. 26* (Györ: Verlag des Regiments, 1909), p. 361. The authorized strength of a regiment in war and peacetime, the number of battalions and companies, etc. was changed in 1816, 1831, and several times after 1848. See Table IV in Appendix.

[45] Wrede, *Geschichte der k.u.k. Wehrmacht* 1:700, 702. In 1830 the 12th Jägers, which had never left the northeast provinces of the empire, once again became Galician and were replaced by the 8th (Austrian) Field–Jägers, stationed in Lombardy since 1822.

[46] Unlike the Field–Jägers, which were elite sharpshooter units recruited on a provincial basis from volunteers and regular infantry conscripts, the Kaiser–Jägers were raised from conscripts in the Tyrol and Vorarlberg, Alpine provinces that traditionally did not supply men to regular infantry units. Because each of the Kaiser–Jäger battalions drew men out of a common pool from the German Tyrol, the Italian Tyrol, and Vorarlberg, no single battalion had an Italian majority. See Wrede, *Geschichte der k.u.k. Wehrmacht*, 1:646.

[47] Gustav Hubka von Czernczitz, *Geschichte des k.u.k. Infanterie-Regiments Graf von Lacy Nr. 22* (Zara: Verlag des Regiments, 1902), p. 249; Wrende, *Geschichte der k.u.k. Wehrmacht*, 1:271. The 22nd also did not have the red–trimmed uniforms common to the Italian regiments, but neither did the converted 16th and

26th Venetian regiments, which retained their traditional colors after becoming Italian in 1817. Coincidentally, the third transplanted Italian regiment, the Lombard 44th, already wore red trim.

[48] Wrede, *Geschichte der k.u.k. Wehrmacht*, 1:207, 278. In 1821 the Hofkriegsrat gave the regiments permission to supplement their conscripted manpower by recruiting "foreigners" (i.e., men from outside of Lombardy and Venetia), but the effects appear to have been minimal. See Buschek, *Markgraf von Baden No. 23*, p. 17.

[49] See Zucchi, *Memorie del Generale Carlo Zucchi*, pp. 85–95 passim.

[50] Frimont to Meternich, Milan, 16 Feb. 1831, HHSA, StK., Prov., L–V, Carton 24: Berichte der kommandierenden L. V. Königreich Frimont und Radetzky 1826–1848 (hereafter cited as Berichte Frimont u. Radetzky), fol. 490–96 passim. Italics added.

[51] Joelson, *Haugwitz 38sten Regiment*, pp. 17–19; Czernczitz, *Graf von Lacy Nr. 22.*, p. 255. For the navy's role in the capture of Zucchi, see p. 71 below.

[52] Czernicczitz, *Graf von Lacy Nr. 22*, pp. 255–56.

[53] Frimont to Metternich, Milan, 13 June 1831, HHSA, StK., Prov., L–V, Carton 24: Berichte Frimont u. Radetzky, fol. 603–6.

[54] Figure from Rothenberg, "The Austrian Army in the Age of Metternich," 163.

[55] Radetzky, "Abschrift . . . welche die Bestimmung der Truppen in Italien enthält . . . ." (n.d.), KA, Nachlass Radetzky, B/1151: A.25. In this document, Radetzky refers to a request for the information in a Hofkriegsrat dispatch of 23 March 1835, exactly three weeks after Francis died.

[56] Figures from tables in Harm–Hinrich Brandt, *Der österreichische Neoabsolutismus: Staatsfinanzen und Politik 1848–1860*, 2 vols. (Göttingen: Vandenhoeck & Ruprecht, 1978), 2:1098, 1106. The army received the lion's share of the military budget; the navy was allocated only around 1.5 million gulden per year prior to 1848.

[57] Figures for 1837 from Count Ignaz von Hardegg (HKR pres.) to Ferdinand, Vienna, 8 Mar. 1837, KA, HKR Akten, Präs. 1837/325, fol.1–12. For an account of the changing national composition of Radetzky's army between 1835 and 1848, see Table V in Appendix.

58 E.g. in his "Uiber das Conscriptionswesen in Italien," (n.d.–pre-1837), KA, Nachlass Radetzky, B/1151: F.55.
59 Mandel, *Graf von Starhemberg Nr. 13*, 2:205.
60 Hartig to Metternich, Prague, 31 Aug. 1833, quoted in Sked, *Survival of the Habsburg Empire*, pp. 42–43.
61 Joelson, *Haugwitz 38sten Regiment*, p. 30. Transport by sea was first employed in June 1841, when the field battalions of the 13th Infantry were sent from Fiume to Dalmatia on steamships rented from the Austrian Lloyd. See Mandel, *Graf von Starhemberg Nr. 13*, 2:220–21.
62 During the Croatian elections of July 1845, a watershed in the development of Croatian nationalism, two battalions of the 13th (Venetian) Infantry clashed with the populace of Zagreb, killing 17 and wounding 54. The troops lost one dead and nine wounded in the riot and had to be confined to their barracks afterward for fear of greater bloodshed. The same regiment earlier had gotten along well with the population of Fiume, which, however, was predominantly Italian. See Mandel, *Graf von Starhemberg Nr. 13*, 2:219, 223–24.
63 Wrede, *Grossfürst von Russland Nr. 26*, pp. 366–67 and Friedrich Dengler, *Kurzgefasste Geschichte des kaiserlichen und königlichen Infanterie-Regimentes Rupprecht Prinz von Bayern Nr. 43* (Vienna: C. W. Stern Verlag, 1908), p. 70. Considering the number of cholera deaths in Lombardy and Venetia during these years (50,000 in 1836 alone), the troops probably faced greater health risks at home. See Tivaroni, *Storia critica del Risorgimento* 3/1:394.
64 Sked, *Survival of the Habsburg Empire*, p. 52.
65 Ferdinand to Hardegg, Schönbrunn, 30 June 1837, KA, HKR Akten, Präs. 1837/1137, fol. 5–10 authorizes the creation of the guard, which was to consist of thirty men from Lombardy and thirty from Venetia. According to Walter Wagner, "Die k. (u.) k. Armee: Gliederung und Aufgabenstellung," in *Die Habsburgermonarchie 1848–1918* vol. 5: *Die Bewaffnete Macht*, Adam Wandruszka and Peter Urbanitsch (eds.) (Vienna: Verlag der österreichischen Akademie der Wissenschaften, 1987), 202, the guard was not officially disbanded until June 1856. On the unpopularity of the guard with the aristocracy see Sked, *Survival of the Habsburg Empire*, p. 176.
66 Figures from Radetzky, "Pia desideria in Bezug auf die Verthei-

digung Italiens, 1840, KA, Nachlass Radetzky, B/1151: A.31, and Radetzky to Hardegg, Milan, 9 Mar. 1844, *ibid.*, A. 67.

[67] Radetzky to Hardegg, Milan, 9 Mar. 1844, *ibid.*

[68] Radetzky to Metternich, Milan, 10 Mar. 1846, HHSA, StK., Prov., L–V, Carton 24: Berichte Frimont u. Radetzky, fol. 742–47. In addition to the hundreds of men on furlough from his Italian units, many of Radetzky's non–Italian regiments were not receiving reinforcements from their home districts and had fallen well under their authorized strength. In the report cited above he discusses the 51st (Transylvanian) Infantry, which had only 915 men in its two field battalions, less than half of its paper-strength of 2,293.

[69] Joelson, *Haugwitz 38sten Regiment*, p. 42. This draft came under a new conscription law promulgated in 1845, providing for a standard eight–year term of service throughout the empire. The law greatly reduced the obligations of recruits from Hungary and the Austrian crownlands by bringing them into line with what had been the rule in Lombardy and Venetia since 1820. The term for the Italian provinces remained unaffected.

[70] According to Sked, *Survival of the Habsburg Empire*, p. 36, the common soldier was paid at a rate of five kreutzer, or around .20 Austrian lire, per day. By comparison, the adult male cotton spinner in 1845 made a daily wage of between .75 and 2.50 Austrian lire, and even a child could earn between .20 and .50 lire per day as a spinner. See Greenfield, *Economics and Liberalism*, p. 124n.

[71] Sked, *Survival of the Habsburg Empire*, pp. 96–99, 106–8.

[72] Referred to in Carl Friedrich Kübeck to Hardegg, 16 Dec. 1847, KA, HKR Akten, Pras. 1847/2200, fol. 2–5. Kübeck, president of the Hofkammer (Court Treasury), balked at the expense of the reinforcement process and refused to appropriate additional funds to send troops to northern Italy by rail or steamship.

[73] Figures based on unit locations given in the *Militär-Schematismus des österreichischen Kaiserthums*, 1847 and 1848, and the regimental histories in Wrede, *Geschichte der k.u.k. Wehrmacht*. For specific units involved see Table V in Appendix.

[74] Nugent to Hardegg (HKR pres.), Granz, 26 Dec. 1847, KA, HKR Akten, Pras. 1847/2193, fol. 2–5. A thorough search of the records reveals no other specific proposals to move Italian troops out of Italy before the revolution.

75 Radetzky to Hardegg, Milan, 12 Dec. 1847, and Radetzky (Wallmoden) to HKR, Milan, 22 Feb. 1848, quoted in Sked, *Survival of the Habsburg Empire*, pp. 55 and 127.

76 Many historians have contended that Radetzky lost 17,000 of 20,000 Italians serving in his army, or 17 of 20 battalions, or "80 percent" of them. These figures, repeated in many Italian works, most likely are based upon two unrelated facts: the number of Italians in Radetzky's army (actually 21 battalions; see Table V in Appendix) and the number of men no longer available to him after March 1848. The latter, however, included a number of non-Italians who were cut off or had surrendered in Venice and other cities. Even Austrian military historians have cited similar figures, e.g. Rudolf Kiszling, "Das Nationalitätenproblem in Habsburgs Wehrmacht 1848–1918," *Der Donauraum* 4 (1959): 83.

Notes to Chapter 3

1 The besieged Hungarian garrison of Komorn (Komarom) did not surrender to the Austrians until 2 October 1849. Piero Pieri, *Storia militare del Risorgimento* (Turin: Giulio Einaudi, 1962), if read judiciously, is the most useful military history of the Italian wars of 1848 and 1849. The official Austrian histories, *Der Feldzug der österreichischen Armee in Italien im Jahre 1848* and *Der Feldzug der österreichischen Armee in Italien im Jahre 1849* (both Vienna: Verlag von Karl Hölzl, 1854) are valuable but understandably partisan accounts.

2 Wrede, *Geschichte der k.u.k. Wehrmacht*, 1:207-8; Mandel, *Graf von Starhemberg Nr. 13*, 2:227-58.

3 Wrede, *Geschichte der k.u.k. Wehrmacht*, 1:229-30; Istvan Deak, *The Lawful Revolution: Louis Kossuth and the Hungarians, 1848-1849* (New York: Columbia University Press, 1979), p. 249.

4 Sked, *Survival of the Habsburg Empire*, pp. 57-58; Wrede, *Geschichte der k.u.k. Wehrmacht*, 1:303-4; Wrede, *Grossfürst von Russland Nr. 26*, pp. 378-98.

5 Dragoni, *Herzog zu Sachsen Nr. 45*, pp. 277-306; Wrede, *Geschichte der k.u.k. Wehrmacht*, 1:436-37.

6 Buschek, *Markgraf von Baden Nr. 23*, 2:40-136; Wrede, *Geschich-*

te der k.u.k. Wehrmacht, 1:278–80.
[7] Joelson, *Haugwitz 38sten Regiment*, pp. 60–243; Wrede, *Geschichte der k.u.k. Wehrmacht*, 1:391–92.
[8] Dengler, *Prinz von Bayern Nr. 43*, pp. 76–86; Wrede, *Geschichte der k.u.k. Wehrmacht*, 1:427.
[9] Branko, *Erzherzog Albrecht Nr. 44*, pp. 245–305; Wrede, *Geschichte der k.u.k. Wehrmacht*, 1:432–33.
[10] Wrede, *Geschichte der k.u.k Wehrmacht*, 1:207–8, 229, 436.
[11] *Ibid.*, 2:576.
[12] Jakob Baxa, *Geschichte des k.u.k. Feldjägerbataillons Nr. 8, 1808–1918* (Klagenfurt: Verlag Carinthia, 1974), pp. 183–201; Wrede, *Geschichte der k.u.k. Wehrmacht*, 1:691–92.
[13] Wrede, *Geschichte der k.u.k. Wehrmacht*, 1:701.
[14] *Ibid.*, 1:723.
[15] Czernczitz, *Graf von Lacy Nr. 22*, pp. 267–93, 347; Wrede, *Geschichte der k.u.k. Wehrmacht*, 1:275–76.
[16] Angeli, *Altes Eisen*, p. 26. Chevaux-Legers carried carbines as well as sabres.
[17] Komers-Lindenbach, *Kaiser von Russland Nr. 11*, pp. 39–169; Wrede, *Geschichte der k.u.k. Wehrmacht*, 3/1:361.
[18] Radetzky to his daughter, Verona, 27 April 1848, in Bernhard Duhr, (ed.), *Briefe des Feldmarschalls Radetzky an seine Tochter Friederike, 1847–1857* (Vienna: Josef Roller & Comp., 1892, p. 80.
[19] Josef Bruna, *Im Heere Radetzkys: Skizzen aus den Jahren 1848 und 1849* (Prague: Verlag von F. A. Credner, 1859), p. 59. Bruna was a lieutenant in the 21st (Bohemian) Infantry. The provisional governments in Lombardy and Venetia failed to exploit the desertions to their advantage. The Venetian rebels sent home all of the troops that deserted during the revolution in Venice, while the Lombard government tactlessly rejected the volunteer spirit and alienated the peasantry by applying the old Austrian conscription system to raise its own troops. See Paul Ginsborg, *Daniele Manin and the Venetian Revolution of 1848–49* (Cambridge: Cambridge University Press, 1979), pp. 153–54, and Sked, *Survival of the Habsburg Empire*, p. 187.
[20] For biographical sketches of Calvi, Monti, Zucchi, and Caedalis, see Appendix. On the "Italian Legion" in Hungary in 1848–49 see Francesco Bettoni-Cazzago, *Gli Italiani nella guerra d'Ungheria 1848–49* (Milan: Fratelli Treves, 1887), Guido Zadei, *Il barone*

colonnello Alessandro Monti e la sua azione in Ungheria nel 1849 (Brescia: Vittorio Gatti, 1929), and Kathrin Sitzler, *Solidarität oder Söldertum: die ausländischen Freiwilligenverbände im ungarischen Unabhängigkeitskrieg 1848–49* (Osnabrück: Biblio Verlag, 1980), pp. 115–45. These sources place the peak strength of the legion at between 900 and 1,200 men in the summer of 1849; it numbered less than 500 when forced to retreat to Turkish soil following the Hungarian defeat. Monti and these remaining rebels were "repatriated" to Sardinia in May 1850.

[21] Sked, *Survival of the Habsburg Empire*, p. 57.

[22] Tivaroni, *Storia critica del Risorgimento*, 3/1:425.

[23] Joelson, *Haugwitz 38sten Regiment*, pp. 42–43.

[24] In 1856 Friulians accounted for 15 percent of the population of Venetia; see Kramer, *Österreich und das Risorgimento*, p. 30. See also Sked, *Survival of the Habsburg Empire*, pp. 58–61. Sked uses the 26th as his example of what went wrong in the typical Italian regiment; he fails to address the Friulian question, however, and gives no evidence of a similarly high percentage of criminals in any other regiment.

[25] Sked, *Survival of the Habsburg Empire*, p. 52.

[26] See Table III in Appendix.

[27] See Sked, *Survival of the Habsburg Empire*, pp. 56–57, and Table II in Appendix.

[28] Repeated, perhaps most recently, by Kramer, *Österreich und das Risorgimento*, p. 31. As for the supposed rebellious nature of the civilian population of Lombardy, John Whittam, *The Politics of the Italian Army, 1861–1918* (London: Croom Helm, 1977), p. 12, cites cases in which Lombard peasants even flooded their fields in 1848 to impede the advance of the Piedmontese army.

[29] Radetzky to his daughter, Verona, 23 Apr. 1848, *Briefe des Feldmarschalls Radetzky*, p. 79.

[30] Sked, *Survival of the Habsburg Empire*, pp. 199–202.

[31] On Francis Joseph's decree of 19 Sept. 1849, see Mandel, *Graf von Starhemberg Nr. 13*, 2:262.

[32] After defeating the Piedmontese at Novara, Radetzky informed Vienna that it would be "impossible" for him to send any of his 108,000 troops to Hungary; the field marshal apparently still had not forgiven Windischgrätz for denying him reinforcements the year before and was in no mood to be helpful. Radetzky to Prince Felix zu Schwarzenberg, Milan, 17 Apr. 1849, HHSA, Politisches

Archiv (hereafter cited as PA), XL. Interna, Carton 64: Korr. mit Radetzky 1849, fol. 195–98; Radetzky to Schwarzenberg, Milan, 22 Apr. 1849, *ibid.*, fol. 207–9.

33 Dengler, *Prinz von Bayern Nr. 43*, p. 99. The loyal 11th Jägers were also allowed to stay until mid–1850.

34 Regimental histories give a variety of dates for this decree, ranging from 23 October to 1 December 1850.

35 For a brief summary of the reforms see Wrede, *Geschichte der k.u.k. Wehrmacht*, 1:20, 50–1, 108. Wagner, "Die k.(u.)k. Armee: Gliederung und Aufgabestellung," 144–324, provides an exhaustive account of all peacetime reforms and restructuring within the army between 1849 and 1866.

36 Wrede, *Geschichte der k.u.k. Wehrmacht*, 3/1:339, 3/2:702; Johann von Naulik, *Geschichte des kais. kön. 55. Linien-Infanterie-Regimentes Baron Bianchi* (Brünn: Carl Winiker, 1863), p. 260; Julius Beran, *Die Geschichte des k.u.k. Infanterie-Regimentes Freiherr von Merkl Nr. 55* (Vienna: Carl Schneid, 1899), p. 297. The 43rd Infantry, displaced from Como and Sondrio, received new grounds in the province of Bergamo from the 38th Infantry.

37 Because the 63rd Infantry had been stationed in the backward eastern regions of the monarchy ever since the Napoleonic wars, as of the mid–1850s many of these officers "had seen neither a railway nor a steamship" and had "only vague notions" about these new modes of transportation, which had been in use in the western regions of the Habsburg Empire for some twenty years. See Angeli, *Altes Eisen*, p. 19. Angeli, serving in the Hungarian 37th Infantry, came into contact with the officers of the 55th during the occupation of Moldavia.

38 Mandel, *Graf von Starhemberg Nr. 13*, 2:267–69.

39 Branko, *Erzherzog Albrecht Nr. 44*, pp. 338–39.

40 Casualty figure from Angeli, *Altes Eisen*, p. 11.

41 Dragoni, *Herzog zu Sachsen Nr. 45*, pp. 313–19; Naulik, *55. Baron Bianchi*, p. 266; Beran, *Freiherr von Merkl Nr. 55*, pp. 302–19; Buschek, *Markgraf von Baden No. 23*, 2:146–47; Rudolf Szutsek, *Chronik des k.k. Infanterie Regimentes Nro. 26, seit seiner Errichtung 1717 bis Ende 1883* (Gran: Druck von Johann Laiszky, 1887), pp. 93–94; Komers-Lindenbach, *Kaiser von Russland Nr. 11*, pp. 181–83. The 22nd (Trieste) Infantry also served in Galicia during the Crimean War; see Czernczitz, *Graf von Lacy Nr. 22*, pp. 304–8. The 11th "Tsarevich" Uhlans

retained their name despite high Austro-Russian animosity; after Alexander became tsar in 1855, the 11th became the "Kaiser von Russland" Uhlans.

[42] E.g. the 13th (Venetian) Infantry in Carinthia in 1851-52, which arrested 500 deserters, conscription evaders and other fugitives. See Mandel, *Graf von Starhemberg Nr. 13*, 2:272.

[43] On the effect of transfer on a regiment see Sked, *Survival of the Habsburg Empire*, p. 52. In the period 1815-48 Lombard and Venetian regiments headquartered in other provinces moved an average of once every 3.8 years; from 1849-59 the average posting was 1.5 years.

[44] Kramer, *Österreich und das Risorgimento* p. 31. The figure includes 5,600 Friulians, most of them in the 26th Infantry, and is so high that it must also include Italians from Trieste, Istria and the southern Tyrol.

[45] The new Jäger battalions were both supported by recruits from Lombardy. The 11th Jägers, traditionally raised from both Lombardy and Venetia, in 1857 became a Lombard battalion. The other Italian Jäger battalions—the 8th and 25th—were recruited in Venetia after 1849. In the cavalry, the 7th Uhlans were drawn from Venetia and the 9th Uhlans from Lombardy. See Wrede, *Geschichte der k.u.k. Wehrmacht*, 1:667, 681, 690, 700, 722; 3/1:191, 345.

[46] William Jenks, *Francis Joseph and the Italians, 1849-1859* (Charlottesville, Va.: University Press of Virginia, 1978), pp. 140, 146-47.

[47] Istvan Deak, "Defeat at Solferino: The Nationality Question and the Habsburg Army in the War of 1859," in Béla K. Király, (ed.), *War and Society in East Central Europe*, vol. 14: *The Crucial Decade: East Central European Society and National Defense, 1859-1870* (New York: Social Science Monographs, Brooklyn College Press, 1984), p. 503.

[48] *Ibid.*, 504.

[49] Mandel, *Graf von Starhemberg Nr. 13*, 2:284-85.

[50] Quoted in Beran, *Freiherr von Merkl Nr. 55*, p. 332. The 3rd (Galician) dragoons were slated to become Venetian, but the war brought the postponement (and eventual cancellation) of the change. See Wrede, *Geschichte der k.u.k. Wehrmacht*, 3/1:201.

[51] Deak, "Defeat at Solferino," 501.

[52] *Ibid.* 505-6. In citing examples of desertions Deak mentions the

Notes   139

13th, 22nd, 26th, 43rd, 45th and 55th regiments—three Venetian, two Lombard, and one from Trieste. The Italian Jäger battalions serving with the *Küstenarmee* (the 6th, 8th, 11th and 25th) also appear to have behaved poorly.

53 The 13th Infantry, stationed in Udine for a brief time in 1854, was the only exception.

54 In early April the fourth battalions were ordered to reinforce the German federal fortresses, but aside from four battalions that made it to Ulm, none reached their destination before the armistice.

55 For the authorized strength of battalions and regiments as of 1859 see Table IV in Appendix. Roughly 33,000 Italians were called back from furlough during the mobilization, most of them going to the 4th, 5th, and depot battalions. These men alone represented a force as large as the entire number of Lombards and Venetians in the Austrian army as of March 1848. Figure from *Der Feldzug 1859 in Italien* (Vienna: Verlag der k.u.k. Kriegsschule, 1898), p. 9.

56 Dragoni, *Herzog zu Sachsen Nr. 45*, pp. 330–31; Wrede, *Geschichte der k.u.k. Wehrmacht*, 1:230, 437.

57 Mandel, *Graf von Starhemberg Nr. 13*, 2:290–92.

58 Dengler, *Prinz von Bayern Nr. 43*, p. 103; Wrede, *Grossfürst von Russland Nr. 26*, pp. 421–22; Deak, "Defeat at Solferino," 506. Renato Giusti, "Il 1859 nel Veneto," *Mitteilungen des österreichischen Staatsarchivs* 31 (1978): 258–70 refers to scattered uprisings occurring in Venetia during the war, but these appear to have had little effect on the men of the Venetian regiments.

59 Beran, *Freiherr von Merkl Nr. 55*, p. 323.

60 Komers-Lindenbach, *Kaiser von Russland Nr. 11*, pp. 190–92; Czernczitz, *Graf von Lacy Nr. 22*, pp. 316–30. Three additional Italian Jäger battalions—the 26th, 27th and 30th—were created in Hungary and Croatia during the war but none saw action. After the war, th 27th and 30th were assigned to non-Italian recruiting grounds while the 26th drew its manpower from Venetia.

61 Buschek, *Markgraf von Bden No. 23*, 2:161–62.

62 Because there were almost 40,000 Lombards in the army by the end of the war, the repatriation was no small undertaking. The 23rd Infantry alone sent home 4,238 men; the 55th (which had suffered few desertions during the war) returned 5,136. See Buschek, *Markgraf von Baden No. 23*, 2:163; Beran, *Freiherr*

von Merkl Nr. 55, p. 324; Dengler, *Prinz von Bayern Nr. 43*, p. 105; Komers-Lindenbach, *Kaiser von Russland Nr. 11*, p. 105.

63 In the two weeks after Magenta, the 45th lost 236 men to desertion. See Deak, "Defeat at Solferino," 506.

64 Wrede, *Geschichte der k.u.k. Wehrmacht*, 1:230, 275–76, 437. Trentinaglia was the only Italian among the officers of the three regiments receiving decorations.

65 *Ibid.*, 1:226.

66 *Ibid.*, 1:585; Carl von Wenzl, *Auszug aus der Geschichte des k.u.k. Infanterie-Regimentes Arnulf Prinz von Bayern Nr. 80* (Lvov: Verlag des Regimentes, 1900), p. 5. The 79th Infantry, for example, was formed from the third and fourth battalions of the 26th Infantry and the third battalion of Trieste's 22nd. The 80th received the third and fourth battalions of the 16th and the fourth battalion of the 13th. The depleted ex–Lombard 38th Infantry was given the fourth battalion of the 45th.

67 Komers-Lindenbach, *Kaiser von Russland Nr. 11*, pp. 194–95; Wrede, *Geschichte der k.u.k. Wehrmacht*, 3/1:339, 3/2:702.

68 In the three Lombard regiments for which figures are available, 350 men decided to stay; the total for the five regiments must have been 500–600. See Buschek, *Markgraf von Baden No. 23*, 2:163; Beran, *Freiherr von Merkl Nr. 55*, p. 324; Dengler, *Prinz von Bayern Nr. 43*, p. 105.

69 Trentinaglia and Cattanei held their commands from 1859 until 1866. The new 79th Infantry also had an Italian commander (Colonel Giulio Bagnalasta) from 1863–66. See Wrede, *Geschichte der k.u.k. Wehrmacht*, 1:226, 391, 586, and Table III in Appendix. The Sardinian (soon to be Italian) army organized three Lombard divisions by the spring of 1860 but, at least initially, had very few officers from Lombardy. By 1866 some 12 to 13 percent of the Italian army's officers were Lombards, but many of these either had never served in the Austrian army or had left it in 1848. See Pieri, *Storia militare del Risorgimento*, pp. 630–32; Edoardo Scala, *La Guerra del 1866 ed altri scritti* (Rome: Tipografia Regionale, 1981), pp. 24–25.

70 Armeeoberkommando (AOK) to Degenfeld, Vienna, 14 Mar. 1860, KA, Centralkanzleiatkten (CK), Präsidialreihe (Präs.) 1860/1334, fol. 1–35 passim. In contrast to these high concentrations of troops, the army had less than 38,000 on garrison duty in all of Hungary.

[71] Order of Battle, 14 Mar. 1860, *ibid.* The 22nd Infantry was also kept from the front, stationed in Graz. See Wrede, *Geschichte der k.u.k. Wehrmacht*, 1:271.

[72] Ministerrat resolution, 23 Mar. 1861, in *Die Protokolle des Österreichischen Ministerrates 1848-1867*, part V, vol. 4, Horst Brettner–Messler (ed.) (Vienna: Österreichischer Bundesverlag, 1977), p. 222. A total of 927 men evaded conscription in Venetia in 1860.

[73] Dragoni, *Herzog zu Sachsen Nr. 45*, p. 342.

[74] Mandel, *Graf von Starhemberg Nr. 13*, 2:297, 302. Statistics from Rothenberg, *The Army of Francis Joseph*, p. 61. The Italian figure includes those in the 22nd Infantry and the Tyrolese Kaiser-Jägers.

[75] Rudolf Streith, *Geschichte des k.u.k. Feldjäger-Bataillons Nr. 26 (1859-1890)* (Innsbruck: Verlag der Wagner'schen Universitäts-Buchhandlung, 1892), pp. 10–12; Wenzl, *Prinz von Bayern Nr. 80*, pp. 6–13; Wrede, *Geschichte der k.u.k. Wehrmacht*, 1:589.

[76] The average posting of an Italian regiment's field battalions in 1859–66 was 2.5 years, up from 1.5 years in 1849–59. See Table II in Appendix.

[77] See Richard Blaas, "Vom Friauler Putsch im Herbst 1864 bis zu Abtretung Venetiens 1866," *Mitteilungen des österreichischen Staatsarchivs* 19 (1966): 264. The unrest occurred in the districts of the 26th and 79th regiments.

[78] Mandel, *Graf von Starhemberg Nr. 13*, pp. 304–15; Wrede, *Grossfürst von Russland Nr. 26*, pp. 427; Dragoni, *Herzog zu Sachsen Nr. 45*, p. 346; Wenzl, *Prinz von Bayern Nr. 80*, p. 14.

[79] Czernczitz, *Graf von Lacy Nr. 22*, p. 366f.

[80] The Italians had over 250,000 men at their disposal for the campaign, counting 38,000 volunteers serving under Garibaldi, while the Austrian forces numbered 113,000, of which around 38,000 were assigned to garrisons or to keep order in the rear. See *Der Feldzug 1866 in Italien* (Vienna: Verlag der k.u.k. Kriegsschule, 1902), pp. 28–34, and Pieri, *Storia militare del Risorgimento*, pp. 754–59. Italy lost 714 killed, 2,576 wounded, 4,101 prisoners and missing at Custoza; Austria lost 1,170 killed, 3,984 wounded, 2,802 prisoners and missing. Rothenberg, *The Army of Francis Joseph*, p. 69, contends that Albrecht's missing were "largely from Italian and Magyar regiments" but at least for the Italians

81 Czernczitz, *Graf von Lacy Nr. 22*, pp. 336–51; Attilio Tamaro, *Storia di Trieste*, 2 vols. (Trieste: Edizioni Lint, 1924; reprint ed. 1976), 2:367–68. this could not have been the case, since none took part.
82 See Table VI in Appendix.
83 Mandel, *Graf von Starhemberg Nr. 13*, 2:368, 390. Colonel Carlo Radaelli was the Italian army attaché in Prussia in charge of establishing contact with Venetian prisoners of war. A native of Venice and veteran of the Austrian navy, Radaelli was a close friend of the Bandiera brothers and a founding member of the Mazzinian sect Esperia in 1840. Four days after Königgrätz he visited 600 Venetian prisoners at Spandau. See Radaelli to Bettino Ricasoli (Italian minister-president), Berlin, 7 July 1866, in Sergio Camerani and Gaetano Arfé (eds.), *Carteggi di Bettino Ricasoli*, vol. 22: *20 giungno – 31 luglio 1866*, no. 81 of *Fonti per la storia d'Italia* (Rome: Istituto storico italiano per l'età moderna e contemporanea, 1967), pp. 183–84, no. 248. On Radaelli's earlier career see chapter 4 below.
84 Streith, *Geschichte . . . Nr. 26*, pp. 24–25.
85 Almost half of the prisoners and missing were from the 80th Infantry, which was trapped by the Prussians after hours of bloody fighting in the Swiep Wald. See Wenzl, *Prinz von Bayern Nr. 80*, pp. 15–19. Statistics available for 16 of the 20 Venetian battalions at Könniggrätz (see Table VI in Appendix) indicate that these units suffered casualties of 729 killed, 1,015 wounded, and 1,989 prisoners or missing, a ratio of killed : wounded : prisoners and missing of 1 : 1.39 : 2.73. The overall Austrian losses were 5,658 killed, 7,574 wounded, and 29,580 prisoners or missing, a ratio of 1 : 1.34 : 5:23. In 1848–49 and 1859, figures for prisoners and missing in some Italian units cast suspicion over their loyalty; in 1866, however, they appear to have done better than the army as a whole.
86 Wrede, *Geschichte der k.u.k. Wehrmacht*, 1:230.
87 *Ibid.*, 1:208, 230, 304, 392, 437, 586–87, 589, 662, 692.
88 Wrede, *Grossfürst von Russland Nr. 26*, pp. 449–50.
89 Giovanni Baptista Falzari, "L'armistizio di Cormons del 1886," *Studi Goriziani* 21 (1957): 10–21.
90 Czernczitz, *Graf von Lacy Nr. 22*, p. 347; Laura Castellazzi, "I rapporti della Guardia Nazionale di Verona sui disordini dal 6 al 12 ottobre 1866," *Il quadrilatero nella storia militare, politica,*

economica e sociale dell'Italia risorgimentale (Verona: Linotipia veronese Ghidini Fiorini, 1967): 135.

[91] Menabrea to Count Max von Wimpffen (Austrian plenipotentiary), Vienna, 27 Sept. 1866, HHSA, PA, XI. Italienische Staaten, Carton 157: Friedensverhandlungen 1866, part 1, fol. 199.

[92] Count Alexander Mensdorff (Austrian foreign min.) to Menabrea, Vienna, 6 Oct. 1866, *ibid.*, fol. 18; Menabrea to Mensdorff, Vienna, 17 Oct. 1866, *ibid.*, fol. 178; Count Friedrich Ferdinand von Beust (Austrian foreign min.) to Count Luigi Rati–Opizzoni (Italian envoy), Vienna, 26 Oct. 1866, *ibid.*, Carton 170; Kgr. Italien, Varia 1866, fol 58–59; Rati–Opizzoni to Mensdorff (sic), Vienna, 28 Oct. 1866, *ibid.*, Carton 157: Friedensverhandlungen 1866, part 1, fol. 174; Archduke Albrecht to Min. des Äussern (memorandum), 29 Oct. 1866, *ibid.*, XL. Interna, Carton 124: Korrespondenz mit Erz. Albrecht und Wimpffen 1866, fol. 170.

[93] Mandel, *Graf von Starhemberg Nr. 13*, 2:377; Anton Werner et al., *Geschichte des kaiserlichen und königlichen Infanterie-Regimentes Freiherr von Mollinary Nr. 38, seit seiner Errichtung 1725 bis 1891* (Budapest: Pester Buchdruckerei–Actien-Gesellschaft, 1892), pp. 431–32.

[94] Mandel, *Graf von Starhemberg Nr. 13*, 2:389.

[95] Luraghi, "Italians in the Habsburg Armed Forces," 227; Wrede, *Grossfürst von Russland Nr. 26*, p. 451.

[96] Quoted in Streith, *Geschichte . . . Nr. 26*, pp. 18–19.

Notes to Chapter 4

[1] Lawrence Sondhaus, *The Habsburg Empire and the Sea: Austrian Naval Policy, 1797–1866* (West Lafayette, Ind.: Purdue University Press, 1989), chapters 2–5, covers the operational and administrative history of the navy during the years 1814–48. On the program that produced the fleet inherited by Austria in 1814, see Sondhaus, "Napoleon's Shipbuilding Program at Venice and the Struggle for Naval Mastery in the Adriatic, 1806–1814," *The Journal of Military History* 53 (1989): 349–62.

[2] Artur von Khuepach and Heinrich von Bayer, *Geschichte der k.u.k. Kreigsmarine* part II: *Die k.k. österreichsche Kriegsmarine in dem Zeitraum von 1797 bis 1848*, vol. 3: *Geschichte der k.k. Kriegsmarine während der Jahre 1814–1847* (Graz: Verlag Hermann Böhlaus Nachfolger, 1966), pp. 33, 41.

3 The Austrian navy did not have admiral's ranks until 1829. Until then, major general (later equated with rear admiral) was the rank above the highest grade of captain.

4 Dandolo's conduct rated in "Etat Nominatif des Officiers de la Marine Italienne," n.d. (1806–1808), The Papers of Prince Eugene de Beauharnais, Princeton University Library, box 34, folder 5.

5 Figures compiled from *Militär-Schematismus des österrichischen Kaiserthums* (1817), appendices of Khuepach, *Geschichte der k.u.k. Kriegsmarine* II/2 and Khuepach and Bayer, *Geschichte der k.u.k. Kriegsmarine* II/3, and Italian roster in "Etat Nominatif des Officiers de la Marine Italienne," Beauharnais Papers, 34/5.

6 In 1814 a proposal to introduce German as an elective at the academy met with defeat, even though its supporters argued that the language would be necessary to facilitate future interaction between the navy and the predominantly-German army officer corps. See Peter Salcher, *Geschichte der k.u.k. Marine-Akademie* (Pola: Carl Gerold's Sohn, 1902), p. 12.

7 The army invariably came in over budget, spending at least 46 million florins in every year between 1819 and 1847. See figures in Brandt, *Neoabsolutismus*, 1:1098.

8 For a biographical sketch of Paulucci, see Appendix.

9 Salcher, *Marine-Akademie*, pp. 14–15, 34–52 passim. The drop in enrollment came in part because of new Austrian classifications. Whereas the Italian navy considered graduated cadets not yet commissioned as ensigns to still be under the wing of the academy, the Austrians made a sharper distinction between a student (*Zögling* or *allievo*) and a cadet, the latter being a recent graduate not yet promoted to ensign. Under the Austrian system, 41 of the 58 students of 1814 would have been cadets. See *ibid.*, p. 11.

10 Salcher, *Marine-Akademie*, pp. 15, 33.

11 Crenneville to Bellegarde (HKR president), Vienna, 20 Dec. 1822, KA, Nachlass Foliot de Crenneville, B/216, no. 14, fol. 361–70 passim.

12 Friedrich Engel-Janosi, *Die Jugendzeit des Grafen Prokesch von Osten*, (Innsbruck: Universitäts-Verlag Wagner, 1938), p. 48. Prokesch served with the navy from 1825 to 1830 before returning to the army. Transfer from the army was the only other means

of entry into the corps until 1838, when a new program made it possible for young men to qualify as sea cadets by taking a one or two year non-resident course and passing a qualifying exam. See Salcher, *Marine-Akademie*, p. 67.

[13] Because the army was reluctant to relinquish able-bodied conscripts, the 13th (Venetian) Infantry and 22nd (Trieste) Infantry always had their share of *seekundige* soldiers.

[14] Engel-Janosi, *Prokesch von Osten*, p. 48.

[15] Khuepach and Bayer, *Geschichte der k.u.k. Kriegsmarine* II/3, p. 58.

[16] Josef Fleischer, *Geschichte der k.u.k. Kriegsmarine*, part II, vol. 3 (Leitmeritz, 1911), KA, Manuskripte/Marine (Ms/Ma) 4, p. 92, provides the most thorough account of this affair. To paper over the incident, Paulucci even had the *Orione* renamed after its next refitting; it returned to sea as the *Oreste*.

[17] See biographical sketch of Dandolo in Appendix. Khuepach and Bayer, *Geschichte der k.u.k. Kriegsmarine* II/3, p. 99, make special reference to Dandolo's differences with Paulucci on the subject of discipline.

[18] Dandolo to Gyulai (HKR president), Vienna, 24 Nov. 1830, KA, HKR Akten, Präs. 1830/1575, fol. 365-67.

[19] On promotion controversy see Friedrich Wallisch, *Die Flagge Rot-Weiss-Rot: Männer und Täten der österreichischen Marine in vier Jahrhunderte* (Graz: Verlag Styria, 1956), p. 52.

[20] Radaelli, *Storia dello Assedio*, pp. 2-3.

[21] FMLt. Count Zichy, military commander in Venice from 1842-48, complained to Metternich about Paulucci's refusal to cooperate with the army. A case involving his own son, artillery captain Antonio Paulucci, sheds some light on the marquis's relations with the Austrian police. Zichy notes on conversation with Metternich (Trieste, August 1844), KA, Nachlass Zichy, B/184:2, fol. 83-86; "Commissions-Vortrag sammt Gutachten," Venice, 27 July 1841, KA, Marineakten (hereafter cited as MA), A/j 7 (1840), no. 5 and 5-a.

[22] See Radaelli, *Storia dello Assedio* p. 3. Attilio's contact with Maroncelli is described in Filippo Nani Mocenigo, *La Marina Veneta e i fratelli Bandiera* (Venice: Tipografia Orfanotrofio di A. Pellizzato), p. 12; Emilio's early activities referred to in Paulucci to Hofkriegsrat, Venice, 30 Apr. 1844, KA, HKR Akten, Präs. 1844/684.

23 Bandiera to Metternich, Venice, 3 Apr. 1831, HHSA, StK., Notenwechsel HKR, Carton 293, a.d. Marine, Teil 2, and Metternich to Bandiera, Vienna, 16 Apr. 1831, *ibid.* contain the captain's report of the operation and the chancellor's praise of its execution.

24 Radaelli, *Storia dello Assedio*, p. 7.

25 Joseph Bergmann, *Erzherzog Friedrich von Oesterreich und sein Antheil am Kriegszuge in Syrien im Jahre 1840* (Vienna: Tendler, 1857), pp. 27–41; Ernesto Simion and Mario Nani Mocenigo, *La campagna navale di Siria del 1840* (Rome: Tip. Ufficio del Capo di Stato Maggiore, 1933), passim. Bergmann, childhood tutor of Frederick, and Simion and Nani, Italian naval officers, give somewhat differing accounts of the details of the campaign; the latter contend that Frederick's heroism was overrated and that Chinca was the "true hero" of Sidon (p. 104).

26 Cf. Bergmann, *Erzherzog Friedrich*, pp. 49–54, and Giuseppe Mazzini, "Ricordi dei fratelli Bandiera" (1845), in *Scritti editi ed inediti di Giuseppe Mazzini* (Edizione Nazionale), 95 vols. (Imola: Cooperativa Tipografico Editrice Paolo Gateati, 1921), 31:24–25. Bergmann (writing in 1857) omitted the names of Moro and other Esperia members from his list of Frederick's subalterns on the *Bellona*. No Austrian work on the navy mentions Moro's role as a messenger to Mazzini. Italian historians usually base their accounts on Mazzini's essay, never mention Frederick, and confuse the circumstances and details of the cruise.

27 Radaelli, *Storia dello Assedio*, p. 9; Emilio Bandiera to Fabrizi, n.p., 30 Aug. 1843, quoted in Franco Della Peruta, "Attilio Bandiera," *Dizionario Biografico degli Italiani*, vol. 5 (Rome: Istituto della Enciclopedia Italiana, 1963), 683.

28 Zichy notes on conversation with Metternich (Trieste, August 1844), KA, Nachlass Zichy, B/184:2, fol. 83–86; Zichy to Hardegg, Venice, 1 June 1844, KA, HKR Akten, Präs, 1844/973, fol. 2–7 discusses a plan by Attilio Bandiera during the winter of 1843–44 to desert to Constantinople, seize an armed steamer and attack the *Bellona* to force his father's hand.

29 Mazzini, "Ricordi dei fratelli Bandiera," *Scritti editi ed inediti* 31:20, makes a point of disclaiming all responsibility for "seducing" the Bandieras to action.

30 This and the following paragraphs are based upon an extensive run of correspondence on the Bandieras in KA, HKR Akten,

Präsidialreihe 1844; only the more significant letters will be cited below.

[31] Stürmer to Metternich, Constantinople, 20 Mar. 1844, HHSA, Die Akten des k.u.k. Ministeriums des Äussern 1848-1918, Administrative Registratur (hereafter cited as HHSA, AR), F 52 – Sicherheitswesen, Carton 1, fol. 257-70 includes the ambassador's first discussion of Attilio's desertion. Radetzky to Hardegg, Verona, 23 Mar. 1844, KA, HKR Akten, Präs. 1844/436, fol. 1, 4 contains Radetzky's first reference to Emilio's flight. Italian sources identify Tito Vespasiano Micciarelli as the agent betraying Attilio Bandiera.

[32] See Emiliana P. Noether, " 'Morally Wrong' or 'Politically Right'? Espionage in Her Majesty's Post Office, 1844-45," *Canadian Journal of History* 22 (1987): 53-54.

[33] Mayersbach (Austrian consul) to Metternich, Corfu, 23 Mar. 1844, HHSA, AR, F 52, Carton 1, fol. 271-75. Mazzini later accused the British government, which was opening his mail at the time, of providing information on the Bandieras to Austria and to Naples, their final destination. The allegations helped spark a political crisis in England. See Noether, "Espionage in Her Majesty's Post Office," 47-49.

[34] Hardegg to Emperor Ferdinand, Vienna, 24 May 1844, KA, HKR Akten, Präs. 1844/1458, fol. 4-19.

[35] See Luigi Carci, *La spedizione e il processo dei fratelli Bandiera* (Modena: Società tipografica modenese, 1939), pp. 10-43; Riccardo Pierantoni, *Storia dei fratelli Bandiera e loro compagni in Calabria* (Milan: Casa Editrice L. F. Cogliati, 1909), pp. 325-96. There are a number of less reliable works on the Bandiera's expedition; all are hagiographic in nature and some even fail to mention that they were Austrian naval officers.

[36] Carci, *La spedizione*, pp. 44-57; Pierantoni, *Storia dei fratelli Bandiera*, pp. 397-417. The king of Naples pardoned Mariani in 1846; he returned to his home in Lombardy and later petitioned Emperor Francis Joseph for a pardon.

[37] Guido Poosch, Baldiserotto proceedings and verdict, Venice, 23 May 1845, KA, MA, A/j 7 (1845), no. 1-b. During the trial, an Italian seaman alleged that Attilio Bandiera had once forced him into a homosexual relationship; from the evidence given, it appears that the homosexual circle aboard the *Bellona* included at least some Esperia members. Karoly's reaction to such behavior,

which of course was not uncommon among sailors, echoed that of Count Prokesch, who criticized the morality of navy officers when serving with the fleet in the late 1820s. See Engel-Janosi, *Prokesch von Osten*, p. 65.

38 HKR circular, Vienna, 10 Jan. 1845, KA, HKR Akten, Präs. 1845/10, fol. 1–164. The admiral's deteriorating health was cited in the decision not to prosecute. He died in 1847, at the age of 62.

39 Radaelli, *Storia dello Assedio*, p. 12.

40 Frederick, only 23 at the time of his appointment, showed questionable judgment in many personnel decisions after 1844. Matticola, considered to be among those most compromised in the Bandiera affair, was exonerated on the strength of the archduke's acquaintance with him and affirmation of his personal honor. Archduke Frederick to Hardegg, Venice, 22 Jan. 1845, Präs. 1845/869, fol. 13–17.

41 South Slavs accounted for 15 percent of the officers and 11 percent of the cadets in 1844, 16 percent of the officers and 10 percent of the cadets in 1848. Figures deduced from *Militär-Schematismus*, 1844 and 1848.

42 Archduke Frederick to Hardegg, Venice, 3 Aug. 1847, KA, HKR Akten, Präs. 1847/1249, fol. 2, 9; HKR circular, Vienna, 8 Aug. 1847, *ibid.*, fol. 1, 10.

43 Max von Sterneck, a future commander of the navy, shared the prevailing view of Marinovich as a cadet in 1847. See Sterneck to mother, Venice, 28 Nov. 1847, in *Admiral Max Freiherr von Sterneck: Erinnerungen aus den Jahren 1847 bis 1897,* Jerolim Benko von Boinik (ed.) (Vienna: A. Hartleben, 1901), p. 50.

44 See Ginsborg, *Daniele Manin and the Venetian Revolution*, pp. 50, 141.

45 Jerolim Benko von Boinik, *Geschichte der k.k. Kriegsmarine*, part III: *Die k.k. österreichische Kriegsmarine, in dem Zeitraume von 1848 bis 1871*, vol. 1: *Geschichte der k.k. Kriegsmarine während der Jahre 1848 und 1849* (Vienna: Verlag des k.k. Reichs-Kriegs-Ministerium, Marine-Sektion, 1884), p. 51n; Hardegg to Martini, 5 Feb. 1848, KA, MA, M/c 27 (1848), no. 278-a (Carton 46); MOKdo. circular, Venice, 12 Feb. 1848, *ibid.*, no. 278.

46 Benko von Boinik, *Geschichte der k.k. Kriegsmarine* III/1, pp. 66–77; Giovanni Minotto, "Particolari sugli avveniment dei 22

Marzo 1848 nell' Arsenale di Venezia" (copy), KA, Nachlass Zichy, B/184:2, fol. 119-22.

47 Robert van Nuffel, "Intorno alla perdita della flotta all'inizio della rivoluzione veneziana," *Rassegna Storica del Risorgimento* 44 (1957): 786-91; Benko von Boinik, *Geschichte der k.k. Kriegsmarine* III/1, pp. 120-21.

48 Officer corps to Dandolo, Venice, 24 Oct. 1847, KA, HKR Akten, Präs. 1847/1907, fol. 4-5.

Notes to Chapter 5

1 Sondhaus, *The Habsburg Empire and the Sea*, chapters 6-9, covers the operational and administrative history of the navy during the years 1848-66.

2 These and the following figures compiled from rosters in *Militär-Schematismus* (1848); Benko von Boinik, *Geschichte der k.k. Kriegsmarine* III/1, pp. 12-13; and C. Randaccio, *Le marinerie militari italiane nei tempi moderni (1750-1850)*, (Turin: Artero e comp., 1864), pp. 133-40. For a further breakdown by nationality, station, and rank, see Table VIII in Appendix.

3 See Benko von Boinik, *Geschichte der k.k. Kriegsmarine* III/1, pp. 127-39 passim.

4 *Ibid.*, pp. 171-90; Adolph Schwarzenberg, *Prince Felix zu Schwarenberg, Prime Minister of Austria 1848-1852* (New York: Columbia University Press, 1950), pp. 18-19.

5 KA, MA, M/c 27 (1848) includes the paperwork for the repatriation of officers, with ample evidence of the variety of conditions under which they were discharged. On the hostage negotiations see Benko von Boinik, *Geschichte der k.k. Kriegsmarine* III/1, pp. 307-16.

6 Turszky (gov. Dalmatia) to Latour (war min.), Zara, 3 July 1848, KA, MA, M/c 27 (1848), no. 93-b (Carton 44); Higgia to MOKdo., Zara, 18 Sept. 1848, *ibid.*, no. 93-a.

7 MOKdo. circular, Trieste, 5 Apr. 1848, KA, MA, M/c 27 (1848), no.174 (Carton 45); Latour to MOKdo., Vienna, 4 Sept. 1848, *ibid.*, no. 170.

8 Benko von Boinik, *Geschichte der k.k. Kriegsmarine* III/1, p. 315.
9 Radaelli, *Storia dello Assedio*, pp. 7–8. In the correspondence among higher officials, Michieli's name appears prominently in Zichy to Hardegg, Venice, 1 Dec. 1844, enclosure to HKR Akten, Präs. 1845/869, and Marinovich to Zichy, Venice, 22 Nov. 1847, fol. 94–95. For a biographical sketch of Michieli, see Appendix.
10 This particular problem, not admitted in Dahlerup's own *In österreichischen Diensten*, 2 vols. (Berlin: Meyer und Jessen, 1911–12), receives coverage in Peter Handel-Mazzetti's manuscript *Geschichte der k.u.k. Kriegsmarine*, part III, vol. 2: *1850–1866* (n.d.), KA, Ms/Ma 19, section I, p. 9.
11 Salcher, *Marine-Akademie*, pp. 19–22.
12 On Austria's role in this German navy project see Lawrence Sondhaus, "*Mitteleuropa zur See?* Austria and the German Navy Question, 1848-52," *Central European History* 20 (1987): 125–44.
13 Martini to Kriegsministerium, Trieste, 6 Sept. 1848, KA, MA, A/j 7 (1848), no. 26; extensive exchanges on Fumanelli in A/j 7 (1850), no. 33.
14 See Benko von Boinik, *Geschichte der k.k. Kriegsmarine* III/1, pp. 646–47n. Austria's envoy in Turin reported that a "great number" of Venetians were trying to enter Sardinian service; they were accepted at their former rank despite the "animosity" caused by the subsequent delay in the promotion of "indigenous officers." Count Rudolph Apponyi to Schwarzenberg, Turin, 28 Feb. 1850, HHSA, PA, XI. Italienische Staaten, Carton 44: Sardinien, Berichte 1850, fol. 84–85.
15 A number of Venetian officers in Venice at the time of the revolution followed the cue of those repatriated from Pola and sought releases from their oaths. Their appeals, filed during the war, were not accepted.
16 In January 1852 Michele Garbizza and Domenico Giaj were hanged after their conviction for Marinovich's murder. Three others, including former naval engineering captain Giuseppe Ponti, were condemned to death *in absentia*. See Tivaroni, *Storia critica del Risorgimento* IV/1, p. 26.
17 Slovenes, hailing from a region between the German and Italian-speaking realms, were well suited for these intermediary roles and eventually accounted for a disproportionate number of the NCOs.

See Miroslav Pahor, *Slovenski mornarji Austrije v obrambi Dalmacije in Istre 1849-1917* (Piran: Pomorske muzej Sergej Mašera, 1978), passim.

[18] Handel-Mazzetti, *Geschichte der k.u.k. Kriegsmarine* (MS) III/2/I: 109-10. The two highest-ranking South Slavs in the corps were also retired at this time, on terms similar to those accorded Salvini.

[19] See Benko von Boinik, *Geschichte der k.k. Kriegsmarine* III/1, p. 721.

[20] See Jenks, *Francis Joseph and the Italians*, p. 68 and Wrede, *Geschichte der k.u.k. Wehrmacht* I, Beilage VII and IX.

[21] Handel-Mazzeti, *Geschichte der k.u.k. Kriegsmarine* (MS) III/2/I: 23-24.

[22] See Table VII in Appendix.

[23] Handel-Mazzetti, *Geschichte der k.u.k. Kriegsmarine* (MS) III/2/I: 27.

[24] Kriegsministerium to MOKdo. (memo), Vienna, 10 Oct. 1861, KA, MA, M/c 28 (1861), no. 11 a-b, fol. 2-3.

[25] Hadik (adjutant) to Ferdinand Max, Trieste, 16 June 1861, KA, MA, M/c 33 (1861), no. 18; MKdo. Trieste to Gubernium-Dalmatia (memo), Trieste, 26 Apr. 1862, *ibid.*, M/c 28 (1862), no. 10, fol. 1. The Italian deserters fled either to Rome or across the Adriatic to Dalmatia, where most of the requests were processed.

[26] Mamula (army cmdr. Dalmatia) to k.k. Festungs- und Insel Kdo. (Lissa), Zara, 12 Jan. 1861, KA, MA, M/c 15 (1861), no. 1, fol. 1; Wüllerstorf (port admiral-Pola) to Bourguignon (squadron cmdr.), Pola, 14 Jan. 1861, *ibid.*, M/c 22 (1861), no. 22, fol. 2.

[27] The term "*Italia irredenta* (unredeemed Italy)" did not gain currency until the late 1870s, and most historians date Irredentism from 1866, but the Venetian revolutionary claim to Istria and Dalmatia was evident in 1848-49. For a concise summary of the development of irredentism up to Italy's entry into World War I, see Dennison I. Rusinow, *Italy's Austrian Hertitage, 1919-1946* (Oxford: Clarendon Press, 1969), pp. 15-40.

[28] Hadik to Ferdinand Max, Trieste, 11 Jan. 1861, KA, MA, M/c 33 (1861), no. 1, fol. 1; Ferdinand Max to Hadik, Vienna, 14 Jan. 1861, *ibid.*, no. 2, fol. 1-2.

29 See Raffaele Fasanari, "Lo spionaggi politico–militare organizzato da Luigi Mongo in territorio austriaco per incarico di Vittorio Emanuele II (1861–1864)," in *Il quadrilatero nella storia militare, politica, economica e sociale dell'Italia risorgimentale* (Verona: Linotipia veronese Ghidini Fiorini, 1967), 182. Spigliatti worked for master spy Luigi Mongo, whose non–Italian correspondents included a number of high–ranking Habsburg officers.

30 Protocol, Pola, 25 June 1862, KA, MA, M/c 15 (1862), no. 1 a–f (with enclosures).

31 See Handel–Mazzeti, *Geschichte der k.u.k. Kriegsmarine* (MS) III/2/II: 173–82; Handel–Mazzetti, "Das Seegefecht bei Helgoland am 9. Mai 1864," *Marine Rundschau* 39 (1934): 193–98; D. Paschen, "Der blutige Tag von Helgoland," *Marine Rundschau* 44 (1939): 470–76.

32 Twenty–nine of 227, or 13 percent, as of 1865. See Table VII in Appendix.

33 "Stand und Armierung der k.k. operativen Eskadre im Jahre 1866," in Josef Fleischer, *Geschichte der k.k. Kriegsmarine*, part III: *Die k.k. österreichsche Kriegsmarine in dem Zeitraume von 1848 bis 1871*, vol. 3; *Geschichte der k.k. Kriegsmarine während des Krieges im Jahre 1866* (Vienna: Verlag des k.u.k. Reichskriegsministeriums, Marinesektion, 1906), pp. 362–63. The best accounts of Lissa are in *ibid.*, pp. 185–299, and Angelo Iachino, *La campagna navale di Lissa 1866* (Milan: Casa editrice Il Saggiatore, 1966), pp. 379–488, both meticulous reconstructions of every facet of the action.

34 See Franco Micali Baratelli, *La marina militare italiana nella vita nazionale (1860–1914)* (Mursia: U. Mursia editore S.p.A., 1983), p. 152.

35 "Stand und Armierung der königlich italienischen Opeationsflotte im Jahre 1866," in Fleischer, *Geschichte der k.k. Kriegsmarine* III/3, pp. 360–61; roster of academy graduates, 7 Mar. 1848, KA, MA, M/c 27 (1848), no. 293 (Carton 46). The Italian *Annuario ufficiale della Marina* indicates that years of service by these Italians in the Austrian navy counted toward their seniority in the Royal Italian navy, as did service in the Sardinian and Neapolitan fleets or in the Venetian navy of 1848–49.

36 Ensign Amilcare Predonzan, naval artillery lieutenants Antonio Rochlitzer–Scordelli and Pietro Pisoni, marine lieutenant Enrico Mercurio, and naval ordnance lieutenant Marco Valtan applied

for their official releases through diplomatic channels, apparently after leaving for Italy without official permission; Italian sources indicate that Valtan became a staff officer in the Italian navy on 24 July 1866, while the war was still in progress. Documentation in Vice Admiral Louis Fautz to Min. des Äussern, Vienna, 17 May 1867, HHSA, AR, F 44 – Marinewesen, Carton 3: Generalia 1860–70, Varia; Fautz to Min. des Äussern, Vienna, 12 July 1867, *ibid.*; *Annuario ufficiale della Marine*, 1873. A comparison of the *Militär-Schematismus* naval officer corps rosters for 1865 and 1868 reveals that ensigns Nicolo Dojmi, Giuseppe Boscarolli, Carlo Marchetti, and Leone Ahsbahs also left the service in the wake of the war, as did Cadet Marquis Ferdinando Paulucci.

Notes to Chapter 6

[1] Nani Mocenigo, *La Marina Veneta*, pp. 28–29.
[2] Sampling of figures given in Gianni Oliva, *Storia degli alpini* (Milan: Rizzoli Editore, 1985), p. 27.
[3] See Table IX in Appendix; conscription information from Rothenberg, *The Army of Francis Joseph*, p. 81. The contention by Luraghi, "Italians in the Habsburg Armed Forces," 227, that the army "still possessed several Italian regiments" after 1866 has no basis in fact.
[4] From *Militärstatistisches Jahrbuch* (1885). The navy had a four-year term of active service, one longer than the army.
[5] 148 "semester hours" based on annual curriculum averaging 37 hours of classroom study per week, as outlined in the *Jahrbuch der k.k. Kriegsmarine* (1871), pp. 66–69. French and English, the languages of the bulk of all naval literature, were as important to the course of study as the Habsburg national tongues.
[6] Salcher, *Marine-Akademie*, p. 40; starting in 1882, students were no longer required to have both English and French but had to take one as an elective.
[7] For a broader depiction of these trends, see Table VII in Appendix. The growth of the other nationalities came at the expense of the German contingent, which fell to less than 50 percent in the late 1880s after peaking at over 60 percent in the late 1860s and early 1870s. The reason for the German decline was the loss, after 1866, of its officer recruiting grounds in the states of the

German Confederation, an important resource during the period of germanization.

8 On the promotions of Morelli, Zaccaria, and Florio, cf. *Militär-Schematismus* and the periodic *Rangs- und Eintheilungsliste der k.k. Kriegsmarine*, passim. Toward the end of the century, Morelli and Florio each received the dignity and pension of rear admiral in retirement, as did Captain Giuseppe Primavesi.

9 Figure from *Militärstatistisches Jahrbuch* (1887). For the influence of Venice on Tegetthoff see Baratelli, *La marina militare italiana*, pp. 96 and 152; on Sterneck's writing see ed. note by Jerolim Benko von Boinik in Sterneck, *Erinnerungen*, p. 94n.

10 See Luraghi, "Italians in the Habsburg Armed Forces," 227.

11 Czernczitz, *Graf von Lacy Nr. 22*, pp. 354–78; Wrede, *Geschichte der k.u.k. Wehrmacht*, 1:275–76. In 1868, a reorganization of the army divided each regiment into three field and two reserve battalions, the latter to be stationed in the regiment's home recruiting district during peacetime.

12 The following paragraphs are based upon Francesco Salata, *Guglielmo Oberdan* (Bologna: Nicola Zanichelli, 1924); Alfred Alexander, *The Hanging of Wilhelm Oberdank* (London: London Magazine Editions, 1977); Giani Stuparich, "Guglielmo Oberdan," *Rassegna Storica del Risorgimento* 58 (1971): 183–98; and Claus Gatterer, *Erbfeindschaft Italien-Österreich* (Vienna: Europaverlag, 1972), pp. 13–25. Salata gives the most extensive of the many Italian treatments of Oberdan's life. Alexander, Stuparich, and Gatterer provide the most recent accounts in English, Italian, and German.

13 Oberdan's illegitimacy has resulted in much disagreement among scholars attempting to define his ancestry. He grew up with his mother's surname Oberdank, dropping the "k" only after his flight to Italy. Salata, writing in the fascist era, insists that Oberdan was "purely Italian," while Alexander contends that he had no Italian blood at all. Most agree that his father, a veteran of the 22nd or 26th Infantry, was of Italian descent.

14 Wrede, *Geschichte der k.u.k. Wehrmacht*, 1:275–76. One battalion of Kaiser–Jägers also fought in Bosnia, and its Lieutenant Giulio Bombiero received the Order of the Iron Crown. See *ibid.*, 1:651. Desertion figure for 22nd Infantry from Gatterer, *Erbfeindschaft*, p. 17.

15 Czernczitz, *Graf von Lacy Nr. 22*, pp. 458–63; Wrede, *Geschichte*

der k.u.k. Wehrmacht, 1:275–76.
16 Czernczitz, Graf von Lacy Nr. 22, p. 517.
17 Wrede, Geschichte der k.u.k. Wehrmacht, 1:608–9.
18 Ibid., 1:609. Exceptions to the district system of stationing came in Vienna, Bosnia–Herzegovina, and Galicia, all of which had greater garrison or defense needs than could be provided by local or regional regiments. See Rothenberg, *The Army of Francis Joseph* p. 111.
19 See Wrede, *Geschichte der k.u.k. Wehrmacht*, 1:713. From 1898 to 1908 Italians accounted for less than 20 percent of the 20th Field–Jägers, and Slovenian temporarily became the only language of the unit. During this same decade, the 97th Infantry had a slightly larger Italian contingent, in some years exceeding 30 percent. See Table IX in Appendix.
20 Czech immigrants made up the third largest national group in the Tyrol; initially, they were concentrated in the 4th Kaiser–Jägers, which had Czech as its second language of command instead of Italian. The army soon abandoned this division and restored Italian as the second language of all Kaiser–Jäger regiments.
21 Figures from *Militärstatistisches Jahrbuch*, 1883, 1893, 1986, 1907.
22 On Montecuccoli's tenure as Marine–Kommandant see Hans Hugo Sokol, *Geschichte der k.u.k. Kriegsmarine* part III: *Die k. k. österreichische Kriegsmarine 1848 bis 1914 ("Abschlußband des Geschichtswerkes der k.u.k. Kriegsmarine")* (Vienna: Amalthea, 1980), pp. 197–231, and Paul Halpern, *The Mediterranean Naval Situation, 1908–1914* (Cambridge: Harvard University Press, 1971), pp. 157–73.
23 Cf. *Jahresbericht der k.u.k Kriegsmarine* 1899 (p. 106), 1905 (p. 98), 1908 (p. 122), 1913 (p. 127). Figures for illiteracy in the native language of recruits show that the Italians were second only to the South Slavs in this category in each of these years.
24 Census statistics cited by Umberto Corsini, "Die Italiener," in *Die Hambsburgermonarchie 1848–1918*, vol. 3: *Die Völker des Reiches*, Adam Wandruszka and Peter Urbanitsch (eds.) (Vienna: Verlag der österreichischen Akademie der Wissenschaften, 1980), 850–60 passim. Navy figures from *Militärstatistisches Jahrbuch* (1910); army statistics from *ibid*, 1911, and Maximilian Ehnl, *Die österreichisch–ungarische Landmacht nach Aufbau, Gliederung, Friedensgarnison, Einteilung und nationaler Zusammensetzung im Sommer 1914*, Ergänzungsheft 9 of Österreich-

Ungarns letzter Krieg (Vienna: Verlag der "Militärwissenschaftlichen Mitteilungen," 1934), passim. Italians traditionally were not used in artillery units, but for a brief time in the early 1900s the 1st Mountain Artillery (*Gebirgsartillerie*) Regiment was 20 percent Italian. When the army reorganized its artillery on the eve of World War I, Italians once again were largely eliminated from this branch.

25 Figures from Gatterer, *Erbfeindschaft*, pp. 138–39. Some estimates have as many as 2,000 Tyrolese fighting in the Italian army. On Battisti's career in Vienna see Angelo Ara, "Governo e parlamento in Austria nel periodo del mandato parlamentare di Cesare Battisti, 1911–1914," in *Fra Austria e Italia: Dalle Cinque Giornate alla questione alto-atesina* (Udine: Del Bianco editore, 1987), 137–53.

26 *Ibid.*, p. 138. The *Landesschützen* were the Alpine equivalent of Landwehr. In 1914 they consisted of three regiments and a cavalry division (half-regiment).

27 Austria, Bundesministerium für Landesverteidigung, *Österreich-Ungarns letzter Krieg 1914–1918*, 8 vols. (Vienna: Verlag der "Militärwissenschaftlichen Mitteilungen," 1930–38), 1:214, 2:51, 75. In June 1914 the 97th Infantry had two battalions at Bjelovar, one at Karlovac and one in Trieste, a deployment it had been in since 1912. The action of 26 August 1914 and the subsequent imprisonment of Italians in Russia are referred to in Hans Weiland and Leopold Kern, (eds.), *In Feindeshand: Die Gefangenschaft im Weltkriege in Einzeldarstellungen*, 2 vols. (Vienna: Bundesverlag der ehemaligen österreichischen Kriegsgefangenen, 1931), I:58–59, 312.

28 Rothenberg, *The Army of Francis Joseph*, pp. 184–85.

29 Gatterer, *Erbfeindschaft*, pp. 138–39, 141.

30 *Ibid.*, p. 148. and *Österreich-Ungarns letzter Kreig*, 2:292.

31 *Österreich-Ungarns letzter Krieg*, 2:290, 4:212, 6:194–97.

32 The only exception came with the German Austrian regiments, which maintained their *Ersatz* units in their own recruiting districts. See Richard Georg Plaschka, Horst Haselsteiner, and Arnold Suppan, *Innere Front: Militärassistenz, Widerstand und Umsturz in der Donaumonarchie 1918* (Munich: R. Oldenbourg Verlag, 1974), 1:39–42.

33 For an extensive bibliography of works on Chiesa see Umberto Corsini, "Damiano Chiesa," *Dizionario Biografico degli Italiani*,

24:706–7.

34 Speaking through his character "the Grumbler (*Der Nörgler*)", Kraus discusses the Battisti case at length, noting that "the special effect of our beastliness is that the enemy propaganda, instead of lying, simply reproduced our reality . . . ." He called the controversial picture "the eternal photograph of our culture," evidence of the depths to which mankind had sunk. See Karl Kraus, *Die letzten Tage der Menschheit* (Vienna: Verlag "Die Fackel," 1919), Act V, scene 32. Gaetano Arfé, "Giuseppe Cesare Battisti," *Dizionario Biografico degli Italiani*, 7:271, provides an extensive bibliography on Battisti.

35 *Österreich-Ungarns letzter Kreig*, 2:100–1, 447, 614; 3:123; 4:23, 369, 421–25, 432–33, 562, 567, 649.

36 De Gasperi quoted in Gatterer, *Erbfeindschaft*, p. 138.

37 Gatterer, *Erbfeindschaft*, pp. 138–39, refers to 5,000 Italian Tyrolese entering Russian service, but this must be a misprint, for he adds this figure to his 700 in the Italian army and comes up with 1,200. A small number of Italians captured in Russia were repatriated in 1916 via Tashkent, British India, and the Suez Canal and went on to serve against Austria in the Alps. See Weiland and Kern, *In Feindeshand*, I:310.

38 Figures from Plaschka, et al., *Innere Front*, 2:341, 347. The *Landesschützen* usually appear in the literature as the *Kaiserschützen*, an honorary designation given them by Emperor Charles in 1917. In June 1914 these units, like the regular Kaiser–Jägers, had Italian contingents of between 38 and 41 percent, corresponding roughly to the 40 percent Italian share of the population of the Tyrol in the census of 1910; see Ehnl, *Die österreichisch-ungarische Landmacht . . . im Sommer 1914*, pp. 79–80.

39 "Southwest" battalions referred to in *Österrich-Ungarns letzter Krieg*, 7:409, 414, 796.

40 Plaschka, et al., *Innere Front*, p. 346; there are no precise figures for the 1918 composition of the 97th.

41 See *ibid.*, 2:335–52. The regiments with Italian minorities of 2 percent or less were the 1st (Silesian), 17th (Carniolan), 29th (Banat), 37th (Hungarian), 47th (Styrian), and 60th (Hungarian), and the new 107th, 122nd, 130th, 135th, and 204th. The 5th (Bohemian) and 24th (Hungarian) Field–Jägers, the 5th (Inner Austrian) Dragoons, the 11th and 37th Landwehr, and the 2nd, 4th, and 5th Mounted Landwehr were also in this category.

42 Some authors (including Plaschka, et al., *Innere Front*, 1:278) place the Habsburg P.O.W. total as high as 2 million. On the controversy over the number of prisoners taken on the eastern front see Gerald H. Davis, "Deutsche Kriegsgefangene im Ersten Weltkrieg in Russland," *Militärgeschichtliche Mitteilungen* (1982), no. 1. On the Italians at Tambov see Weiland and Kern, *In Feindeshand*, I: 312.

43 Quoted in Plaschka, et al., *Innere Front*, 1:346.

44 *Ibid.*, 1:346–56, 2:70n.

45 *Österreich-Ungarns letzter Krieg*, 7:126, 148, 409, 538, 799. Among the so-called "Southwest" battalions, the 4th-stationed in Wallachia in the summer and fall of 1918—suffered the most desertions. See *ibid.*, 7:796.

46 1918 figures from Hans Hugo Sokol, *Österreich-Ungarns Seekrieg* (Vienna: Amalthea Verlag, 1930), p. 692.

47 Richard Georg Plaschka, *Cattaro – Prag: Revolte und Revolution* (Graz: Verlag Hermann Böhlaus Nachfolger, 1963), p. 13. The following paragraphs are based upon Plaschka's account of the Cattaro mutiny in *ibid.*, pp. 13–192; more condensed versions of the same story appear in his *Matrosen, Offiziere, Rebellen: Krisenkonfrontationen zur See 1900–1918*, 2 vols. (Vienna: Verlag Herman Böhlaus Nachfolger, 1984), 2:155–278, and *Innere Front*, 1:107–48.

48 On the strikes of January 1918 in Pola and the shipyards of Trieste see Plaschka, et al., *Innere Front*, 1:61–76.

49 Quoted in Plaschka, *Cattaro – Prag*, p. 26.

50 Quoted in *ibid.*, p. 107.

51 Only one officer, Dalmatian Croat ensign Antun Sešan, openly sided with the rebels; on the last day of the mutiny, he commandeered a seaplane and fled to Italy.

52 Statistics in Plaschka, *Cattaro – Prag*, p. 190n.

53 Quoted in *ibid.*, p. 183.

54 See Plaschka, et al., *Innere Front*, 1:415–20.

55 *Ibid.*, 2:224–39.

56 See prisoner figures in Emil Ratzenhofer, "Der Waffenstillstand von Villa Giusti und die Gefangennahme Hunderttausender," in *Österreich-Ungarns letzter Krieg*, Ergänzungsheft 1 (Vienna: Verlag der "Militärwissenschaftlichen Mitteilungen," 1931), 50.

57 *Österreich-Ungarns letzter Krieg*, 7:800.

[58] Romania reentered the war on the side of the Entente only on November 9, well after the Habsburg army had ceased to function.

Notes to Epilogue

[1] The population of Lombardy and Venetia stood at just under 4 million in 1817, just over 5 million in 1847; see figures in Corsini, "Die Italiener," 848. The army and navy kept roughly 40,000 Italians under arms throughout this period.

[2] The number of infantry battalions raised in the provinces climbed to 41 from the pre-revolutionary level of 31, while the demands for cavalry manpower rose from eight squadrons to 38. The population of Lombardy and Venetia reached 5.15 million by 1857, up from 5 million a decade earlier; see Corsini, "Die Italiener," 849n.

[3] Over 50,000 Venetians fought in the war, of a total population of 2.5 million. Latter figure from *ibid.*, 849.

[4] Quoted in Gatterer, *Erbfeindschaft*, p. 170.

[5] See John W. Cole and Eric R. Wolf, *The Hidden Frontier: Ecology and Ethnicity in an Alpine Valley* (New York: Academic Pess, 1974), p. 16. Their work on the Trentino and South Tyrol, and Feliks Gross's *Ethnics in a Borderland* (Wesport, Conn.: Greenwood Press, 1978) on Trieste and the former Austrian Küstenland, confirm that national identity is still a confusing matter in these regions.

BIBLIOGRAPHY

I. Unpublished Documents

Haus- Hof- und Staatsarchiv, Vienna
    Administrative Registratur
        F 44 – Marinewesen
        F 52 – Sicherheitswesen
    Politisches Archiv
        XI. Italienische Staaten
        XL. Interna
    Staatskanzlei
        Notenwechsel mit dem Hofkriegsrat
        Provinzen
            Lombardo-Venezien
Kriegsarchiv, Vienna
    Centralkanzleiakten
        Präsidialreihe
    Hofkriegsrat Akten
        Präsidialreihe
    Manuskripte
    Marineakten
        Administrative Akten (A/j)
        Militärische Akten (M/c)
    Nachlässe
        Folliot de Crenneville
        Radetzky
        Zichy
Princeton University Library
    The Papers of Prince Eugene de Beauharnais
        Box 34

II. Published Documents, Memoirs, Personal Accounts

Angeli, Moriz von. *Altes Eisen: Intimes aus Kriegs- und Friedensjahren.* Stuttgart: J. G. Cotta'sche Buchhandlung Nachfolger, 1900.

Brettner-Messler, Horst,(ed.) *Die Protokolle des Österreichischen Ministerrates 1848–1867,* part V, Vol. 4. Vienna: Österreichischer Bundesverlag, 1977.

Bruna, Josef. *Im Heere Radetzkys: Skizzen aus den Jahren 1848 und 1849.* Prague: Verlag von F. A. Credner, 1859.

Camerani, Sergio, and Arfé, Gaetano, (eds.), *Carteggi di Bettino Ricasoli,* vol. 22: *20 giungno – 31 luglio 1866.* No. 81 of *Fonti per la storia d'Italia.* Rome: Istituto storico italano per l'età moderna e contemporanea, 1967.

Dahlerup, Hans Birch von. *In österreichischen Diensten.* 2 vols. Berlin: Meyer und Jessen, 1911-12.

Duhr, Bernhard, (ed.) *Briefe des Feldmarschalls Radetzky an seine Tochter Friederike, 1847–1857.* Vienna: Josef Roller & Comp., 1892.

Mazzini, Giuseppe. *Scritti editi ed inediti di Giuseppe Mazzini.* Edizione Nazionale. 95 vols. Imola: Cooperativa Tipografico Editrice Paolo Galeati, 1921.

Radaelli, Carlo Alberto. *Storio dello Assedio di Venezia negli anni 1848-1849.* Venice: Tipografia Antonelli, 1875.

Sterneck zu Ehrenstein, Maximilian Daublebsky von. *Admiral Max Freiherr von Sterneck: Erinnerungen aus den Jahren 1847 bis 1897.* Jerolim Benko von Boinik (ed.). Vienna: A. Hartleben, 1901.

Zucchi, Carlo, *Memorie del generale Carlo Zucchi.* Nicodeme Bianchi (ed.). Milan: M. Guigoni, 1861.

III. HANDBOOKS, GUIDES, STATISTICAL SOURCES

Austria/Austria-Hungary. *Jahrbuch der k.k. Kriegsmarine.*

———. *Jahresbericht der k.u.k. Kriegsmarine.*

———. *Militär-Schematismus des österreichischen Kaisterthums.* Annual, title varies.

———. *Militärstatistisches Jahrbuch.*

———. *Rangs- und Eintheilungsliste der k. k. Kriegsmarine.* Irregular periodical.
Dizionario Biografico degli Italiani.
Italy. *Annuario ufficiale della Marina.*

IV. REGIMENTAL HISTORIES

Baxa, Jakob. *Geschichte des k.u.k. Feldjägerbataillons Nr. 8, 1808–1918.* Klagenfurt: Verlag Carinthia, 1974.
Beran, Julius. *Die Geschichte des k.u.k. Infanterie-Regimentes Freiherr von Merkl Nr. 55.* Vienna: Carl Schneid, 1899.
Branko, Franz von. *Geschichte des k.k. Infanterie-Regimentes Nr. 44 Feldmarschall Erzherzog Albrecht, von seiner Errichtung 1744 bis 1875.* Vienna: k. k. Hof- und Staatsdruckerei, 1875.
Buschek, Wilhelm, et al. *Geschichte des k.u.k. Infanterie-Regiments Markgraf von Baden No. 23.* 2 vols. Budapest: Im Selbstverlag des Regiments, 1911.
Czernczitz, Gustav Hubka von. *Geschichte des k.u.k. Infanterie-Regi- ments Graf von Lacy Nr. 22.* Zara: Verlag des Regiments, 1902.
Dengler, Friedrich. *Kurzgefasste Geschichte des kaiserlichen und königlichen Infanterie-Regimentes Rupprecht Prinz von Bayern Nr. 43.* Vienna: C. W. Stern Verlag, 1908.
Dragoni von Rabenhorst, Alfons. *Geschichte des k.u.k. Infanterie-Regimentes Prinz Friedrich August Herzog zu Sachsen Nr. 45 von der Errichtung bis zur Gegenwart.* Brünn: Rudolf M. Rohrer, 1897.
[Joelson, Moriz von]. *Geschichte des k.k. Feldmarschalleutnant Eugen Graf Haugwitz 38sten Linien-Infanterie-Regimentes seit seiner Errichtung im Jahre 1814 bis zu Gegenwart.* Leitmeritz: C. W. Medau, 1865.
Komers-Lindenbach, Hugo von. *Geschichte des k.k. Uhlanen-Regimentes Alexander II., Kaiser von Russland Nr. 11 (vormals 7. Chevauxlegers Regiment) von seiner Errichtung 1814 bis Ende 1877.* Vienna: Ludwig Mayer, 1878.
Mandel, Friedrich. *Geschichte des k.u.k. Infanterie-Regiments Guidobald Graf von Starhemberg Nr. 13.* 2 vols. Cracow: W. L. Anczyc & Comp., 1893.
Naulik, Johann von. *Geschichte des kais. kön. 55. Linien-Infanterie-Regimentes Baron Bianchi.* Brünn: Carl Winiker, 1863.

Streith, Rudolf. *Geschichte des k.u.k. Feldjäger-Bataillons Nr. 26 (1859-1890).* Innsbruck: Verlag der Wagner'schen Universitäts-Buchhandlung, 1892.
Szutsek, Rudolf. *Chronik des k. k. Infanterie Regimentes Nro. 26, seit seiner Errichtung 1717 bis Ende 1883.* Gran: Druck von Johann Laiszky, 1887.
Wenzl, Carl von. *Auszug aus der Geschichte des k.u.k. Infanterie-Regimentes Arnulf Prinz von Bayern Nr. 80.* Lvov: Verlag des Regimentes, 1900.
Werner, Anton, et al. *Geschichte des kaiserlichen und königlichen Infanterie-Regimentes Freiherr von Mollinary Nr. 38, seit seiner Errichtung 1725 bis 1891.* Budapest: Pester Buchdruckerei-Actien-Gesellschaft, 1892.
Wrede, Alphons von. *Geschichte des k.u.k. Infanterie-Regimentes Michael Grossfürst von Russland Nr. 26.* Györ: Verlag des Regiments, 1909.

V. OTHER SECONDARY WORKS CITED

Alexander, Alfred. *The Hanging of Wilhelm Oberdank.* London: London Magazine Editions, 1977.
Ara, Angelo. "Governo e parlamento in Austria nel periodo del mandato parlamentare di Cesare Battisti." *Fra Austria e Italia: Dalle Cinque Giornate alla questione alto-atesina* (Udine: Del Bianco editore, 1987): 137-53.
Austria. Bundesministerium für Landesverteidigung. *Österreich-Ungarns letzter Krieg 1914-1918.* 8 vols. Vienna: Verlag der "Militärwissenschaftlichen Mitteilungen," 1930-38.
———. Kriegsministerium. *Der Feldzug der österreichischen Armee in Italien im Jahre 1848.* Vienna: Verlag von Karl Hölzl, 1854.
———. *Der Feldzug der österreichischen Armee in Italien im Jahre 1849.* Vienna: Verlag von Karl Hölzl, 1854.
Austria-Hungary. Kriegsministerium. *Der Feldzug 1859 in Italien.* Vienna: Verlag der k.u.k. Kriegsschule, 1898.
———. *Der Feldzug 1866 in Italien.* Vienna: Verlag der k.u.k. Kriegschule, 1902.
Baratelli, Franco Micali. *La marina militare italiana nella vita nazionale (1860-1914).* Mursia: U. Mursia editore S.p.A., 1983.
Barker, Thomas M. *Army, Aristocracy, Monarchy: Essays on War, Society, and Government in Austria, 1618-1780.* Boulder, Colo.:

East European Monographs, 1982.

———. *The Military Intellectual and Battle: Raimondo Montecuccoli and the Thirty Years' War*. Albany, N.Y.: State University Press of New York, 1975.

Benedikt, Heinrich. *Kaiseradler über dem Apennin: Die Österreicher in Italien 1700 bis 1866*. Vienna: Verlag Herold, 1964.

Benko von Boinik, Jerolim. *Geschichte der k. k. Kriegsmarine*, part II: *Die k.k. österreichische Kriegsmarine in dem Zeitraume von 1848 bis 1871*, vol. 1: *Geschichte der k.k. Kriegsmarine während der Jahre 1848 und 1849*. Vienna: Verlag des k.k. Reichs-Kriegs-Ministerium, Marine-Sektion, 1884.

Bergmann, Joseph. *Erzherzog Friedrich von Oesterreich und sein Antheil am Kriegszuge in Syrien im Jahre 1840*. Vienna: Tendler, 1857.

Bettoni-Cazzago, Francesco. *Gli Italiani nella guerra d'Ungheria 1848-49*. Milan: Fratelli Treves, 1887.

Blass, Richard. "Vom Friauler Putsch im Herbst 1864 bis zur Abtretung Venetiens 1866." *Mitteilungen des österreichischen Staatsarchivs* 19 (1966): 264-338.

Borus, Joszef M. "Hungarian Regiments, Officers and Soldiers of the Habsburg Army during the French Revolutionary and Napoleonic Wars," in Béla K. Király, (ed.), *War and Society in East Central Europe*, vol. 4: *East Central European Society and War in the Era of Revolutions, 1775-1856* (New York: Social Science Monographs, Brooklyn College Press, 1984): 32-46.

Brandt, Harm-Hinrich. *Der österreichische Neoabsolutismus: Staatsfinanzen und Politik 1848-1860*. 2 vols. Göttingen: Vandenhoeck & Ruprecht, 1978.

Braubach, Max. *Prinz Eugen von Savoyen: Eine Biographie*. 5 vols. Munich: R. Oldenbourg, 1963-65.

Carci, Luigi. *La spedizione e il processo dei fratelli Bandiera*. Modena: Società tipografica modenese, 1939.

Castellazzi, Laura. "I rapporti della Guardia Nazionale di Verona sui disordini dal 6 al 12 ottobre 1866." *Il quadrilatero nella storia militare, politica, economica e sociale dell'Italia risorgimentale* (Verona: Linotipia veronese Ghidini Fiorini, 1967): 133-73.

Cole, John W. and Wolf, Eric R. *The Hidden Frontier: Ecology and Ethnicity in an Alpine Valley*. New York: Academic Press, 1974.

Corsini, Umberto. "Die Italiener," in *Die Habsburgermonarchie 1848-1918*, vol. 3: *Die Völker des Reiches*, Adam Wandruszka and

Peter Urbanitsch (eds.) (Vienna: Verlag des österreichischen Akademie der Wissenschaften, 1980): 839–79.
Dallolio, Alberto, (ed.). *I moti del 1820 e del 1821 nelle carte Bolognesi*. Bologna: Nicola Zanichelli, 1923.
Davis, Gerald H. "Deutsche Kriegsgefange im Ersten Weltkrieg in Russland," in *Militärgeschichtliche Mitteilungen* (1982), no. 1.
Deak, Istvan. "Defeat at Solferino: The Nationality Question and the Habsburg Army in the War of 1859," in Béla K. Király, (ed.), *War and Society in East Central Europe*, vol. 14: *The Crucial Decade: East Central European Society and National Defense, 1859–1870* (New York: Social Science Monographs, Brooklyn College Press, 1984): 496–516.
―――. *The Lawful Revolution: Louis Kossuth and the Hungarians, 1848–1849*. New York: Columbia University Press, 1979.
Duffy, Christopher. *The Army of Maria Theresa: The Armed Forces of Imperial Austria, 1740–1780*. London: David & Charles, 1977.
Ehnl, Maximilian. *Die österreichisch-ungarische Landmacht nach Aufbau, Gliederung, Friedensgarnison, Einteilung und nationaler Zusammensetzung im Sommer 1914*. Ergänzungsheft 9 of *Österreich-Ungarns letzter Krieg*. Vienna: Verlag der "Militärwissenschaftlichen Mitteilungen," 1934.
Engel-Janosi, Friedrich. *Die Jugendzeit des Grafen Prokesch von Osten*. Innsbruck: Universitäts-Verlag Wagner, 1938.
Falzari, Giovanni Battista. "L'armistizio di Cormons del 1866." *Studi Goriziani* 21 (1957): 10–21.
Fasanari, Rafaele. "Lo spionaggio politico–militare organizzato da Luigi Mongo in territorio austriaco per incarico di Vittorio Emanuele II (1861–1864)." *Il quadrilatero nella storia militare, politica, economica e sociale dell'Italia risorgimentale* (Verona: Linotipia veronese Ghidini Fiorini, 1967): 177–201.
Fleischer, Josef. *Geschichte der k.k. Kriegsmarine*, part III: *Die k.k. österreichische Kriegsmarine in dem Zeitraume von 1848 bis 1871*, vol. 3: *Geschichte der k.k. Kriegsmarine während des Krieges im Jahre 1866*. Vienna: Verlag des k.u.k. Reichskriegsministeriums, Marinesektion, 1906.
Gatterer, Claus. *Erbfeindschaft Italien-Österreich*. Vienna: Europaverlag, 1972.
Ginsborg, Paul. *Daniele Manin and the Venetian Revolution of 1848–49*. Cambridge: Cambridge University Press, 1979.

Giusti, Renato. "Il 1859 nel Veneto." *Mitteilungen des österreichischen Staatsarchivs* 31 (1978): 258–70.
Greenfield, Kent Roberts. *Economics and Liberalism in the Risorgimento: A Study of Nationalism in Lombardy, 1814–1848*. Baltimore, Md.: The Johns Hopkins Press, 1934; rev. ed. 1965.
Gross, Feliks. *Ethnics in a Borderland*. Westport, Conn.: Greenwood Press, 1978.
Halpern, Paul. *The Mediterranean Naval Situation, 1908–1914*. Camridge: Harvard University Press, 1971.
Handel–Mazzetti, Peter. "Das Seegefecht bei Helgoland am 9. Mai 1864." *Marine Rundschau* 39 (1934): 193–98.
Iachino, Angelo. *La campagna navale di Lissa 1866*, Milan: Casa editrice Il Saggiatore, 1966.
Jenks, William. *Francis Joseph and the Italians, 1849–1859*. Charlottesville, Va.: University Press of Virginia, 1978.
Khuepach, Artur von. *Geschichte der k.u.k. Kriegsmarine*, part II: *Die k. k. österreichische Kriegsmarine in dem Zeitraume von 1797 bis 1848*, vol. 2: *Geschichte der k.k. Kriegsmarine während der Jahre 1802 bis 1814*. Vienna: Staatsdruckerei Wien, 1942.
Khuepach, Artur von, and Bayer, Heinrich von. *Geschichte der k.u.k. Kreigsmarine*, part II: *Die k.k. österreichische Kriegsmarine in dem Zeitraum von 1797 bis 1848*, vol. 3: *Geschichte der k.k. Kriegsmarine während der Jahre 1814–1847*. Graz: Verlag Hermann Böhlaus Nachfolger, 1966.
Kiszling, Rudolf. "Das Nationalitätenproblem in Habsburgs Wehrmacht, 1848–1918." *Der Donauraum* 4 (1959): 82–93.
Kramer, Hans. *Österreich und das Risorgimento*. Vienna: Bergland Verlag, 1963.
Kraus, Karl. *Die letzten Tage der Menschheit*. Vienna: Verlag "Die Fackel," 1919.
Lehnert, Josef von. *Geschichte der k.u.k. Kriegsmarine*, part II: *Die k.k. österreichische Kriegsmarine in dem Zeitraume von 1797 bis 1848*, vol. 1: *Geschichte der österreichisch–venetianischen Kriegsmarine während der Jahre 1797 bis 1802*. Vienna: Gerold & Comp., 1891.
Luraghi, Raimondo. "Italians in the Habsburg Armed Forces, 1815–1849," in Béla K. Király,(ed.), *War and Society in East Central Europe*, vol. 4: *East Central European Society and War in the Era of Revolutions, 1775–1856* (New York: Social Science Monographs, Brooklyn College Press, 1984): 219–29.

Nani Mocenigo, Filippo. *La Marina Veneta e i fratelli Bandiera*. Venice: Tipografia Orfanotrofio di A. Pellizzato, 1907.

Noether, Emiliana P. " ' Morally Wrong' or 'Politically Right'? Espionage in Her Majesty's Post Office, 1844–45." *Canadian Journal of History* 22 (1987): 41–57.

Nuffel, Robert van. "Intorno alla perdita della flotta all'inizio della rivoluzione veneziana." *Rassengna Storica del Risorgimento* 44 (1957): 786–91.

Oliva, Gianni. *Storia degli alpini*. Milan: Rizzoli Editore, 1985.

Pahor, Miroslav. *Slovenski mornarji Austrije v obrambi Dalmacije in Istre 1849–1917*. Piran: Pomorske muzej Sergej Mašera, 1978.

Paschen, D. "Der blutige Tag von Helgoland." *Marine Rundschau* 44 (1939): 470–76.

Pierantoni, Riccardo. *Storia dei fratelli Bandiera e loro compagni in Calabria*. Milan: Casa Editrice L. F. Cogliati, 1909.

Pieri, Piero. *Storia militare del Risorgimento*. Turin: Giulio Einaudi, 1962.

Plaschka, Richard Georg; Haselsteiner, Horst; and Suppan, Arnold. *Innere Front: Militärassistenz, Widerstand und Umsturz in der Donaumonarchie 1918*. Munich: R. Oldenbourg Verlag, 1974.

Plaschka, Richard Georg. *Cattaro – Prag: Revolte und Revolution*. Graz: Verlag Hermann Böhlaus Nachfolger, 1963.

———. *Matrosen, Offiziere, Rebellen: Krisenkonfrontationen zur See 1900–1918*. 2 vols. Vienna: Verlag Hermann Böhlaus Nachfolger, 1984.

Randaccio, C. *Le marinerie militari italiane nei tempi moderni (1750–1850)*. Turin: Artero e comp., 1864.

Ratzenhofer, Emil. "'Der Waffenstillstand von Villa Giusti und die Gefangennahme Hunderttausender." In Ergänzungsheft 2 of *Österreich-Ungarns letzter Krieg*. Vienna: Verlag der "Militärwissenschaftlichen Mitteilungen," 1931.

Rauchensteiner, Manfried. *Kaiser Franz und Erzherzog Carl: Dynastie und Heerwesen in Österreich, 1796–1809*. Vienna: Verlag für Geschichte und Politik, 1972.

Rechberger von Rechkron, Josef. *Geschichte der k.k. Kriegsmarine*, part I: *Österreichs Seewesen in dem Zeitraume von 1500–1797*. Vienna: Verlag des k.k. Reichs–Kriegs–Ministeriums, Marine-Section, 1882.

Rothenberg, Gunther E. *The Army of Francis Joseph*. West Lafayette, Ind.: Purdue University Press, 1976.

---. "The Austrian Army in the Age of Metternich." *Journal of Modern History* 40 (1968): 155–65.

Rusinow, Dennison I. *Italy's Austrian Heritage, 1919–1946.* Oxford: Clarendon Press, 1969.

Salata, Francesco. *Guglielmo Oberdan.* Bologna: Nicola Zanichelli, 1924.

Salcher, Peter. *Geschichte der k.u.k. Marine-Akademie.* Pola: Carl Gerold's Sohn, 1902.

Scala, Edoardo. *La Guerra del 1866 ed altri scritti.* Rome: Tipografia Regionale, 1981.

Schwarzenberg, Adolph. *Prince Felix zu Schwarzenberg, Prime Minister of Austria 1848–1852.* New York: Columbia University Press, 1950.

Sella, Domenico, and Capra, Carlo. *Il ducato di Milano dal 1535 al 1796.* Turin: U.T.E.T., 1984.

Sked, Alan. *The Survival of the Habsburg Empire: Radetzky, the Imperial Army and the Class War, 1848.* London: Longman, 1979.

Simion, Ernesto, and Nani Mocenigo, Mario. *La campagna navale di Siria del 1840.* Rome: Tip. Ufficio del Capo di Stato Maggiore, 1933.

Sitzler, Kathrin. *Solidarität oder Söldertum: Die ausländische Freiwilligenverbände im ungarischen Unabhängigkeitskrieg 1848–49.* Osnabrück: Biblio Verlag, 1980.

Sokol, Hans Hugo. *Geschichte der k.u.k. Kriegsmarine*, Part III: *Die k.k. österreichische Kriegsmarine 1848 bis 1914 ("Abschlußband des Geschichtswerkes der k.u.k. Kriegsmarine").* Vienna: Amalthea Verlag, 1930.

Sondhaus, Lawrence. "*Mitteleuropa zur See?* Austria and the German Navy Question, 1848–52." *Central European History* 20 (1987): 125–44.

---. "Napoleon's Shipbuilding Program at Venice and the Struggle for Naval Mastery in the Adriatic, 1806–1814." *The Journal of Military History* 53 (1989): 349–62.

---. *The Habsburg Empire and the Sea: Austrian Naval Policy, 1797–1866.* West Lafayette, Ind.: Purdue University Press, 1989.

Stuparich, Giani. "Guglielmo Oberdan." *Rassegna Storica del Risorgimento* 58 (1971): 183–98.

Szabo, Franz. "Unwanted Navy: Habsburg Armaments under Maria Theresa." *Austrian History Yearbook* 17–18 (1981–82): 29–53.

Tamaro, Attilio. *Storia di Trieste*. 2 vols. Trieste: Edizioni Lint, 1924; reprint ed. 1976.
Tivaroni, Carlo. *Storia critica del Risorgimento Italiano*. 9 vols. Turin: Le Roux, 1888–97.
Wagner, Walter. "Die k.(u.)k. Armee: Gliederung und Aufgabenstellung," in *Die Habsburgermonarchie 1848–1918*, vol. 5: *Die bewaffnete Macht*, Adam Wandruszka and Peter Urbanitsch (eds.) (Vienna: Verlag der österreichischen Akademie der Wissenschaften, 1987): 142–633.
Wallisch, Friedrich. *Die Flagge Rot-Weiss-Rot: Männer und Täten der österreichischen Marine in vier Jahrhunderte*. Graz: Verlag Styria, 1956.
Weiland, Hans, and Kern, Leopold, (eds.). *In Feindeshand: Die Gefangenschaft in Weltkriege im Einzeldarstellungen*. 2 vols. Vienna: Bundesverlag der ehemaligen österreichischen Kriegsgefangenen, 1931.
Whittam, John. *The Politics of the Italian Army, 1861–1918*. London: Croom Helm, 1977.
Wrede, Alphons von. *Geschichte der k.u.k. Wehrmacht: Die Regimenter, Corps, Branchen und Anstalten von 1618 bis Ende des XIX. Jahrhunderts*. 7 vols. Vienna: L. W. Seidel & Sohn, 1893–1900.
Zadei, Guido. *Il barone Colonnello Alessandro Monti e la sua azione in Ungheria nel 1849*. Brescia: Vitt. Gatti, 1929.
Zorzi, Alvise. *Venezia Austriaca 1798–1806*. Bari: Editori Laterza, 1986.

APPENDIX

BIOGRAPHICAL INDEX

Note: The following sketches of Italian Habsburg officers include only those of sufficient significance whose personal stories have not received adequate coverage within the body of the text.

BANDIERA, Francesco. Born in Venice in 1785, to a family of Dalmatian Italian descent. Bandiera entered service in 1801 as a cadet in the Austrian navy and passed into Napoleonic Italian service at the beginning of 1806. One French observer characterized him as "an officer of good deportment, but not much of a sailor"; nevertheless, he was promoted to ensign and, in 1808, received a minor command in Dalmatian waters. The same year he married Anna Marsich, daughter of a Venetian naval official; their children included his celebrated sons Attilio (born 1810) and Emilio (born 1819). Bandiera was captured at sea by the British in 1810 but released shortly thereafter. He returned to Austrian service in 1814 and soon won promotion to lieutenant. After reaching captain's rank in the mid-1820s, he earned widespread respect in his conduct of a mission against Moroccan pirates (1828–30), then was elevated to the hereditary nobility for his role in capturing Carlo Zucchi in the Adriatic after the central Italian revolution of 1831. During Austria's subsequent deportation of Polish refugees, Bandiera led expeditions to New York (1833–34), Algiers (1835), and Toulon (1836). Promoted to rear admiral in 1839, he commanded the Austrian contingent in Levantine waters during the Near Eastern crisis of 1840. He was still in command of the Levant squadron in 1844, when the desertions of his sons exposed the Mazzinian conspiracy within the fleet, and had to resign his commission after it was revealed that he had had prior knowledge of their plotting. In early 1845, Hofkriegsrat officials cited his poor health in justifying their decision not to press charges against him. Contrary to Austrian legend, his remorse over the treason and execution of his sons did not drive him to commit suicide. Bandiera died of natural causes at his home in Carpeneto di Mestre in 1847.

CALVI, Pietro Fortunato. Born near Padua in 1817, the son of a Habsburg bureaucrat. A good student in his youth, Calvi received a scholarship to the military engineering academy in Vienna. After completing his studies in 1836, he was commissioned as an officer in the 13th (Venetian) Infantry. He eventually came into contact with patriotic circles and embraced the Italian cause. Calvi was stationed with the 13th at Graz, with the rank of first lieutenant, when word arrived of the March 1848 revolution in Vienna. Anticipating an upheaval in Italy, he resigned his commission and returned home to help organize the defense of the Veneto against the Austrians. As a captain in rebel service, he commanded the Venetian "Cacciatori delle Alpi" in 1849, then went into exile in Greece following the fall of Venice. Calvi moved to Turin in 1850 but was expelled by the Sardinians after being suspected as an organizer of the aborted 6 February 1853 uprising in Milan. In September 1853 he launched a rebel expedition to the Venetian Alps from his new home in Switzerland, only to be captured en route by the Austrians. Calvi was imprisoned at Mantua, tried before a special military court, convicted of high treason in January 1855, and executed six months later. He was the only Italian Habsburg officer to be executed for treasonous activity in the wake of the revolution of 1848.

CAVEDALIS, Giambattista. Born near Pordenone in 1794, Cavedalis studied engineering during the Napoleonic era and was an engineer officer in the Italian army when Austria reacquired his native Venetia. He secured an engineering commission in the Habsburg army in 1817 but resigned from the service five years later. After a distinguished career as a civilian engineer, Cavedalis became one of the leading political figures in the Venetian revolution of 1848–49 and held colonel's rank in the rebel army. In 1850 he petitioned Vienna for the right to return from exile; after Radetzky intervened on his behalf, he was granted clemency and ended up designing one of the last stretches of the *Südbahn* (Vienna–Trieste railway), which opened in 1857. Cavedalis retired to his family home in time to see it annexed to Italy, and died there in 1878.

DANDOLO, Sylvestro. Born in Venice in 1766, to an aristocratic family of ancient lineage; his ancestors included four doges. Dandolo entered the Venetian navy in 1780 and rose to captain's rank by the fall of the republic. A captain in the Austrian navy from 1797 to 1805, he served as Marine–Kommandant for four months during the War of 1805. He passed into Napoleonic Italian service after the subsequent peace treaty forced him to resign his Habsburg commission; the French doubted his loyalties and never entrusted him with a significant command. Dandolo returned to Austrian service in 1814 and commanded the Levant squadron during the Greek War of Independence in the 1820s. Promoted to rear admiral in 1829, he became vice admiral and second in command to his bitter rival, Paulucci, seven years later. When Archduke Frederick became Marine–Ober–Kommandant in 1844, Dandolo was placated with the prestigious Order of the Golden Fleece. He took command of the service following Frederick's death in the fall of 1847, forty-two years after his first tenure in the office, but died only four weeks later.

FONTANELLI, Achille. Born in Modena in 1775, Fontanelli began his military career in the late 1790s under the Cisalpine Republic. He went on to achieve high rank in the army of the Napoleonic kingdom of Italy, serving briefly in 1811 as war and naval minister to Eugene Beauharnais. Fontanelli subsequently fought under Napoleon in Russia and, in 1814, was one of the highest ranking Italian officers taken into Habsburg service. His career as an Austrian Feldmarshalleutnant ended shortly thereafter, with his voluntary retirement from the army. He died in Milan in 1838.

MAZZUCCHELLI, Luigi. Born in Brescia in 1776, Mazzucchelli likewise began his military career in the late 1790s under the Cisalpine Republic. He rose to general's rank in the Napoleonic Italian army, seeing most of his action as a subordinate commander in Spain during the Peninsular War. Mazzucchelli was taken into the Austrian army as a major general and eventually earned a promotion to Feldmarschalleutnant. His willingness to serve the Habsburgs earned him the enmity of later patriotic Italian historians. He retired to Milan and finally died in 1868, ironically living to see the Austrians lose northern Italy.

MICHIELI, Carlo. Born in Venice, c. 1823, Michieli ultimately became one of the more enigmatic figures in the history of the Austrian navy. After attending the naval academy in Venice from 1836 to 1841, he served as a cadet in the Levant squadron and was among the original members of the Mazzinian sect Esperia. He remained under suspicion after the Bandiera affair of 1844 but showed no further signs of revolutionary convictions. In March 1848 Michieli was the only Esperia alumnus to remain loyal to the Austrians; he promptly vindicated their trust in the sensitive post of courier between Feldmarschalleutnant Gyulai at Trieste and Captain Buratovich at Pola. He was promoted to ensign in 1848 and lieutenant in 1849; two years later, he was named to the coveted post of personal adjutant to the emperor's brother, Archduke Ferdinand Max. Michieli helped groom the archduke to command the navy, but the extent of his influence on his young charge remains open to speculation. He did not see his own career benefit significantly after Ferdinand Max became Marine-Ober-Kommmandant in 1854. Michieli rose to captain's rank and was commanding a frigate when he died prematurely in 1860, most likely from the effects of syphillis.

MONTI, Alessandro. Born in Brescia in 1818, Monti attended the military engineering academy in Vienna. Like Calvi, he did not become an engineer officer upon graduation, opting instead for a more socially prestigious branch of the service. He eventually settled with the 2nd (Bohemian) Chevaux-Legers and reached the rank of first lieutenant by 1842. On leave in Brescia in March 1848, Monti resigned his commission and took command of local rebels. He led Alpine and Italian Tyrolese contingents in the summer of 1848, fleeing to Piedmont after the Italian defeat at Custoza. After considering him for a commission in their army, the Sardinians sent him on a diplomatic mission to the Balkans. Between December 1848 and March 1849 he travelled to Serbia and Turkey in an effort to stir up support for the Italian cause, but his mandate was cancelled following the defeat at Novara. Monti then went to Hungary on his own initiative and took command of a legion of Italian deserters from Austrian service (Mostly veterans of the 16th Infantry). In August 1849 he followed Kossuth and other Hungarian loyalists into exile in Turkey; he was "repatriated" to Sardinia the following May, along with the remainder of the Italian legion. He subsequently rejected a commission in the Sardinian army, which refused to recognize the colonel's rank he had held under Kossuth. Late in 1850 he turned down a tempting offer to organize Italian volunteers in Uruguay for duty against Argentina. Poverty ultimately drove him to take a job as a prison director in Piedmont, a post he held for only one year before dying in 1854. Monti was the only Italian Habsburg veteran to play a significant role fighting against the Austrians outside of Italy during the revolutions of 1848–49.

PAULUCCI delle Roncole, Marquis Amilcare. Born in Modena in 1773, Paulucci's earliest service was in the Neapolitan and French navies. A colorful character, the experiences of his youth included a brief period as a slave in North Africa, after being captured by Barbary pirates; later, he was rumored to have been the lover of the queen of Naples. He commanded the Napoleonic Italian navy from 1804 until its expansion in 1806, after the Italian acquisition of Venice. Thereafter, he served as commander of its active squadron until being captured at sea by the British in 1808. Paulucci was imprisoned in Malta until 1812, when he was paroled after pledging not to serve against Britain again. He interpreted his oath in the narrowest sense (that it permitted service on land, against allies of Britain) and spent the remainder of the war in the Italian army, rising to the rank of major general. The Austrians granted him the same dignity in 1814, and ten years later he was officially transferred to the navy to begin a long tenure as Marine–Ober–Kommandant. Paulucci was personally responsible for many of the conditions which permitted the growth of the Mazzinian conspiracy within the fleet. He was forced to retire in disgrace after the Bandiera affair of 1844 and died the following year.

ZUCCHI, Carlo. Born in Reggio in 1777, Zucchi, like Fontanelli and Mazzucchelli, began his military career as a young volunteer under the Cisalpine Republic. He rose to the rank of lieutenant general in the Napoleonic Italian army and was personally close to Eugene Beauharnais. His participation in last ditch efforts to save the viceroy's throne aroused the suspicions of the Austrians, who arrested him briefly in 1814; he was quickly released, though, and offered a commission as Feldmarschalleutnant. Zucchi served briefly in Bohemia before retiring, discouraged by postings far from home and by the suspicion with which the Habsburg army treated its Italian soldiers. In the wake of the revolutions of 1820, he was implicated in a

Carbonari plot and imprisoned from 1823 to 1826. Five years later, he came out of retirement to lead the central Italian revolution, only to be defeated and captured by the Austrians. After years of confinement in the interior of the monarchy, consideration for Zucchi's advancing age and declining health led Habsburg officials to transfer him to a prison in Palmanova, Venetia, which fell to rebel forces in March 1848. Freed from captivity, Zucchi served as one of the commanders of the Venetian army in 1848–49. He then retired from public life, and died in 1863.

APPENDIX

Statistical Tables

Table I

The table below, compiled from a number of regimental histories, gives the approximate Napoleonic Italian origin of the new Austrian Italian units formed in 1814. (IR = infantry regiment)

Italian Infantry

Regt. dei Veliti (Foot Guards)	to Light Battalion #1(*)
Regt. Cacciatori (Guards Rifles)	to Light Battalion #1(*)
Grenadier guards battalion (+)	to new IR #1
1st volunteer IR	to new IR #1
2nd volunteer IR	to new IR #2
1st line IR	to new IR #1
2nd line IR	to new IR #2
3rd line IR	to new IR #2
4th line IR	to new IR #3
5th line IR	to new IR #3
6th line IR	to new IR #4
7th line IR	to new IR #4
"Colonial" battalion "Elba"(+)	to new IR #4
1st light IR	to Light Battalion #3
2nd light IR	to Light Battalion #2
3rd light IR	to Light Battalion #4
4th light IR	to Light Battalion #4

Cavalry units (all to 1st Austro–Italian Chevaux–Legers):
  Guards Dragoons regiment ("guardi Reale" or Horse Guards)
  King's Dragoons regiment ("del Re")
  Queen's Dragoons regiment ("della Regina")
  1st regiment chausseurs
  2nd regiment chausseurs
  3rd regiment chausseurs
  4th regiment chausseurs

(*) - also contributed troops to new IR #1
(+) - referred to as "regiment" in some accounts

In November 1814 the Austro–Italian infantry regiments received the following numbers in the regular line of Habsburg infantry: IR #1 = #13; IR #2 = #23; IR #3 = #38; IR #4 = #43. The 1st Austro–Italian Chevaux–Legers became the 7th Chevaux–Legers. In 1816 the four light battalions were combined to form another line infantry regiment, #45.

Table II

These charts, compiled from the *Militär-Schematismus* and Wrede's *Geschichte der k.u.k. Wehrmacht* and checked against the regimental histories, give the locations of the headquarters of each Italian infantry regiment during the period 1814–1859.

Venetian regiments, 1815–1848: (1–3 battalions to 1825, 1–2 from 1825–1848)

13th (Padua)	16th (Treviso)	26th (Udine)	45th (Verona)
Brünn 1815	(ex-Styrian IR)	(ex-Carthinian IR)	(from light inf.)
Vienna 1815–16	**TREVISO 1817–30**	**UDINE 1817–33**	**PADUA 1816–18**
Ljubljana 1816–18	**VENICE and**	**VENICE 1833–38**	**VERONA 1818–21**
Klagenfurt 1818–22	**TREVISO 1830–38**	**UDINE 1836–38**	Pressburg 1821–30
VICENZA 1882–24	**MANTUA 1838–39**	Zagreb 1838–40	Fiume 1830–35
VERONA 1824–25	Olmütz 1839–45	Graz 1840–45	Zara 1835–39
Olmütz 1825–30	Graz 1845–46	Innsbruck 1845–48	**UDINE 1839**
Graz 1830–40	Pest 1846–48	Salzburg 1848	**MANTUA 1838–40**
Fiume 1840–41	***	***	**VERONA 1840–42**
Zara 1841–43	2nd battalion	1st battalion	**VICENZA 1842–43**
Fiume 1843–44	in Cattaro from	in Cattaro from	**PADUA 1843–46**
Zagreb 1844–46	1836–39	1829–36	**TREVISO 1846–47**
Graz 1846–48	***	***	**VERONA 1847–48**
***	3rd battalion	3rd battalion	**BERGAMO 1848**
3rd battalion	in or near Treviso	in or near Udine	***
in Padua or	after 1825	after 1825	2nd battalion in
Venice after			Cattaro from 1846
1825			***
			3rd battalion in
			Verona after 1825
34 years or	31 years or	31 years or	32 years or
102 batt. yrs.	93 batt. yrs.	93 batt. yrs.	96 batt. yrs.
3 L–V (1st)	*22 L–V (1st)	*14 L–V (1st)	14 L–V (1st)
3 L–V (2nd)	+19 L–V (2nd)	*21 L–V (2nd)	12 L–V (2nd)
+26 L–V (3rd)	+31 L–V (3rd)	+31 L–V (3rd)	28 L–V (3rd)
32 b.y. L–V	62 b.y. L–V	66 b.y. L–V	54 b.y. L–V
(31.4%)	(66.6 %)	(70.9%)	(56.2%)

\+ – deserted en masse in 1848
* – suffered serious desertions in 1848
b.y., batt. yrs. – battalion/years
L–V – years spent in Lombardy–Venetia
Bold type – garrison in Lombardy–Venetia

Appendix 181

Table II continued

Lombard regiments, 1815–1848: (1–3 battalions to 1825, 1–2 from 1825–48)

23rd (Lodi)	38th (Brescia)	43rd (Como)	44th (Milan)
Prague 1815–20	Graz 1815–30	Buda 1814–16	(ex-Galician IR)
Pressburg 1820–21	BRESCIA 1830–31	Pressburg 1816–18	MILAN and PAVIA
Pest 1821–24	Ancona 1831	Zagreb 1818–23	1817–21
Buda 1824–30	CREMONA 1831–32	Kosice 1823–29	LODI 1821
Zagreb 1830–31	BRESCIA 1832–33	Pest 1829–30	Alessandria
Peterwardein 1831–36	CREMONA 1833–34	Zara 1830–36	1821–22
	MANTUA 1834–37	Fiume 1836–37	PAVIA 1822–23
Buda 1836–48	VERONA 1837–38	Zagreb 1837–38	Prague 1823–30
***	CREMONA 1838–39	UDINE 1838–39	Teschen 1830–31
3rd battalion	Zara 1839–41	BRESCIA 1839–40	Wadowice 1831–32
in or near Lodi	Fiume 1841–43	BERGAMO 1840–48	Neutitschein
after 1825	UDINE 1843–46	***	1832–35
	VICENZA and	2nd battalion in	Olmütz 1835–39
	PADUA 1846–47	Cattaro 1841–42/3	UDINE 1839–41
	LEGNAGO and	***	VERONA 1841–42
	MANTUA 1847–48	3rd battalion	PALMANOVA 1842–3
	***	in or near Como	CREMONA 1843–48
	3rd battalion in	after 1825	***
	Brescia after 1825		1st battalion in
			Cattaro 1842/3–6
			***
			2nd battalion in
			Cattaro 1839–41
			***
			3rd battalion in
			Milan after 1825
34 years or	34 years or	34 years or	31 years or
102 batt. yrs.	102 batt. yrs.	102 batt. yrs.	93 batt. yrs.
0 L–V (1st)	14 L–V (1st)	10 L–V (1st)	+11.5 L–V (1st)
0 L–V (2nd)	14 L–V (2nd)	*8.5 L–V (2nd)	+13 L–V (2nd)
+23 L–V (3rd)	*23 L–V (3rd)	+23 L–V (3rd)	29 L–V (3rd)
23 b.y. L–V (22.5%)	51 b.y. L–V (50%)	41.4 b.y. L–V (40.7%)	53.5 b.y. L–V (57.5%)

\+ – deserted en masse in 1848
* – suffered serious desertions in 1848
b.y., batt. yrs. – battalion/years
L–V – years spent in Lombardy–Venetia
Bold type – garrison in Lombardy–Venetia

Table II continued

Venetian regiments, 1849-1859: (1-3 battalions)

13th (Padua)	16th (Treviso)	26th (Udine)	45th (Verona)
Prague 1849-50	Olmütz 1849-51	Temesvar 1849-50	Zara 1849-52
Theresienstadt 1850-51	Brünn 1851-54	Klausenburg 1850	Zagreb 1852-53
Budweis 1851	Vienna 1854-55	Debreczin 1850-51	Fiume 1853-54
Klagenfurt 1851-52	Prague 1855-59	Kosice 1851-52	Bucharest 1854-55
Esseg 1852-53	***	Buda 1852-54	Krajova 1855-56
Zagreb 1853-54	4th battalion:	Tarnopol 1854-55	Fiume 1856-58
UDINE 1854	no data 1850-52	Pest 1855-56	Vienna 1858-59
Trieste 1854-55	w/1-3 1852-55	Graz 1856-58	***
Graz 1855-56	**TREVISO 1855-59**	Olmütz 1858-59	4th battalion:
Komorn 1856-58	***	***	Carinthia 1850-52
Pressburg 1858-59	Depot battalion:	4th battalion:	**VERONA 1852-53**
***	**TREVISO 1852-55**	Upper Austria 1850-52	w/1-3 1853-54
4th battalion:		w/1-3 1852-55?	Fiume 1854-55
Celje 1850-51		**UDINE 1855-59**	**VERONA 1855-59**
PADUA 1851-52		***	***
w/1-3 1852-55		Depot battalion:	Depot battalion:
PADUA 1855-59		**UDINE 1852-55**	**VERONA 1852-55**
***			
Depot battalion:			
PADUA 1852-55			
10 years or	10 years or	10 years or	10 years or
42 batt. yrs.	42 batt. yrs.	42 batt. yrs.	42 batt. yrs.
.5 L-V (1st)	0 L-V (1-3)	0 L-V (1-3)	0 L-V (1-3)
.5 L-V (2nd)	4 L-V (4th)	4 L-V (4th)	5 L-V (4th)
.5 L-V (3rd)	3 L-V (dpt)	3 L-V (dpt)	3 L-V (dpt)
5.5 L-V (4th)	--	--	--
3 L-V (dpt)	7 b.y. L-V	7 b.y. L-V	8 b.y. L-V
---	(16.7%)	(16.7%)	(19%)
10 b.y L-V			
(23.8 %)			

b.y., batt. yrs. - battalion/years
L-V - years spent in Lombardy-Venetia
BOLD TYPE - garrison in Lombardy-Venetia

Appendix

Table II continued

Lombard regiments, 1849–1859: (1–3 battalions)

23rd (Lodi, ex. 1852-Cremona)	38th (Brescia)	43rd (Como, Lodi 1852, Bergamo-53)	44th (Milan)
Vienna 1849-50	Teplitz 1849-50	MILAN 1849-50	Bludenz 1849-50
Prague 1850-51	Komotau 1850	CREMONA 1850	(Germany 1850-51)
Josephstadt 1851-54	Theresienstadt 1850-51	Graz 1850-51	Ratzeburg 1851
Bochnia 1854-55	Eger 1851	Königgrätz 1851-54	Pilsen 1851
Vienna 1855-58	Prague 1851	Brünn 1854-56	Theresienstadt 1851-52
Fiume 1858-59	Linz 1851-59	Prague 1856-59	Budweis 1852-53
***	***	***	Prague 1853-55
4th battalion:	4th battalion:	4th battalion:	Innsbruck 1855-9
LODI(?) 1850-51	BRESCIA 1850-52	COMO/LODI 1850-52	***
Judenburg 1851	w/1-3 1852-55	w/1-3 1852-55	4th battalion:
CREMONA 1851-52	BRESCIA 1855-59	BERGAMO 1852-55	MILAN 1850-52
w/1-3 1852-55	***	***	w/1-3 1852-55
LODI(?) 1855-59	Depot battalion:	Depot battalion:	MILAN 1855-59
***	BRESCIA 1852-55	LODI 1852-53	***
Depot battalion:		BERGAMO 1853-55	Depot battalion:
CREMONA 1852-53			MILAN 1852-55
LODI 1853-55			
10 years or <u>42 batt. yrs.</u>	10 years or <u>42 batt. yrs.</u>	10 years or <u>42 batt. yrs.</u>	10 years or <u>42 batt. yrs.</u>
0 L-V (1-3)	0 L-V (1-3)	0 L-V (1-3)	0 L-V (1-3)
5.5 L-V (4th)	6 L-V (4th)	6 L-V (4th)	6 L-V (4th)
3 L-V (dpt)	3 L-V (dpt)	3 L-V (dpt)	3 L-V (dpt)
---	--	--	--
8.5 b.y. L-V (20.2%)	9 b.y. L-V (21.4%)	9 b.y. L-V (21.4%)	9 b.y. L-V (21.4%)

55th (Monza-1853): 1-4 batt. Hermannstadt 1853, Temesvar 1853-54;
1-3 batt. Jassy 1854-55, Braila 1855-56, Pest 1856-57, Graz 1857-59;
4th batt. Temesvar 1854-55, MONZA 1855-59; depot MONZA 1853-55.
6 years or <u>26 batt. yrs.</u>: 6 b.y. l-V (23.1%)

---

b.y., batt. yrs. - battalion/years
L-V - years spent in Lombardy-Venetia
BOLD TYPE - garrison in Lombardy-Venetia

Table III

The figures below indicate the percentage of Italian-surnamed officers appearing in the Lombard and Venetian regimental lists of the *Militär-Schematismus* in the years indicated. Regiments only briefly drawing upon northern Italy for manpower (such as the cavalry regiments of the 1850s) are not shown.

Regiment	1815	1827	1837	1847	1850	1859	1860	1866
IR #13	86	45	36	29	18	18	17	22
IR #16	9+	30	28	27	19	16	18	19
IR #23	82	61	37	31	22	19	7**	--
IR #26	23+	24	27	18	16	19	19	18
IR #38	87	45	41	39	29	18	17	16
IR #43	95	48	38	30	19	15	4**	--
IR #44	7+	30	23	25	13	18	4**	--
IR #45	59*	35	39	33	31	17	13	12
IR #55	--	--	--	--	3@	20	4**	--
IR #79	--	--	--	--	--	--	20	23
IR #80	--	--	--	--	--	--	14	17
cavalry	87	46	48	27	19	31	21**	--

(*) 1817
(+) 1818
(@) 1853
(**) regiments converted to non-Italian manpower in 1860

Table IV

The chart below, arranged from tables in Wrede's *Geschichte der k.u.k. Wehrmacht*, traces the fluctuations in the official "paper" strength and composition of Habsburg infantry regiments after 1814. The years at left are those in which decrees or laws brought a significant redefinition of the size of a regiment. Prior to 1848, Hungarian battalions were slightly larger, and "German" Austrian regiments also had Landwehr formations.

1816 – Peacetime:	3 battalions x 756 men (Total 2,268) and 2 companies (272 men) detached for service in grenadier battalion with similar contingents from one or two other regiments. Officer corps: 73.
Mobilized:	3 battalions x 1,308 men (Total 3,924) and 2 companies (348 men) detached for service with grenadiers. Officer corps: 75.
1831 – Peacetime:	3 battalions x 1,235 men (Total 3,708) and 2 companies (356 men) detached for service with grenadiers. Officer corps: 71.
Mobilized:	same as peacetime. Officer corps: 74.
1852 – Peacetime:	4 battalions x 1,320 men (5,280 men) including 4 companies (880 men) serving as grenadiers (one with each battalion of the regiment). Cadres for another 4 companies (560 men) detached as depot battalion in home recruiting center. (Total 5,280 + 560 = 5,840 men). Officer corps: 152.
Mobilized:	same as peacetime, except 4 grenadier companies brought together to form a grenadier battalion for each regiment. These men were to be replaced in each battalion by a new company of regular infantry (Total 5,280 + 880 = 6,160 men).

Table IV continued

1855 – Peacetime:	3 battalions x 774 men (2,322 men). Depot battalion abolished and replaced by former 4th field battalion reduced to cadre strength (414 men). Companies of grenadiers as in 1852, but reduced to total of 516 in peacetime. (Total 2,322 + 414 = 2,736 men).
Mobilized:	same as 1852 peacetime and mobilized (4 battalions x 1,320 men) and grenadier battalion (Total 5,280 + 880 = 6,160).
1857 – Peacetime:	same as 1855 peacetime (2,322 + 414 = 2,736 men), with 94 officers.
Mobilized:	4 battalions x 1,320 men (5,280) plus 880 grenadiers, plus a restored depot battalion of 532 men. (Total 5,280 + 880 + 532 = 6,692 men), w/166 officers.
1860 – Peacetime:	3 battalions x 534 (Total 1,602 men). Officer corps: 88
Mobilized:	3 battalions x 1,188 men (3,564) plus 2 depot companies of 198 men apiece (Total 3,564 + 396 =3,960 men), with 134 officers.
1861 – Peacetime:	4 battalions x 1,008 men (Total 4,032). Officer corps: 160. (4th battalion not formed immediately in many regts.)
Mobilized:	same as peacetime. (The Venetian regts. each had a 5th battalion in 1866).
1867 – Peacetime:	5 battalions x 432 men (Total 2,160). Officer corps: 93
Mobilized:	6 battalions x 912 men (5,472) plus a depot of 456 men. (Total 5,472 + 456 = 5,928 men), with 218 officers.

Table IV continued

1869 – Peacetime: 5 battalions x 380 men (Total 1,900). Officer corps: 111.
Mobilized: 5 battalions x 944 men (4,700) plus a depot battalion of 1,140 men. (Total 4,720 + 1,140 = 5,860 men) w/231 officers.
1882 – Peacetime: 4 battalions x 344 men (Total 1,376). Officer corps: 106. Battalions detached for occupation duty in Bosnia raised to 524 men.
Mobilized: 5 battalions x 944 men (Total 4,720). Officer corps: 211.
1890 – Peacetime: same as 1882 peacetime.
Mobilized: same as 1882 mobilized, except for 1 5th (reserve or *Ersatz*) battalion slightly smaller (932 men) than the other four but expandable to 1,092 men.
1895 – Peacetime: 4 battalions x 388 men (Total 1,552). Officer corps: 112. Battalions detached for occupation duty in Bosnia raised to 532 men.

Table V

The strength and national composition of Radetzky's army in the years leading up to 1848 has been the subject of much scholarly comment and misperception. The chart below is based on periodic figures in KA, Nachlass Radetzky, measured against unit locations given in Wrede's *Geschichte der k.u.k. Wehrmacht*, the *Militär-Schematismus*, and various regimental histories. Years shown represent status at middle of year except in last four columns (see key).

Infantry

IR #1	(B-M)	1st bat.	1835	1837	1840	1844	1847-S	1847-N	1848-J	1848-M
IR #1	(B-M)	2nd bat.	1835	1837	1840	1844	1847-S	1847-N	1848-J	1848-M
IR #4	(AUS)	1st bat.	1835	--	--	--	--	--	--	--
IR #4	(AUS)	2nd bat.	1835	--	--	--	--	--	--	--
IR #7	(INA)	1st bat.	1835	--	--	--	1847-S	1847-N	1848-J	1848-M
IR #7	(INA)	2nd bat.	1835	--	--	--	1847-S	1847-N	1848-J	1848-M
IR #12	(GAL)	1st bat.	1835	--	--	--	--	--	--	--
IR #12	(GAL)	2nd bat.	1835	--	--	--	--	--	--	--
IR #12	(GAL)	3rd bat?	1835	--	--	--	--	--	--	--
IR #13	(L-V)	3rd bat.	1835	1837	1840	1844	1847-S	1847-N	1848-J	1848-M
IR #14	(AUS)	1st bat.	1835	1837	--	--	--	--	--	--
IR #14	(AUS)	2nd bat.	1835	1837	--	--	--	--	--	--
IR #15	(GAL)	1st bat.	1835	--	--	--	--	--	--	--
IR #15	(GAL)	2nd bat.	1835	--	--	--	--	--	--	--
IR #15	(GAL)	3rd bat?	1835	--	--	--	--	--	--	--
IR #16	(L-V)	1st bat.	1835	1837	--	--	--	--	--	--
IR #16	(L-V)	2nd bat.	1835	--	--	--	--	--	--	--
IR #16	(L-V)	3rd bat.	1835	1837	1840	1844	1847-S	1847-N	1848-J	1848-M
IR #17	(INA)	1st bat.	1835	--	--	--	--	1847-N	1848-J	1848-M
IR #17	(INA)	2nd bat.	1835	--	--	--	--	1847-N	1848-J	1848-M
IR #18	(B-M)	1st bat.	1835	1837	1840	1844	1847-S	1847-N	1848-J	1848-M
IR #18	(B-M)	2nd bat.	1835	1837	1840	1844	1847-S	1847-N	1848-J	1848-M
IR #21	(B-M)	1st bat.	1835	1837	1840	1844	1847-S	1847-N	1848-J	1848-M
IR #21	(B-M)	2nd bat.	1835	1837	1840	1844	1847-S	1847-N	1848-J	1848-M
IR #22	(INA)	1st bat.	1835	1837	1840	--	--	--	--	--
IR #23	(L-V)	3rd bat.	1835	1837	1840	1844	1847-S	--	--	--
IR #26	(L-V)	1st bat.	--	1837	--	--	--	--	--	--
IR #26	(L-V)	2nd bat.	1835	1837	--	--	--	--	--	--
IR #26	(L-V)	3rd bat.	1835	1837	1840	1844	1847-S	--	--	--
IR #27	(AUS)	1st bat.	1835	--	--	--	--	--	1848-J	1848-M
IR #27	(AUS)	2nd bat.	1835	--	--	--	--	--	1848-J	1848-M
IR #32	(HUN)	1st bat.	1835	1837	1840	1844	1847-S	--	1848-J	1848-M
IR #32	(HUN)	2nd bat.	1835	1837	1840	1844	1847-S	--	1848-J	1848-M
IR #33	(HUN)	1st bat.	1835	1837	1840	--	--	1847-N	1848-J	1848-M
IR #33	(HUN)	2nd bat.	1835	1837	1840	--	--	1847-N	1848-J	1848-M
IR #38	(L-V)	1st bat.	1835	1837	--	1844	1847-S	1847-N	1848-J	1848-M
IR #38	(L-V)	2nd bat.	1835	1837	--	1844	1847-S	1847-N	1848-J	1848-M
IR #38	(L-V)	3rd bat.	1835	1837	1840	1844	1847-S	1847-N	1848-J	1848-M
IR #43	(L-V)	1st bat.	--	--	1840	1844	1847-S	1847-N	1848-J	1848-M
IR #43	(L-V)	2nd bat.	--	--	1840	1844	1847-S	1847-N	1848-J	1848-M
IR #43	(L-V)	3rd bat.	1835	1837	1840	1844	1847-S	1847-N	1848-J	1848-M

Appendix

Table V continued

Unit									
IR #44 (L-V) 1st bat.	--	--	1840	--	1847-S	1847-N	1848-J	1848-M
IR #44 (L-V) 2nd bat.	--	--	--	1844	1847-S	1847-N	1848-J	1848-M
IR #44 (L-V) 3rd bat.	1835	1837	1840	1844	1847-S	1847-N	1848-J	1848-M
IR #45 (L-V) 1st bat.	--	--	1840	1844	1847-S	1847-N	1848-J	1848-M
IR #45 (L-V) 2nd bat.	--	--	1840	1844	--	--	--	--
IR #45 (L-V) 3rd bat.	1835	1837	1840	1844	1847-S	1847-N	1848-J	1848-M
IR #47 (INA) 1st bat.	1835	1837	1840	1844	1847-S	1847-N	1848-J	1848-M
IR #47 (INA) 2nd bat.	1835	1837	1840	1844	1847-S	1847-N	1848-J	1848-M
IR #48 (HUN) 1st bat.	--	--	--	--	--	--	1848-J	1848-M
IR #48 (HUN) 2nd bat.	--	--	--	--	--	--	1848-J	1848-M
IR #51 (H-T) 1st bat.	1835	1837	1840	1844	1847-S	--	--	--
IR #51 (H-T) 2nd bat.	1835	1837	1840	1844	1847-S	--	--	--
IR #52 (HUN) 1st bat.	1835	1837	1840	1844	1847-S	1847-N	1848-J	1848-M
IR #52 (HUN) 2nd bat.	1835	1837	1840	1844	1847-S	1847-N	1848-J	1848-M
IR #61 (H-B) 1st bat.	1835	1837	1840	1844	1847-S	1847-N	1848-J	1848-M
IR #61 (H-B) 2nd bat.	1835	1837	1840	1844	1847-S	1847-N	1848-J	1848-M
Kaiser-Jäger 1st bat.	1835	1837	--	--	--	--	1848-J	1848-M
Kaiser-Jäger 2nd bat.	1835	--	--	--	--	--	1848-J	1848-M
Kaiser-Jäger 3rd bat.	1835	--	--	--	--	--	1848-J	1848-M
Kaiser-Jäger 4th bat.	1835	--	--	--	--	--	--	--
3rd Jäger bat. (AUS)	1835	1837	--	--	--	--	--	--
8th Jäger bat. (L-V)	1835	1837	--	1844	1847-S	1847-N	1848-J	1848-M
9th Jäger bat. (AUS)	1835	1837	1840	--	--	--	1848-J	1848-M
10th Jäger bat. (AUS)	1835	--	1840	1844	1847-S	1847-N	1848-J	1848-M
11th Jäger bat. (L-V)	--	--	1840	1844	1847-S	1847-N	1848-J	1848-M
Gren. 27-47 (INA)	1835	1837	--	--	--	--	--	--
Gren. 7-17-22 (INA)	1835	--	--	--	--	--	--	--
Gren. 33-52-61 (H-B)	1835	1837	1840	1844	1847-S	1847-N	1848-J	1848-M
Gren. 38-43-45 (L-V)	1835	1837	1840	1844	1847-S	1847-N	1848-J	1848-M
Gren. 16-26 (L-V)	1835	1837	1840	1844	1847-S	1847-N	1848-J	1848-M
5th garrison (L-V)	1835	1837	1840	1844	1847-S	1847-N	1848-J	1848-M
6th garrison (L-V)	1835	1837	1840	1844	1847-S	1847-N	1848-J	1848-M
1 bat. 2nd Grenz (SS)	--	--	--	--	--	--	1848-J	1848-M
1 bat. 3rd Grenz (SS)	--	--	--	--	--	--	1848-J	1848-M
1 bat. 4th Grenz (SS)	--	--	--	--	--	--	1848-J	1848-M
1 bat. 5th Grenz (SS)	--	--	--	--	--	--	--	1848-M
1 bat. 6th Grenz (SS)	--	--	--	--	--	--	--	1848-M
1 bat. 7th Grenz (SS)	--	--	--	--	--	--	--	1848-M
1 bat. 8th Grenz (SS)	--	--	--	--	--	--	--	1848-M
1 bat. 9th Grenz (SS)	--	--	--	--	--	--	--	1848-M
1 bat.10th Grenz (SS)	--	--	--	--	--	--	--	1848-M
1 bat.11th Grenz (SS)	--	--	--	--	--	--	--	1848-M
Total battalions:	63	44	40	39	41	43	54	61

Cavalry

Unit									
1.C-Legers 8sq. (AUS)	1835	--	--	--	--	--	--	--
4.C-Legers 8sq. (B-M)	--	--	--	--	--	1847-N	1848-J	1848-M
5.C-Legers 6sq. (B-M)	--	--	--	--	--	--	1848-J	1848-M
2.Dragoons 6sq. (AUS)	1835	1837	1840	1844	1847-S	1847-N	1848-J	1848-M
4.Dragoons 6sq. (B-M)	1835	--	--	--	--	--	--	--
5.Hussars 8sq. (HUN)	1835	1837	1840	1844	1847-S	1847-N	1848-J	1848-M
7.Hussars 8sq. (HUN)	1835	1837	1840	1844	1847-S	1847-N	1848-J	1848-M
4.Uhlans 6sq. (GAL)	--	--	--	--	--	--	--	1848-M
Total squadrons:	36	22	22	22	22	30	36	42

Key

bat.	battalion
sq.	squadrons
1847–S	spring of 1847
1847–N	end of November 1847
1848–J	end of January 1848
1848–M	outbreak of revolution, March 1848
Gren.	grenadier battalion (with numbers of IRs contributing troops)
(L–V)	Lombard and Venetian (Italians)
(AUS)	German Austrians
(B–M)	Bohemian–Moravian (Germans and Czechs)
(HUN)	Hungarians
(H–T)	Hungarian–Transylvanian (predominantly Hungarian and Romanian)
(H–B)	Hungarian–Banat (predominantly Hungarian and Serbian
(GAL)	Galician (Polish and Ruthenian)
(INA)	Inner Austrian (German & Slovene; Italian & Slovene in IR #22)
(SS)	South Slav (Croatians and Serbs)
?	(two battalions unaccounted for in 1835, most likely the 3rd battalions of IR #12 and IR #15).
C–Legers	Chevaux–Legers (light cavalry)

Recapitulation

1835:	63 battalions (18 Italian)	36 squadrons (0 Italian)
1837:	44 battalions (18 Italian)	22 squadrons (0 Italian)
1840:	40 battalions (18 Italian)	22 squadrons (0 Italian)
1844:	39 battalions (21 Italian)	22 squadrons (0 Italian)
1847 (spr.):	41 battalions (21 Italian)	22 squadrons (0 Italian)
1847 (Nov.):	43 battalions (21 Italian)	30 squadrons (0 Italian)
1848 (Jan.):	54 battalions (21 Italian)	36 squadrons (0 Italian)
1848 (Mar.):	61 battalions (21 Italian)	42 squadrons (0 Italian)

65 of the units (43 battalions and 22 squadrons) that were with Radetzky in 1848 also had been with his army in 1835; 49 units (27 battalions and 22 squadrons) were stationed under him throughout the period 1835–48.

Note: In some documents Radetzky claimed his Pioneer (construction) battalion as an infantry battalion, distorting the figures by one.

Table VI

The following illustration of Venetian losses in the War of 1866 includes figures for 16 of the 20 Venetian battalions in Benedek's field army and partial figures for a 17th battalion (the 8th Jägers). Statistics are not available for the 3 battalions of the 16th Infantry (Mainz to Aschaffenburg) or for the 7 fourth battalions and 7 fifth battalions stationed in the rear (illness losses, etc.). Figures given by regiment or Jäger battalions, per battle. Other gaps in data are indicated.

Hühnerwasser (26 June)
#38 (no data)

Trautenau (27 June)
#13 lost   93 killed   417 wounded   122 pris./missing
                         (110 p.w.)   (30 p., 92 m.)

Nachod (27 June)
#38 (no data)

Pokitai (27 June)
#38 (no data)

Münchengrätz (28 June)
#38 lost   35 killed   109 wounded   403 pris./missing
                                        (39 m., 364 p.)

Sobotka (28 June)
#45 lost   47 killed   232 wounded   123 pris./missing

Kost (29 June)
#26J lost   28 killed   51 wounded

Jičin (29 June)
#45 lost   54 killed   167 wounded   0 pris./missing
26J lost   37 killed   58 wounded   0 pris./missing
#38   (no data)

Schweinschädl (29 June)
8.J lost   38 killed   23 wounded   0 pris./missing
                         (10 p.w.)

Horič (30 June)
#38 (no data)
#79 (no data)

Kukus (30 June)
#80 (no data - "many wounded and dead")

Königgrätz (3 July)

#13 lost	15 killed	51 wounded	48 pris./missing
			(23 m., 9 p., 16 p.w.)
#26 lost	61 killed	233 wounded	392 pris./missing
			(28 p., 364 m. or p.w.)
#38 list	352 killed	297 wounded	445 pris./missing
#45 lost	65 killed	161 wounded	159 pris./missing
#79 (no data)			
#80 lost	193 killed	155 wounded	945 pris./missing
8.J. (no data)			
26J lost	43 killed	118 wounded	? pris./missing
Total:	729*	1,015*	1,989* (16 of 20 btn.)

Tobitschau (15 July)

#38 lost	16 killed	14 wounded	25 pris./missing

Miscellaneous and unspecified losses (recorded)

8.J lost; killed, wounded, pris./m.: 688 more
26J lost; 5 wounded

Königgrätz	729*	1,015*	1,989*
Non–Kgrtz.	348*	1,076*	673*
Totals	1,077*	2,091*	2,662* + 688 = 6518*

(*) – all totals partial (i.e. only for units listed above)
k. – killed; w. – wounded; p.w. – prisoners wounded
m. – missing 8.J, 26J – 8th and 26 Jäger battalions
Regiments listed by number (#13, #26, #38, #45, etc.)

Table VII

The Austrian naval officer corps evolved from a predominantly Italian institution to a predominantly German one, with the most decisive changes coming immediately after 1848. The principal sources for this chart are rosters in the *Geschichte der k.(u.)k. Kriegsmarine* for the years 1802–1809, rosters in the *Militär-Schematismus* for 1817–71, and tables in the *Militärstatistisches Jahrbuch* for 1885–1911. Figures from the latter include sea cadets; all others are for commissioned sea officers only.

Nat./pct.	1802	1805	1809	1817	1824	1829	1834	1838	1844
Italians	60	59	44	73	72	68	64	63	59
Germans	6	6	15	5	3	5	8	11	17
S. Slavs+	18	19	22	18	17	17	14	14	15
Others*	16	16	19	4	8	10	14	12	9

Nat./pct.	1848	1850	1853	1856	1859	1862	1865	1868	1871
Italians	60	18	17	11	12	14	13	9	9
Germans	15	37	45	53	60	58	60	62	64
S. Slavs+	16	16	17	12	4	4	5	6	5
Others*	6	29	21	24	24	24	22	23	22

Nat./pct.	1885	1887	1893	1896	1899	1901	1904	1907	1910
Italians	9.7	9.2	7.6	8.5	9.2	9.3	9.6	10.6	9.8
Germans	44.9	46.8	52.8	55.0	54.4	54.5	54.6	51.5	51.0
S. Slavs+	10.3	9.9	8.9	7.6	7.4	7.4	7.6	8.9	9.8
Magyars	14.7	14.6	11.5	10.9	11.6	11.9	11.9	12.3	12.9
Czechs	12.3	11.5	10.9	9.9	9.4	8.9	8.9	9.3	9.2
Poles	4.0	3.5	3.4	3.3	3.5	3.3	3.2	3.0	2.8
Slovenes+	4.0	4.5	4.8	4.7	4.5	4.7	4.2	4.2	4.2
Romanians	—	—	0.1	0.1	—	—	—	0.2	0.3

(*) – "Others" includes all nationalities not listed, as well as officers whose nationality cannot be defined

(+) – South Slav figures include Croatians and Dalmatians only. There were no Slovenes in the officer corps prior to 1850; Slovenes listed under "Others" from 1850–71.

1802 statistics are for May; 1805 for the end of the year; 1809 for the spring (pre-war); 1817–71 for the beginning of the year; 1885–1911 for the end of the year. Because of the imprecise nature of the figures from the years 1802–71, all have been rounded off to the nearest whole percentage.

Table VIII

The dispersal of Austrian naval officers in March and April of 1848, for the corps as a whole and by station, rank, and year of graduation from the naval academy.

All sea Officers	No.	% Of Whole	Released by Navy	to Venice Navy	Still w/Aust.	% Left
Italians	94	(60%)	75	67	19	(35%)
Germans	23	(15%)	3	3	20	(36%)
S. Slavs	27	(16%)	19	18	7+	(13%)
Others*	13		4	5	9	

w/Active Squadron	No.	% Of Whole	Released by Navy	to Venice Navy	Still w/Aust.	% Left
Italians	20	(46%)	15	15	5	(24%)
Germans	8	(19%)	0	–	8	(24%)
S. Slavs	9	(20%)	5	5	4	(19%)
Others*	6		2	2	4	

On Other Stations	No.	% of Whole	Released by Navy	to Venice Navy	Still w/Aust.	% Left
Italians	74	(65%)	60	52	14	(41%)
Germans	15	(13%)	3	3	12	(35%)
S. Slavs	18	(16%)	14	13	3+	(9%)
Others*	7		2	2	5	

Officers by Rank	No.	% of Whole	Released by Navy	to Venice Navy	Still w/Aust.	% Left
Captains	17		11	11	5+	(9%)
Lieutenants	56		34	32	22	(41%)
Ensigns	83		56	49	27	(50%)

Academy Class	No.	Active in '48	Released by Navy	Pct. Released	to Venice Navy	Still w/Aust
Pre–28 or None:		(78)	(45)	(58%)	(na)	(32)
1828	4	3	2	(66%)	2	1
1829	14	4	3	(75%)	3	1
1830	0	–	–	–		
1831	8	3	2	(66%)	2	1

Table VIII continued

Academy Class	No.	Active in '48	Released by Navy	Pct. Released	to Venice Navy	Still w/Aust.
1832	20	10	7	(70%)	7	3
1833	9	7	5	(71%)	3	2
1834	6	3	2	(66%)	1	1
1835	2	0	–	–	–	–
1836	9	3	3	(100%)	2	0
1837	10	7	5	(71%)	5	2
1838	10	6	6	(100%)	5	0
1839	3	3	1	(33%)	1	2
1840	12	9	5	(56%)	4	4
1841	9	8	5	(62%)	5	3
1842	5	2	1	(50%)	(1?)	1
1843	7	5	4	(80%)	4	1
1844	9	6	5	(83%)	5	1
TOTAL Officers	(137)	(79)	(56)	(71%)		(23)
Cadets ('48)						
1845	2	2	1	(50%)	1	1
1846	5	5	1	(20%)	1	4
1847	19	19	11	(58%)	9	8
TOTAL Grads.	(163)	(105)	(69)	(66%)		(36)

(+) – Figure less by one because of murder of Captain Marinovich in March 1848

(*) – "Others" includes all nationalities other than Italian, German, and South Slav, as well as all officers whose origin could not be defined.

% Left – Percentage breakdown of those still with the navy

Table IX

Italians in the Armed Forces of the Dual Monarchy
Post–1867

Overall Manpower

	ARMY		NAVY	
Year	Total	Italians (%)	Total	Italians (%)
1872	856,062	7,803 (0.9)	na	na
1877	806,259	6,267 (0.8)	na	na
1882	874,074	6,355 (0.7)	na	na
1882	885,617	7,683 (0.9)	17,291	5,775 (33.4)
1891	1,015,612	10,285 (1.0)	20,561	6,489 (31.5)
1895	1,162,622	15,098 (1.3)	21,537	6,053 (28.1)
1899	1,433,203	21,535 (1.5)	22,070	6,118 (27.7)
1903	1,495,684	23,223 (1.5)	24,087	6,089 (25.3)
1907	1,497,829	20,501 (1.4)	29,491	7,120 (24.2)
1911	1,462,866	19,528 (1.3)	35,942	6,283 (17.5)

na – Figures for navy not available prior to 1885

Italian Factions in Army Units

Year	IR #97	1st KJ	2nd KJ	3rd KJ	4th KJ	20th FJB
1985	22%	36%	38%	37%	(*)	22%
1988	31	32	40	41	33	(*)
1903	28	40	42	38	42	(*)
1907	24	42	42	41	38	(*)
1911	20	38	41	38	38	31

(*) – Italian contingent below 20% (no figures available)
IR – Infantry regiment
KJ – Kaiser–Jäger regiment
FJB – Field–Jäger battalion

Source: *Militärstatistisches Jahrbuch*

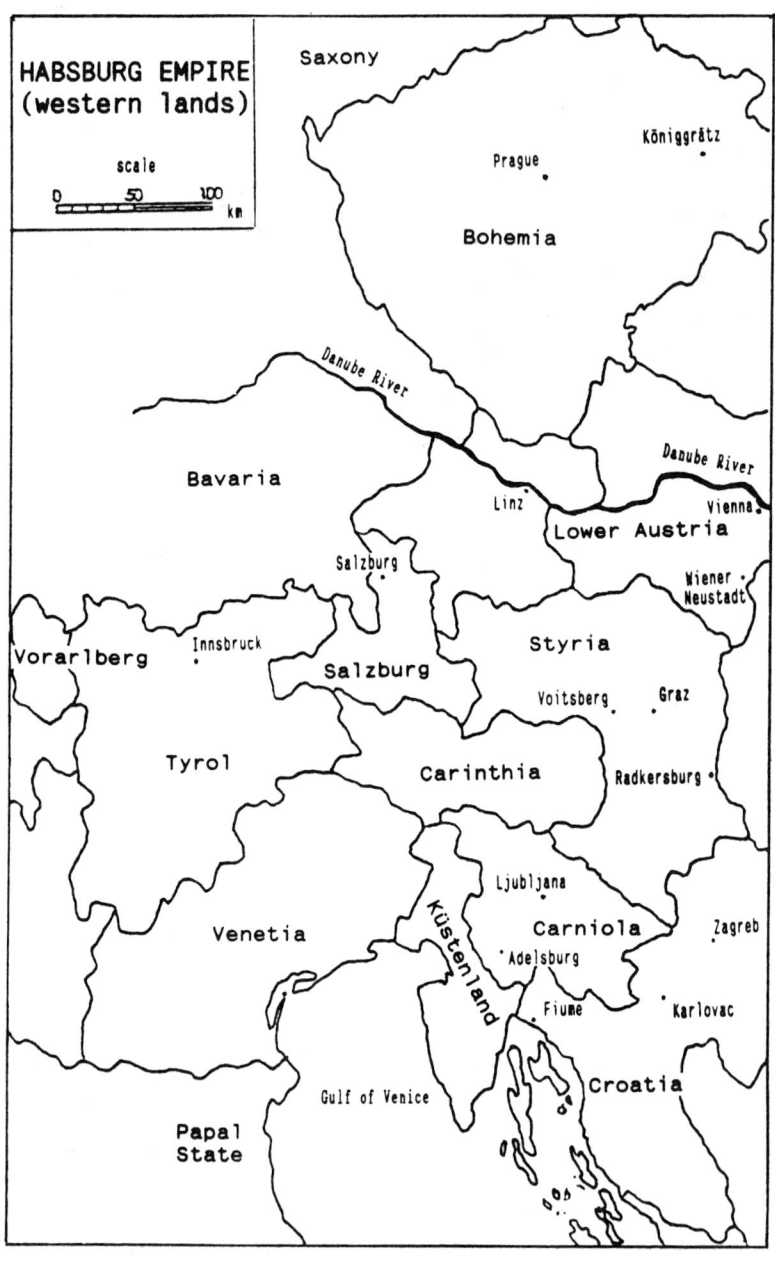

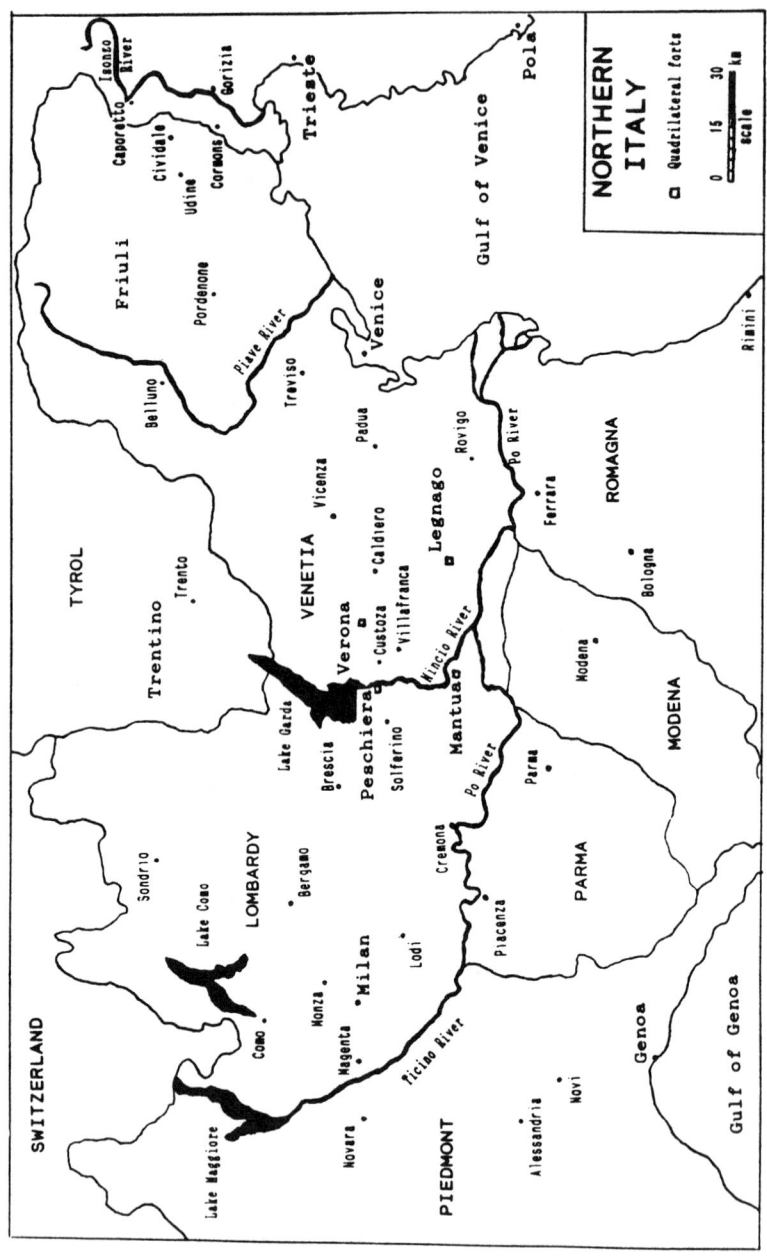

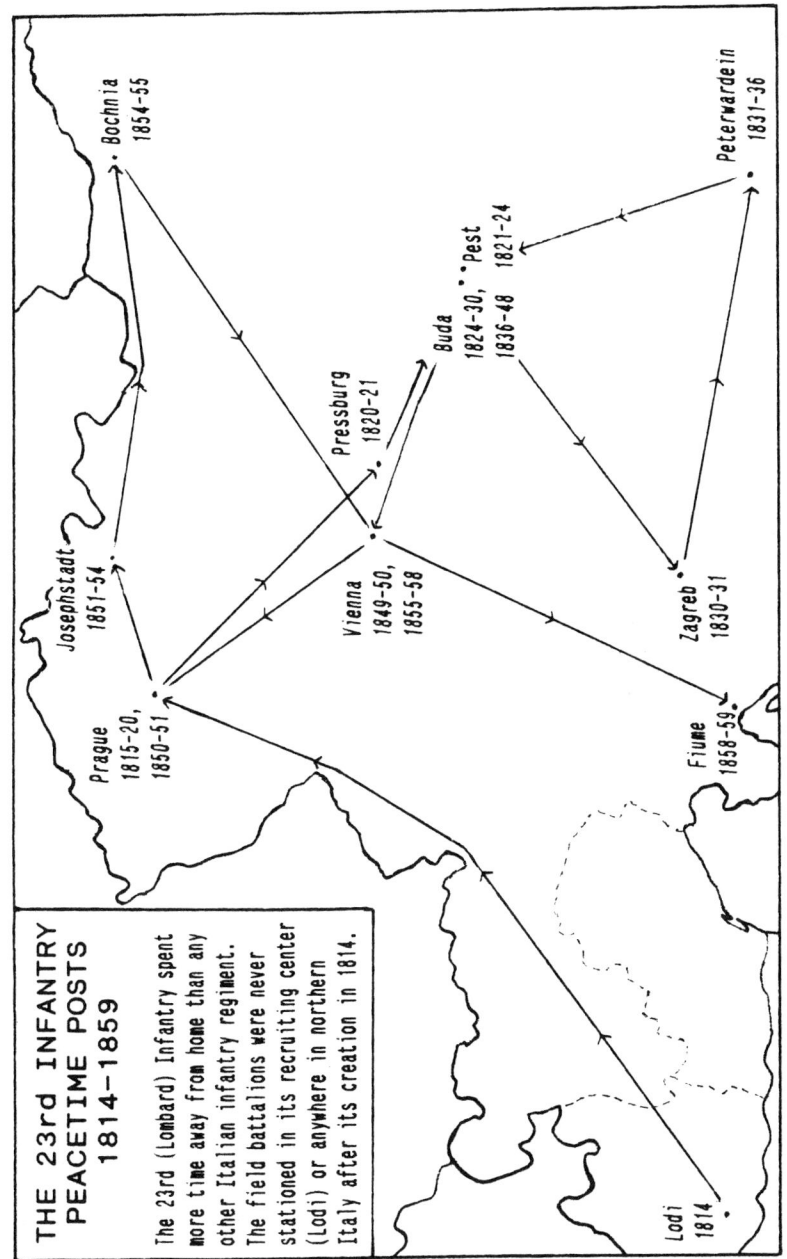

INDEX

Adelsburg (Postojna), 101
Adrario, Biagio, navy officer, 92
Afan de Rivera, Gaetano, navy officer, 114
Ahsbahs, Leone, navy officer, 153n.36
Alberti, Alberto, army officer, 41
Alberti de Poya, Count Bartolomeo, army officer, 18, 22
Alberti, Gastone degli, navy officer, 114
Alberti, Giovanni, navy officer, 68
Albini, Giuseppe, Italian admiral, 93
Albrecht, Archduke, 50-51, 57-59
Alcaudete, Count Antonio, army officer, 3
Alessandria, 23
Ancona, 26
Angeli, Moriz von, army officer, viii, 137n.37
Army, Austrian. *See* entries under Battalions; Regiments; Reserve formations; *see also* individual officers and soldiers
Artillery, 155n.24
Austrian Lloyd, 87, 132n.61
Austrian Succession, War of the (1740-48), 3
Austro-Turkish War (1737-39), 3
Austro-Turkish War (1787-92), 6-7

Bagnalasta, Giulio, army officer, 59, 140n.69
Bagno, Guido di, army officer, 4
Baldiserotto, Francesco, navy officer, 77, 79, 93
Bandiera, Attilio, navy officer, 70-76 passim, 96, 117, 146n.28, 147n.37
Bandiera, Emilio, navy officer, 70-76, 83, 93, 96, 117
Bandiera, Francesco, admiral, 69, 70, 73-77 passim
Baratelli, Franco Micali, historian, 93
Barison, Giuseppe, soldier, 35
Battalions, infantry:
    1st Garrison (Lombard-Venetian, 1853-55), 47, 49;
    5th Garrison (Venetian, 1816-53), 39, 46, 47;

6th Garrison (Lombard, 1830-53), 39-40, 46, 47, 80;
6th Jägers (Lombard-Venetian, 1857-59), 50, 139n.52;
8th Jägers (Lombard, 1830-49; Venetian, 1849-66), 40, 54, 59, 61, 130.n.45, 139n.52;
11th Jägers (Lombard-Venetian, 1823-57; Lombard, 1857-59), 24, 137n.33, 139n.52;
12th Jägers (Lombard-Venetian, 1823-30), 24, 130n.45;
18th Jägers (Lombard-Venetian, 1857-59), 50;
20th Jägers (Trieste, 1886-1918), 102, 104, 106, 109, 155n.19;
25th Jägers (Venetian, 1849-59), 40, 138n.45, 139n.52;
26th Jägers (Venetian, 1859-66), 54, 56, 58, 59, 61, 139n.60;
Grenadiers, 6, 7, 15, 39, 46, 47, 80, 125n.15
Battisti, Cesare, Italian patriot, 104, 107, 108
Bavaria, 3, 48
Bavarian Succession, War of the (1778–79), 5-6
Beauharnais, Prince Eugene de, Viceroy of Italy, 12, 62
Belluno, 56
Benedek, Ludwig August von, general, 57, 58, 59
Benigni, Enrico, army officer, 37
Bergamo, 25, 36, 38, 47, 137n.36
Berti, Renato, sailor, 114
Boccheciampe, Pietro, 76, 77
Bohemia, 6, 26, 29, 48, 52, 54, 55, 57, 58, 59, 61, 88
Bologna, 26, 38
Bombiero, Giulio, army officer, 154n.14
Bordini, Andrea, navy officer, 78, 86
Bordolo di Boreo, Giovanni, general, 98
Boscarolli, Giuseppe, 153n.36
Bosnia, 3, 99, 113
Bossi, Marquis Giovanni, army officer, 6
Braila, 49
Brenner Pass, 117
Brescia, 18, 34, 36, 37, 44
Brest-Litovsk, Peace of (1918), 110, 112
Brünn (Brno), 15, 88
Bua, Giuseppe, navy officer, 75, 77
Bubna, Count Ferdinand, general, 20-23, 26
Bucchia, Tommaso, navy officer, 93
Buda, 15, 37, 99; *see also* Pest
Budget and finances: army, 27-28, 29-30, 47, 49; navy, 64-65, 67-68,

79, 131n.56, 133n.72
Bujacovich, Alexander, admiral, 74
Bukovina, 112
Buratovich, Johann von, admiral, 79, 81, 84

Calabria, 75
Calafati, Guglielmo, navy officer, 92
Caldiero, Battle of (1805), 8
Calligaris, Marcello, sailor, 114
Calvi, Pietro, army officer, 42-43
Campoformio, Treaty of (1797), 8, 9
Canal, Giulio, navy officer, 73
Caporetto, Battle of (1917), 109
Carbonari, 16, 23, 26, 66, 98, 129n.36
Carinthia, 23, 87
Carlsbad Decrees (1819), 20
Carniola, 87, 101
Cassini, Count Oscare, admiral, 103
Cattanei di Momo, Baron Carlo, army officer, 55, 140n.69
Cattaro (Kotor), 29, 36, 99, 112-14
Calvary. *See* Regiments, cavalry
Cavedalis, Giambattista, army officer, 43
Cavour, Count Camillo Benso di, Sardinian minister, 50
Ceccopieri, Count Ferdinando, army officer, 13-14
Cerri, Carlo, navy officer, 114
Charles, Archduke, 8, 9, 125n.29
Charles, Emperor of Austria and King of Hungary, 108, 115
Charles V, King of Spain and Holy Roman Emperor, 1
Charles VI, Holy Roman Emperor, 3, 9
Charles Albert, King of Sardinia-Piedmont, 31, 34
Cheracci, Oreste, navy officer, 114
Chiesa, Damiano, Italian patriot, 107
Chinca, Domenico, navy officer, 71, 93, 146n.25
Cicoli, Alfredo, admiral, 115
Cisalpine Republic, 8
Cividale, 25, 47
Clerici, Marquis Giorgio, army officer, 3
Colli, Baron, army officer, 7
Colonna, Fabrizio, general, 1
Colonna, Prospero, general, 1

Como, 18, 38, 48, 79
Confalonieri, Federico, 70, 129n.36
Conninck, August de, navy commandant, 63, 64, 66, 68
Conscription policies, 19-20, 29-31, 46, 49-50, 55, 89, 105, 133n.69, 141n.72
Corfu, 73-76 passim
Cormons, Armistice of (1866), 59
Cosenza, 75
Cremona, 6, 37, 38, 46
Crenneville, Count Louis Folliot de, general, 66
Crimean War (1854-56), 48-49
Croatia, 29, 105; see also Dalmatia; Istria
Crotone, 75
Cuneo, Battle of (1744), 3
Custoza, Battle of (1848), 34, 38, 40, 45, 82
Custoza, Battleof (1866). 58. 59. 141n.80

Dahlerup, Hans Birch von, navy commandant, 83, 87, 88, 89
Dalmatia, 29, 36, 40-41, 78, 86, 91, 99, 113; manpower for army from, 101; manpower for navy from, 67, 79, 84, 87, 89, 93, 94; officers for navy from, 9,10, 83
Dandolo, Sylvestro, admiral, 63, 64, 68-69, 70, 73, 79, 114n.4
Danubian Principalities, 48-49; see also Moldavia, Wallachia
Deak, Istvan, historian, 51
De Gasperi, Alcide, Italian politician, 108
Degenfeld, Count August von, general, 55
Delucca, Sebastiano, navy officer, 85, 86
Diseases, and fear of: affecting regiments, 23-24, 29, 48-49, 132n.63
Discipline, in peacetime: in the army, 13, 17; in the navy, 67-68, 91-92; see also Carbonari; Mazzinian activity
Döbeln, Battle of (1762), 4
Dojmi, Nicolo, navy officer, 153n.36
Dukla Pass, Battle of (1915), 105

Economic conditions, 20-21, 31, 133n.70
Education. See Naval academy; Regimental schools; Wiener Neustadt Military Academy
Esperia. See Mazzini, Giuseppe
Eugene of Savoy, Prince, 2, 9, 124n.6

Fabrizi, Nicola, Italian patriot, 72-73, 75
Fahrdorf-Lopstedt, Battle of (1864), 56

Farnese, Duke Alessandro, general, 1
Ferdinand, Emperor of Austria, 27
Ferdinand Max, Archduke (later Maximilian of Mexico), 49, 89-92
Feretti, Francesco de, army officer, 4
Ferrara, 31
Ferrari di Grado, Federico, army officer, 37
Filzi, Fabio, Italian patriot, 107
Fincati, Luigi, navy officer, 93
Fiume, 25, 29, 57, 67, 88, 91, 93, 94, 97, 101, 107, 132n.62
Florio, Marco, navy officer, 92, 98
Florio, Riccardo, navy officer, 114, 154n.8
Fontanelli, Count Achille, general, 15
Foscolo, Vincenzo, navy officer, 94
Francis I, Emperor of Austria, 9, 13-16, 25, 27, 125n.29
Francis Joseph, Emperor of Austria and King of Hungary, 42, 46, 47, 51, 56, 60, 88, 89, 100, 108
Frederick, Archduke, navy commandant, 71-73, 76, 78-79, 81
French Revolution and Napoleon, wars of the (1792-1815), 7-16 passim
Frimont, Count Johann, general, 22-23, 25-27, 28
Friuli and Friulians, 44, 54, 56, 136n.24, 138n.44
Fumanelli, Antonio, navy officer, 88
Funes, Angelo, soldier, 35

Galicia, 8, 29, 48-49, 54-55, 105, 108, 109, 110
Garbizza, Michele, arsenal worker, 150n.16
Garibaldi, Giuseppe, 58, 91, 99, 100
Gerelli, Carlo, army officer, 37
German Confederation, 20, 56, 153n.7
Giaj, Domenico, arsenal worker, 150n.16
Giurgevo (Giurgiu), 7
Gogola, Antonio, navy officer, 93
Gorizia, 25, 101, 102, 116
Graz, 15, 25, 28, 32, 35, 46
Graziani, Leone, navy officer, 74, 80
Grünne, Count Karl Ludwig, general, 50-51
Guards regiment (Lombard-Venetian *Leibgarde*), 30, 132n.65
Gyulai, Count Franc, general, 81, 84

Hardegg, Count Ignaz von, general, 76
Hartig, Count Franz, Austrian administrator, 28-29

Helgoland, Battle of (1864), 92
Higgia, Matteo, navy officer, 86
Hochkirch, Battle of (1758), 4
Hofkriegsrat (Court War Council), 2, 32; orders of, affecting army, 13, 15-16, 19-20, 22, 24; orders of, affecting navy, 63, 65-69 passim, 73, 74, 79
Hübner, Count Joseph von, Austrian diplomat, 50
Hungary: Italians garrisoned in, 3, 15, 29, 41, 48, 49, 50, 52, 60, 99; Italians deployed in (1848-49), 35-37, 40-43

Innsbruck, 36, 52
Isonzo River, 59, 101
Istria, 41, 91, 99, 107; manpower for army from, 25, 53, 99, 101; manpower for navy from, 67, 93, 94; officers for navy from, 10
Italian army, 57-61, 91, 92, 96, 99, 107, 109, 115, 116
Italian navy, 91, 93-94, 96, 104, 107, 152n.35
Italian Legion (in Hungary, 1848-49), 43, 136n.20
Italy, Kingdom of, 56, 57, 60, 99, 100, 103-4, 106, 108-9; *see also* Napoleonic kingdom of Italy; Italian army; Italian navy

Jassy (Iasi), 49
Jellačić, Baron Josip, Ban of Croatia, 37, 41
Jičin, Battle of (1866), 58
John, Archduke, 9
Joseph II, Holy Roman Emperor, 6, 7, 9
Julian Alps, 117

Kaiser-Jäger regiments, 15, 25, 61, 96, 102-6 passim, 108-9, 116, 130n.46, 155n.20
Karlovac, 25
Karolyi, Count Ladislaus, army officer, 77
Khevenhüller, Ludwig Andreas, general, 2
Kolowrat, Count Franz, Austrian minister, 27
Königgrätz, Battle of (1866), 58-59, 142n.85
Kraus, Karl, Austrian writer, 107, 156n.34
Kübeck, Adolf, army officer, 77
Kudriaffsky, Ludwig, navy officer, 78, 82
Küstenland, 67, 101, 115; *see also* Istria

Lake Maggiore, 79
Lamberti, Count Camillo, general, 9
Language policies and problems: in the army, 14, 17, 44; in the navy,

64, 66, 78, 88, 90, 97-98, 144n.6
Lemberg (Lvov), 105
Leopold I, Holy Roman Emperor, 2
Leopold II, Holy Roman Emperor, 7
Leuthen, Battle of (1757), 4
Liechtenstein, Prince Alois, general, 15
Lilia, Count Carlo di, general, 98
Linz, 55
Liparachi, Dionisio, navy officer, 94
Lissa, Battle of (1866), 92-94, 98, 103
Ljubljana, 86
Loano, Battle of (1795), 7
Lodi, 18, 37
Lombardy: manpower for army from, 3, 4-5, 6, 10-11, 12-15, 37-40, 42, 45, 51-55, 61, 139n.62, 140n.68; manpower for navy from, 78-79, 84; officers for army from, 5, 13, 55
London, Treaty of (1915), 104, 117
Lopresti, army officer, 7
Ludwig, Archduke, 27
Lunéville, Treaty of (1801), 8
Lussin (Losinj), 91

Magenta, Battle of (1859), 52-53, 54
Mainz, 56, 57, 59
Malta, 72, 75, 77
Manin, Daniele, Italian patriot, 79-80
Mantua, 5, 7, 16, 37, 38, 40, 92
Marchesi, Count Luigi, 101
Marchetti, Carlo, navy officer, 153n.36
Maria Theresa, Habsburg empress, 3, 4, 5
Mariani, Paolo, sailor, 73, 76, 78-79, 147n.36
Marines, Austrian, 3, 124n.10
Marinovich, Johann, navy officer, 79, 80, 83, 88, 150n.16
Maroncelli, Pietro, Italian patriot, 70, 129n.36
Marsich, Giuseppe, navy officer, 77
Martini, Anton von, navy commandant, 79-80, 85, 87
Martini, Giuseppe, army officer, 38
Martini, Cavaliere Francesco, army officer, 3
Masotti, Gustavo, navy officer, 92
Matticolo, Luigi, navy officer, 74, 77, 78, 79, 148n.40

Index

Mauro, army officer, 7
Mazzini, Giuseppe, and Mazzinian activity, 28, 69-78, 80, 86, 146n.26, 147n.33
Mazzucchelli, Count Luigi, general, 15
Mazzuchelli, Ippolito, navy officer, 72, 73, 78
Mehemet Ali, Pasha of Egypt, 71
Menabrea, Luigi, Italian general, 60
Mercurio, Enrico, navy officer, 152n.36
Metternich, Count (later Prince) Clemens von, Austrian chancellor, 20-22, 26-27, 64, 71, 75, 76
Michieli, Count Carlo, navy officer, 86, 89-90
Milan, 5, 17, 18, 19, 20, 22, 25, 28, 31, 34, 36, 38, 44, 85
Mincio River, 34, 92
Minutillo, Baron Francesco, admiral, 92, 103
Modena, 25, 51
Moldavia, 48-49
Mongo, Luigi, Italian spy, 152n.29
Montebello, Battle of (1859), 52
Montecuccoli, Count Raimondo, general, 2, 9
Montecuccoli, Count Rudolf, navy commandant, 103-4
Montenuovo, Count Guglielmo di, army officer, 41-42
Monti, Alessandro, army officer, 42-43
Monza, 48
Morari, Antonio, navy officer, 75, 77
Moravia, 15, 24, 36
Morelli, Domenico Adriano, navy officer, 98, 154n.8
Moreschi, Luigi, army officer, 41
Moretti, army officer, 127n.15
Moreschi, Luigi, army officer, 41
Moretti, army officer, 127n.15
Moro, Domenico, navy officer, 71-72, 75-77, 83, 85, 93-94, 96
Moro, Giovanni, navy officer, 85, 94
Murat, Joachim, King of Naples, 16, 17, 22-23

Naples, 2, 3, 18, 22-23, 76, 84-85, 86, 90-91, 96, 124n.10
Napoleonic Kingdom of Italy, 10; army of, 12-14, 126n.3; navy of, 62-63
Napoleonic Wars. *See* French Revolution and Napoleon, wars of the
Naval academy, 64, 65-66, 69-71, 73, 78, 83, 87, 97, 98, 153n.5
Navy, Austrian: eighteenth-century antecedents of, 3, 9; during the

Napoleonic era, 9-10; under Italian domination, 62-80 passim; during revolutions of 1848-49, 41, 80-88; post-1848 policies toward Italians, 88-92, 97-98, 103-4; in War of 1864, 92; in War of 1866, 92-94; during World War I, 112-15
Near Eastern Crisis (1839-40), 71
Nikolsburg, Peace of (1866), 59
Non-commissioned officers: in Italian regiments, 17, 21-22, 43-44, 47, 55
Novara, Battle of (1849), 34, 36, 40, 45, 82, 83
Novi, Battle of (1800), 8
Nugent, Count Laval, general, 32

Oberdan, Guglielmo, Italian patriot, 99-101, 154n.13
Olini, army officer, 127n.15
Olmütz, 24, 36, 57
Omati, army officer, 4

Padua, 18, 35, 50-51
Paris Peace Conference (1919), 117
Parma, 25, 26
Paroi, Giovanni, Chibo, sailor, 114
Paulucci delle Roncole, Marquis Amilcare, navy commandant, 65, 68-70, 72-76, 145n.21
Paulucci, Antonio, navy officer, 80, 145n.21
Paulucci, Ferdinando, navy officer, 153n.36
Paulucci, Guglielmo, navy officer, 93
Pergen, Count Anton, army officer, 38, 43-44
Persano, Count Carlo Pellion de, Italian admiral, 93
Peschiera, 18
Pest, 15, 29, 35
Piave River, 109, 115, 116
Piccolomini Ottavio, 2, 9
Piedmont, 7, 23, 24, 36, 38, 39, 40; *see also* Sardinia; Sardinian army; Sardinian navy
Pisoni, Pietro, navy officer, 152n.36
Pius IX, Pope, 30
Plombières, Treaty of (1858), 50
Pöck, Friedrich von, navy commandant, 98
Pola (Pula), 41, 79-86 passim, 92, 94, 102, 107, 112-16 passim
Ponti, Giuseppe, navy officer, 150n.16
Porcia, Count Leopoldo, army officer, 38

Pordenone, 54
Pozzo, Cesare, navy officer, 92
Prague, 15, 24, 57
Predonzan, Amilcare, navy officer, 152n.36
Pressburg (Bratislava), 29
Pressburg, Treaty of (1805), 63
Pretis–Cagnodo, Sisino de, Austrian administrator, 100
Primavesi, Giuseppe, navy officer, 154n.8

Quadrilateral forts, 34, 57; see Legnago; Mantua; Peschiera; Verona

Radaelli, Carlo Alberto, navy officer, viii, 69-71, 86, 142n.83
Radetzky, Count Joseph, general, 21, 26-32, 34-40, 42-43, 45-46, 49, 55, 74, 82, 136n.32
Radkersburg, 110, 111
Rainer, Archduke, Viceroy of Lombardy-Venetia, 19, 79
Regimental schools (*Erziehungshäuser*), 6, 17, 21, 25, 47
Regiments, cavalry:
  7th Chevaux-Legers (Lombard-Venetian, 1814-52), 13, 16, 17-18, 22, 41-42, 49, 127n.13, 137n.41;
  8th Dragoons (Lombard-Venetian, 1854-59), 48, 54–55;
  6th Uhlans (Venetian, 1853-59), 47-48;
  7th Uhlans (Venetian, 1857-59), 50, 138n.45;
  9th Uhlans (Lombard, 1857-59), 50, 138n.45;
  11th Uhlans (Lombard, 1853-59), 47, 49, 51, 55;
Regiments infantry:
  13th (part–Venetian, 1801-5), 8;
  13th (Venetian, 1814-66), 14-15, 18, 22, 23-24, 28, 32, 35, 39, 42-43, 50-51, 52, 54, 58, 59, 61, 80, 132n.61, 132n.62, 138n.42, 139n.53, 145n.13;
  16th (Venetian, 1817-66), 18, 22, 23, 24, 35-36, 37, 39, 43, 44, 48, 51, 52, 53-54, 55, 56, 57, 59, 61, 131n.47;
  22nd (Trieste, 1817-74), 25, 26, 40-41, 52-53, 57, 58, 60, 61, 86-87, 89, 96, 99, 101, 130n.47, 137n.41, 141n.71, 145n.13;
  23rd (Lombard, 1814-59), 15, 18, 22, 26, 37, 39, 48, 49, 51, 52, 53, 54, 59, 61, 139n.62;
  26th (Venetian, 1817-66), 18, 22, 23, 24, 29, 36, 39, 44, 49, 51, 52, 57,59, 61, 131n.47, 136n.24, 138n.44;
  38th (Lombard, 1814-59; Venetian, 1860-66), 15, 18, 22, 37-38, 39, 40, 43-44, 48, 51, 52, 53, 54, 55, 59, 60, 61, 137n.36; 140n.66
  43rd (Lombard, 1814-59), 15, 18, 22, 28, 38, 39, 46, 51, 52, 53, 54,

59, 61, 137n.36;
44th ("Regiment Clerici"), 3, 4-5, 6-8, 124n.12;
44th (Lombard, 1817-59), 18, 22, 23, 24, 38-39, 44, 45, 48, 51, 52, 53, 54, 59, 61, 128n.23, 131n.47;
45th (Venetian, 1816-66), 18, 22, 23, 29, 36-37, 39, 45, 48-49, 51, 52, 53, 54, 58, 59, 61, 140n.63;
46th (Venetian, 1801-5), 8;
48th ("Regiment Alcaudete"), 3, 4-5, 6-7;
55th (Lombard, 1852-59), 48-49, 51, 52, 53, 54, 137n.37, 139n.62;
63rd (Venetian, 1801-5), 8;
79th (Venetian, 1860-66), 54, 59, 61, 140n.66, 140n.69;
80th (Venetian, 1860-66), 54, 56, 59, 60, 61, 91, 140n.66;
97th (Trieste, 1883-1918), 101-2, 104-6, 108, 109-12, 115, 115n.19, 156n.27;
"Regiment Marulli," 3, 4, 5;
see also Kaiser-Jäger regiments; Reserve formations; Battalions
Reserve formations:
5th Landwehr (*Schützenregiment*), 102, 105, 106, 108, 110, 112, 115;
Trieste *Jungschützbataillon*, 106;
Tyrolese *Landesschützen*, 105, 108-9, 156n.26, 157n.38;
Tyrolese *Standschützen*, 106
Revolutions of 1820-21, 22-23
Revolutions of 1830-32, 25-26, 27, 71
Revolutions of 1848-49, 31-45 passim, 80-88
Rijeka. *See* Fiume
Rimini, 26
Rochlitzer-Scordelli, Antonio, navy officer, 152n.36
Romagna, 25, 31
Romania, 108, 112, 116, 158n.58; *see also* Moldavia; Wallachia
Rovigo, 54

Sauro, Nazario, Italian patriot, 107-8
Sagredo, Giovanni, navy officer, 84
Salvini, Matteo, navy officer, 88-89, 90
Salvini, Osvaldo, navy officer, 113
Salzburg, 36
Sambucco, Battle of (1795), 7
Sandri, Antonio, navy officer, 94
Sandri, Luigi, navy officer, 86

Santa Lucia, Battle of (1848), 34, 36, 38, 39, 40, 45
Sardinia, 2; see also Piedmont
Sardinian army, 34
Sardinian navy, 82-83, 88, 150n.14
Sarracca, Emerico de, army officer, 101
Schleswig-Holstein, 56
Schönbrunn, Treaty of (1809), 10
Schwarzenberg, Prince Felix zu, Austrian statesman, 85
Schweidnitz, Battle of (1757), 4
Serbia, 3
Seven Years' War (1756-63), 4
Šibenik (Sebenico), 114
Sicily, 3, 91
Sked, Alan, historian, 43, 44, 45, 136n.24
Slavonia, 3
Sobotka, Battle of (1866), 58
Solferino, Battle of (1859), 52–53
Sommariva, Marquis Annibale, general, 13, 14, 127n.6
Sondrio, 48
Spanish Succession, War of the (1701-13), 2
Spannocchi, Count Lelio, general, 115
Spigliatti, Alberto, navy officer, 92
Spinola, Ambroglio, general, 1
Stadion, Count Franz, Austrian finance minister, 64
Stationing policies, 14-15, 18-19, 24, 25, 27-32, 46-47, 49, 52, 55-56
Sterneck, Max von, navy commandant, 98, 148n.43
Strassoldo, Count Giovanni, army officer, 8
Stürmer, Count Bartolomäus von, Austrian diplomat, 74
Styria, 15, 32, 87, 110
Substitutes, hiring of, 128n.24
Székesfehérvár (Stuhlweissenburg), 111

Taaffe, Count Eduard, Austrian minister-president, 100
Tambov (prisoner of war camp, 1914-17), 105, 110
Tegetthoff, Wilhelm von, navy commandant, 92, 98
Temesvar, and Banat of, 3, 6, 36, 49
Thirty Years' War, 1-2
Thugut, Baron Franz Amadeus, Habsburg minister, 9
Tipaldo, Emilio, naval academy professor, 69, 78
Tivaroni, Carlo, historian, 43

Tommaseo, Niccolo, 80
Transylvania, 3, 42, 98, 116
Trautenau, Battle of (1866), 58
Trentinaglia, Giovanni, army officer, 53, 55, 140n.64, 140n.69
Trentino, 96, 99, 104, 105, 106, 108, 116; see also Tyrol
Trento, 107, 116
Treviso, 18, 22, 35-36
Trieste, 3, 8, 10, 68, 70, 73, 77, 80-81, 82, 84, 87, 88, 89, 91, 99-101, 104, 116; manpower for army from, 25, 40-41, 52-53, 57, 101, 102, 106, 115; manpower for navy from, 67, 89, 94; officers for navy from, 9, 10, 97, 103
Triple Alliance, 100, 101
Turina, Rafaele, sailor, 114
Tyrol, 51, 52, 55, 58; Italian manpower for army from, 15, 24-25, 96, 102, 104-5, 106, 108-9, 130n.46

Ubaldini, Paolo, 114
Udine, 18, 22, 36, 44, 54, 139n.53
Ukraine, 108, 109, 112, 115
Umberto, King of Italy, 100

Vacca, Giovanni, Italian admiral, 93
Valentiani, Francesco, army officer, 4
Valtan, Marco, navy officer, 152n.36
Vascotto, Giovanni, sailor, 113
Venetia: manpower for army from, 8, 12-15, 35-37, 39-40, 42, 45, 51-59, 60-61, 142n.83; manpower for navy from, 62, 67, 78-79, 84, 88, 93, 94; officers for army from, 13; officers for navy from, 9-10, 63-64, 66-70, 83-88, 93-94, 150n.15
Venetian Republic, 8, 9-10, 62, 93
Venice, 8, 31-32, 34, 35, 38, 39, 62, 64-67, 69-70, 74-75, 79-88 passim, 91, 96, 107, 115
Venice Arsenal, 64, 80, 85, 88
Verona, 18, 34, 36, 38, 39, 60
Vicenza, 54
Vienna: Italians garrisoned in, 15, 39, 41, 52, 55, 56, 60
Vienna, Treaty of (1866), 60
Villafranca, Armistice of (1859), 53
Voitsberg, 109, 111
Vojvodina, 42
Vorarlberg, 48, 96, 102, 130n.46

Wallachia, 48-49, 109
Wallenstein, general, 2
War of 1859, 50-54, 139n.55
War of 1864, 56
War of 1866, 57-61
Warships, Austrian:
    Abbondanza, corvette, 71;
    Adria, corvette, 72, 75;
    Bellona (I), frigate, 68-69;
    Bellona (II), frigate, 72-73, 76-77;
    Büffel, tugboat, 114;
    Clemenza, corvette, 72;
    Cyclop, auxiliary ship, 114;
    Erzherzog Friedrich, steam frigate, 92;
    Erzherzog Rudolph, harbor-watch ship, 114;
    Gäa, auxiliary ship, 114;
    Guerriera, frigate, 84-85, 36;
    Helgoland, cruiser, 114;
    Hussar, brig, 89;
    Kaiser Karl VI, cruiser, 113;
    Kerka, gunboat, 92;
    Novaro, cruiser, 113;
    Orione, brig, 67-68, 145n.16;
    Pola, ex-*Veneto*, brig, 87;
    Santa Lucia, paddle steamer, 92;
    Seehund, gunboat, 92;
    Torpedoboat 11, 12;
    Torpedoboat 15, 114;
    Triest, ex-*Venezia*, brig, 87;
    Tritone, brig, 72;
    Veloce, corvette, 75;
    Venere, frigate, 87
    Venus, ex-*Venere*, frigate, 87;
    Veneto, brig, 87;
    Venezia, brig, 84, 87;
    Vulcano, paddle steamer, 84-85, 87;
    Vulkan, ex-*Vulcano*, paddle steamer, 87;
Welden, Baron Franz von, general, 36
Wiener Neustadt Military Academy, 21, 65, 79
Wimpffen, Count Franz, general, 88-89

Windischgrätz, Prince Alfred, general, 35, 136n.32
World War I (1914–18), 104-16
Young Italy. *See* Mazzini, Giuseppe
Young, Joseph von, army officer, 127n.18
Zaccaria, Gustavo, navy officer, 98
Zagreb, 29, 114, 132n.62
Zara (Zadar), 29, 86
Zichy, Count Ferdinand, general, 75, 76, 77, 79, 80, 145n.21
Zucchi, Count Carlo, general, 25-26, 43, 71
Zürich, Treaty of (1859), 53, 55